WALKING
MIRACLE

A Vision for Asia, A Prayer for Healing

ART SANBORN

Jeremiah 17: 7-8
Blessings,

YWAM
PUBLISHING
P.O. BOX 55787   SEATTLE, WA 98155

YWAM Publishing is the publishing ministry of Youth With A Mission. Youth With A Mission (YWAM) is an international missionary organization of Christians from many denominations dedicated to presenting Jesus Christ to this generation. To this end, YWAM has focused its efforts in three main areas: (1) training and equipping believers for their part in fulfilling the Great Commission (Matthew 28:19), (2) personal evangelism, and (3) mercy ministry (medical and relief work).

For a free catalog of books and materials, contact:

YWAM Publishing
P.O. Box 55787, Seattle, WA 98155
(425) 771-1153 or (800) 922-2143
www.ywampublishing.com

Walking Miracle: A Vision for Asia, A Prayer for Healing
Copyright © 2008 by Art Sanborn

13 12 11 10 09 08   10 9 8 7 6 5 4 3 2 1

Published by YWAM Publishing
P.O. Box 55787, Seattle, WA 98155

ISBN-13: 978-1-57658-455-2
ISBN-10: 1-57658-455-0

Library of Congress Cataloging-in-Publication Data

Sanborn, Art.
  Walking miracle : a vision for Asia, a prayer for healing / Art Sanborn.
    p. cm.
  ISBN-13: 978-1-57658-455-2 (pbk.)
  ISBN-10: 1-57658-455-0
  1. Sanborn, Art. 2. Missionaries—Biography. 3. Missions—Asia. 4. Youth With a Mission, Inc. I. Title.
  BV3705.S26A3 2008
  266.0092—dc22
  [B]   2007037140

Other International Adventures

Adventures in Naked Faith

Against All Odds

Bruchko

A Cry from the Streets

Dayuma

Imprisoned in Iran

Living on the Devil's Doorstep

Lords of the Earth

The Man with the Bird on His Head

Peace Child

Taking the High Places

Tomorrow You Die

Torches of Joy

Totally Surrounded

To my family:
Ellen, Sean, Anne, Calah, and David who lived it.
This is their story, too.

Contents

ONE

Almost the End

I'M PARALYZED. The terrifying realization swept over me as the ocean's undercurrents thrashed me about.

I willed my arms and legs to propel me to the surface, but they refused to obey. Soon the tide carried me to calmer waters, and face-down my body drifted lifelessly up to the ocean's surface. I tried desperately to turn my head for air. Impossible. I no longer had any command over my body.

Lord, I'm at Your mercy. Surely with so many people at this beach, someone would help me soon.

Okay, stay calm. I started counting. One Mississippi, two Mississippi, three Mississippi, four Mississippi… I wondered how long I could hold my breath. *Maybe this is the end. Maybe I've taken my last breath. Maybe…* No. I knew I mustn't dwell on such thoughts.

The seconds relentlessly labored along. Ninety Mississippi, ninety-one Mississippi… What was taking so long? Couldn't anyone see me out there?

It was December 13, 1998. We had just arrived in Kona, Hawaii, to teach at Youth With a Mission's (YWAM) University of the Nations. My wife, Ellen, and I always looked forward to these times of sharing our passion for ministry with new generations of missionaries. This week we would be teaching on how to relate sensitively and effectively to different cultures.

We had especially looked forward to this particular trip. Ellen's mother, Liz, was joining us, and our youngest son, David, had managed to synchronize the tour of his one-man show, *Song of the Shepherd*, with our travel schedule. That morning we had joined a few hundred others in David's audience, laughing and crying in awe of David's brilliant singing, dancing, and dramatic transformations into twenty different characters.

Afterwards, we ate and talked late into the afternoon. By around five o'clock we realized that we had better hurry if we wanted to hit the waves before sunset. When we arrived at the beach, Ellen and Liz settled down on the sand to bask in the rays that poured from the incandescent blue and coral-hued sky. As spectacular as the view was, David and I had no time for that. We raced to the water.

The waves that day were ideal for bodysurfing, a sport that I had enjoyed for more than forty years. After several smooth rides to the shore, I noticed an approaching wave that surpassed all the other waves. I prepared for it in eager expectation as it swelled and rolled toward me.

Out of the corner of my eye I noticed that David was going to miss this one. He had apparently become hypnotized by the sunset, and it took only a glance upward for me to realize why. The entire sky seemed to drip with the rich and creamy swirls of rainbow sorbet.

Perhaps one more wave, and then I'll go watch the sunset with Ellen. It would be the perfect ride to cap off a perfect day.

I swam into the wave's crest and rested into the powerful tide as it drove me toward the shore. Without warning, the body of the wave sucked back, and the crest slammed my head onto the callous ocean floor. A loud crack sounded in my ears, and pain washed over me in black sheets. I barely managed to retain consciousness as the ocean swells began tossing me about like a rag doll.

I struggled to retain the air in my lungs, but time was running out. I knew I couldn't hold on much longer.

Ninety-four Mississippi, ninety-five Mississippi…

Suddenly, I felt two little hands trying to turn my head. Just a couple of inches more, and I'd be able to grab a breath of air. But the little hands gave up and let go.

Wait, come back! Please… One hundred nine Mississippi, one hundred ten Mississippi. *Jesus, help me.*

I felt my lungs give way and uncontrollably prepare for a suctioning in of water. At that very moment, my whole body was somehow flipped over. Whirling into my lungs came not water but marvelous, life-supporting air. I strained to look behind me. I could see that my arms were being pulled by a Hawaiian lifeguard. How surreal. I knew those were my arms, but I could not feel them.

The lifeguard shouted for someone to call 911 and then looked down at me. "You're gonna be okay, buddy."

I continued to gasp for air, incredibly grateful to still be conscious. And alive. "My wife and son…" Breathe. "Name…Sanborn…"

The kids who had alerted the lifeguard to my predicament now went to search for my family. Within moments, Ellen, Liz, and David were by my side.

"It's going to be all right, honey. The ambulance is on its way," Ellen said. She urged me to stay alert and talk about what had happened.

"I…I'm…" I couldn't seem to steady my breathing. "So…cold."

"We need more towels," David shouted to the crowd that had gathered.

The sun was going down, and the tide was coming in. A chilling combination. Where was the ambulance, and why couldn't anyone move me away from the water?

The lifeguard cradled my head in a viselike grip. "Hey, bro, this happened to me once. I was surfing at this very beach and hit my head. I was paralyzed for six hours, but hey, in no time at all, I was back on my surfboard."

I moved my eyes to Ellen. "What about class? I'm supposed to teach—"

"Don't worry, sweetheart. I'll teach for the next few days, and then you can finish out the week. I'll call the director from the hospital."

Ellen was so amazingly calm. But what if this paralysis wasn't temporary?

One woman kept asking me, "Can you feel this?"

I felt nothing. *What's she talking about?*

The lifeguard said to the woman, "Ma'am, please don't touch him."

"Why can't I feel anything?" I asked.

The woman called for others to come and help move me away from the water's edge.

The lifeguard knew better. "No, stop!" he said. "Ma'am, we are not moving him. Just, please, back off."

I tried to focus. A scripture verse I had read that very morning came to mind. "Then they cried out to the LORD in their trouble, and He brought them out of their distress. He stilled the storm to a whisper; the waves of the sea were hushed" (Psalm 107:28–29, NIV).

High tide was approaching. The waves slithered closer and closer toward my head.

The lifeguard held fast his firm grip on my head. "The tide's coming in, but we can't move him. I need everyone with a surfboard to come over here and block the waves."

Standing between me and the waves, several people planted their surfboards into the sand. After what seemed like an eternity, the medics finally arrived.

"Careful with his neck," one said. "It may be broken."

The medics fastened a neck brace on me, transferred me to a stretcher, and lifted me into the ambulance.

Ellen kept a close watch on every move. A man approached her and asked, "Is that your husband?"

She nodded.

"I know exactly what you're going through," he said. "My father had the exact same injury at this very beach last year. Here's my number. Call me if you need any encouragement."

"How is your father doing now?" Ellen asked.

"Oh, he died."

Needless to say, she never called on him for another dose of that brand of encouragement.

We arrived at the hospital around seven thirty. Even though it was a Sunday night, the hospital's director was on duty in the emergency room. He ordered X-rays and a CT scan. He then telephoned the head of orthopedics and asked him to rush over.

Ellen stayed by my side the whole night. I tried to look as though I was sleeping, but I just could not rest. I had no control of my body, and despite the best efforts of the hospital staff, the only parts of my body that I could feel, my head and neck, were shrill with pain.

The next morning, my doctor made arrangements to transfer me by medical air evacuation to Kaiser Permanente Hospital in Honolulu, one of only two hospitals in the state of Hawaii that had the facilities to tend to a spinal cord injury as severe as mine. It was clear from the initial tests that even with surgery, I would most likely spend the rest of my life as a quadriplegic.

My physician in Kona called Kaiser and dictated my details to a neurosurgery resident. As the resident carefully repeated each of the details, his department's chairman, Dr. Bernard Robinson, was nearby, finishing up some paperwork. I learned later that Dr. Robinson's ears perked up when he overheard that the patient was fifty-three years old. *What a coincidence,* he thought. *He's the same age as I am.* He then heard that the patient was from Tampa, Florida. *My hometown. Another coincidence.* He then heard that the patient was a Christian missionary. A strong Christian himself and an elder in his church, he prayed, "Okay, God, You have my attention."

Dr. Robinson had already finished his last surgery and had informed the hospital that he was going with his family to Tampa for Christmas for the first time in ten years and would, under no circumstances, take another patient. The suitcases were packed, and he was ready to go. But now he felt God leading him to perform just one more surgery.

My first stop at Kaiser Hospital was the radiology department.

"Welcome to the tunnel," the radiology tech said. "We have all the greatest hits from the seventies, eighties, nineties, and today. You name it, we got it. What would you like to listen to?"

"Do you have any jazz?" I asked.

"You got it, bro."

He placed the Walkman headset over my ears, and Kenny G's smooth saxophone washed over my frayed nerves and buffered the threat of claustrophobia for the hour or so that I spent in the MRI tunnel.

Afterward, Dr. Robinson introduced himself and told me that he had reviewed all the tests. "You're very lucky to be alive," he said. I had broken the third and fourth cervical vertebrae in my spine. Apparently, one more pound of pressure from the rogue wave would likely have killed me. Or if anyone had rotated my head after the accident, that also could have killed me.

I breathed another prayer for that lifeguard, who I found out later had actually been off-duty when my accident occurred and had just happened to be there at the beach at the right moment.

Dr. Robinson explained that he would probably need to surgically remove bone from my hip to help repair the bones that were broken in my neck. He had scheduled me for immediate surgery.

After the six-hour operation, I awoke to find myself hooked up to all kinds of tubes and machines—my life support. A dear, sensitive friend and missionary colleague had flown to Honolulu to pray for me. He walked into the room, took one horrified look at me, and began to weep. Unable to speak, he rushed out of the room. The next time I opened my eyes, I saw Dr. Robinson leaning over me. He asked if I could move any part of my body. I tried but could not.

"As I expected," he said.

He sent me downstairs for another MRI. The technician had queued up Kenny G for me, and once again I entered the imposing MRI tunnel.

Afterward I rejoined Ellen and David, who were waiting at the ICU. Since I was not too clear on what was going on, Ellen called our daughter, Michelle, who was in her last year of internal medicine residency at the University of Florida Medical Center. Ellen held up the phone to my ear so that Michelle could explain in lay terms what was happening to me. Those medical school debts were beginning to pay off.

"I'll be on the next plane to Hawaii, Dad," Michelle said. She then proceeded to tell me that Dr. Robinson had called her to explain my condition. During the operation, Dr. Robinson had discovered that I had ossification of the posterior longitudinal ligament (OPLL). An unusual condition, it could have been missed by another surgeon, but it just so happened that Dr. Robinson was one of the world's leading experts on the treatment of OPLL. People flew in from all over Asia to receive his expert treatment.

The disease is usually found in Asians and is thought to be the result of a genetic predisposition. In this disease, one of the ligaments encasing the spinal cord slowly ossifies, thickening as it turns into bone. The ligament thus crowds the area surrounding the spinal cord and eventually chokes the life out of the spinal cord. In my case, the usual fourteen-millimeter space that surrounds the spinal cord had shrunk to only four millimeters at the narrowest point, the C3 and C4 vertebrae, the site of my injury.

This condition had made it more likely for a severe injury of the spinal cord to occur when I hyperextended my neck against the sandbar. If this traumatic injury had not occurred, the OPLL could have caused a slow impingement of the spinal cord over years, with a gradual onset of unusual neurological deficits, making it difficult to diagnose. I could have slowly become a quadriplegic without knowing why. It is unlikely that doctors would have suspected this particular condition, since I'm not Asian. The wave had delivered a small blessing in disguise. I would still be a quadriplegic for the rest of my life, but at least now the doctors and I knew why. That not-knowing could have been fairly exasperating.

I received a second little blessing in disguise. Michelle told me that after Dr. Robinson had removed all of the harmful bone buildup from around my spinal cord, he had a surplus of bone to fuse my broken vertebrae. This meant that he didn't have to cut into my hip to extract extra bone. Michelle finished her explanation by telling me that the surgery had been a success. Dr. Robinson had purged my neck of the disease while safely fusing the bones back together. I would continue my life as a quadriplegic, but at least my life had been spared. Everyone seemed optimistic about my chances of obtaining some degree of recovery. In time, I might even be able to breathe on my own.

From the first time that I heard the hospital personnel referring to me as a quadriplegic, I kept hoping that I would soon wake up from this nightmare to tell Ellen, "Wow, what a horrible dream I just had. By the way, I've decided to give up bodysurfing."

Others now had complete control of my life, deciding how much oxygen went into my lungs, how much fluid ran in and out of my body. No one even asked permission to take my blood. I figured I had plenty to spare, but it would have been nice to at least have been asked.

"Excuse me, would you mind terribly if I borrowed a pint of your blood? We seem to have run out."

"Not a problem. Take all you want. Are you sure a pint will suffice?"

"I wouldn't want to impose."

"Not an imposition at all, really. Here. Why don't you take half a gallon, and if you need any more than that, you can always come back for more."

"I'm sure that will be plenty. Now, you're sure you don't mind?"

"Not at all. My pleasure. In fact, why not take out some fat while you're at it?"

But no one asked me. And because I had oxygen tubes going down my throat, it would have been unrealistic for anyone to expect an answer from me. My only way of communicating was by blinking: one blink meant yes; two blinks meant no. Any question that required more than a yes or a no answer resulted in miscommunication.

I felt my spirit fighting to stay alive. I had seen others die before, and I knew that when a life hangs by a thread, the patient's level of determination is often what makes the difference. *But why fight it?* If I survived this ordeal, I would only live to be a full-time burden on my family. And besides, living with a twenty-four-hour-a-day migraine and no ability to move wouldn't really be living.

Struggling against these thoughts, I turned my focus toward Jesus. As I worshiped Him, He filled me with the will to persevere. I reflected on scriptures that I had memorized, and those scriptures gave light to my present situation. The thought had been nagging me: *What can I possibly do in this situation to be productive?* Then it occurred to me that I could use this time to pray and intercede for others, and I spent much of my waking hours doing just that. I knew I was robbing Satan of any little victory he might have gained from the destruction of my spinal cord.

A deep joy engulfed me as I envisioned the godfather of the under-world slapping around his demons and saying, "All right, youse guys. Whose bright idea was dis, anyway? Come on, we go da all dis effort to provide as many distractions as possible, and then one of youse wise guys gets da genius proposition to take a man away from all dem distrac-tions to a sichee-ation where he has nuttin' to do but pray? Wha'samata you? Come on, fess up. Screwtape? It was you? Aah, you broke my heart. You broke my heart."

At this point, I had no sensation or bodily capacity from my neck down, but my mind was as clear and functional as it had ever been (which, of course, isn't saying much), but I determined that I would be grateful for whatever I did have, even if I had to spend the rest of my life in bed. That said, I would still continue to pray for healing in my body, since the miraculous power of Jesus has no limits.

Ellen told me one day that the office of Joni Eareckson Tada had called to inform me that they had heard about my accident. Joni wanted me to know that she was praying for me and would be happy to talk to me if I needed some encouragement.

I remembered reading about this amazing woman before we left for the mission field. As a teenager, Joni had broken her neck. Even though she has been wheelchair-bound ever since, she has had a profound impact on thousands of lives around the world. She celebrates life with a contagious, unshakable peace and joy that goes beyond circumstances and points directly to her Lord and Savior Jesus Christ. She's also a living reminder of how God can often work through a person to produce much more tremendous results by choosing not to heal her physical ailments.

I prayed, "Lord, there is no possibility that I could ever match what this courageous woman has done with her life in a wheelchair. So if I can't improve on what Joni has done, how about doing something different with me? I mean, healing me, for instance. Now, that would be a wonderful testimony, don't You think?"

After ten days the ICU staff weaned me off the ventilator, which had caused a lung infection that would take two months to heal. To my relief I could finally speak, though my voice was still rather weak and gravelly. Oxygen still flowed from a tank to my nostrils by a plastic tube, which after only one day caused my nose to become red, chapped, and irritated.

I said to my wife, "Ellen, could you please remove this tube from my nose? It's really uncomfortable."

"Honey, we can all see how your nose is reacting to the plastic tubing, so the hospital personnel have tried numerous times to free you from the oxygen tank. So far, though, every time the tubes have been removed, your blood oxygen has quickly dropped to a dangerous level. I'm afraid you can't be weaned off the oxygen tank yet, but we'll find some medication to soothe your poor nose."

What Ellen did not say was that it was unlikely I would ever be weaned off the oxygen tank.

I said, "In what position is my body lying?"

"You're lying flat on your back," she said. "Why?"

"I have the strangest sensation that I am lying in the fetal position."

When Michelle arrived in Honolulu, she sent David out to buy me some high-top basketball shoes to wear at all times so as to prevent my ankles from getting locked straight out. She knew this would be important if in fact I was miraculously able to walk someday. Some of the nurses understandably complained that this was a waste of their time. It was clearly impossible for me to ever walk again. So even though this chore was on my chart, it fell to Ellen, David, and Michelle to continually carry out the task.

Ellen asked me one day, "Honey, why do you think God allowed this to happen?"

"I don't know," I said. "I don't know why, but I do know that this has not taken God by surprise."

David said, "What about all those e-mails we've been getting that say, 'You must be learning so much through this time of trial.' I know the people mean well, but have you been learning anything?"

"I don't know. Maybe someday we'll look back on this and glean some great, significant truth, but I don't know. I can't even read the Bible anymore, unless you read it to me. And though I think it's certainly good to ask, 'What can I learn from this?' I think the more important question is 'How can I respond to this in a way that will glorify God?' That's what really matters."

Perhaps it would be stating the obvious to say that I had been thinking about the biblical story of Job. Though Job lost everything, he refused to sin by charging God with wrongdoing. This had become my creed during this trial. I knew I must measure my success or purpose for living not by prosperity, power, or health but rather by how cheerfully and faithfully I honor God. I believe that He can turn even tragedies for His glory, especially if we keep our attitudes in check.

On the eleventh day, my doctor transferred me from the ICU to my own, private room, just in time for Christmas. Though our children are grown and Ellen and I are constantly on the road, we still do whatever we can to get together as a family for Christmas. This year, Sean, our oldest son, and his wife, Anne, were visiting Anne's family in Australia for the first time since they were married three years before.

We therefore purposely withheld the more discouraging details of my injury from them, convinced that they would have flown to us in a heartbeat if they had known.

Ellen's mother, Liz, had already arranged to be with Ellen's siblings on the mainland for Christmas, but Michelle, David, Ellen, and I celebrated in my tiny hospital room. Though hospital policy forbade the use of Christmas tree lights, we had a small plastic tree (courtesy of our dear friend Pastor Fili), some last-minute gifts, and, most of all, each other. It was a precious time.

For the next two weeks, this room became my universe. I remained totally dependent on others for everything. They fed me, brushed and flossed my teeth, shaved me, changed me, and dressed me. If I had an itch, Ellen, David, or Michelle had to scratch it for me. After a couple of weeks, Michelle had to return to her residency in Florida, but David was able to cancel most of his performance itinerary to help Ellen care for me.

Pekka, my physical therapist, began exercising my lifeless limbs to ward off atrophy. My family had been massaging my limbs since day one, but now Pekka taught them how to also rotate my arms and legs to stimulate the muscular and sensory nervous system. Ellen faithfully did this daily for the next few months.

Pekka also gave me a spirometer to measure the strength of my breathing. She advised me to practice with the device as much as possible. The thought of having a respirator forced down my throat again gave me all the incentive I needed to exercise my lungs several times each day.

On two occasions, my physical therapist tried to sit me up in a wheelchair, but each time I suffered from tremendous pain and light-headedness. On New Year's Eve, two male nurses lifted me up and transferred me onto a wooden board. They strapped me in and cranked the board up into a vertical position. It felt good to be upright after lying horizontal for so long. That first day I stayed vertical for only fifteen minutes, but each day my time on the board increased. By day twenty-three, I was placed upright twice a day for short intervals.

Every day the medical staff tested me to see if I could move one of my fingers, since that remained a slight possibility. To all of our surprise and delight, on the twenty-first day, I managed to move my left index finger a fraction of an inch.

For the first three weeks, I had not been able to use the nurse call button next to my bed. If someone else was in the room with me, I could ask that person to press it when I needed something. But I could now lightly squeeze a couple of the fingers on my left hand, and I could utilize an ultrasensitive call button, as long as it was taped to my hand.

Every night, Ellen or David taped the call button to my left hand. But when the staff came later to turn me over to reduce the risk of bed sores, they would take it off and place it on the table next to my bed. They might as well have shipped it to Afghanistan. Each morning, I had to wait for Ellen to arrive to tape it back to my hand.

Some of the less sensitive orderlies would set up my dinner for me and then walk out of the room, saying, "Enjoy." Funny how little the mouth actually has to do with eating. My mouth muscles were in full working order but somehow that didn't seem to make a bit of difference. Drab as it was, I looked longingly at the food as my lips strained forward in a futile attempt to bridge the divide between my mouth and the food. The orderly would then return an hour or so later and say, "Mr. Sanborn, aren't you hungry? You didn't touch your food."

As my dry, unwatered throat attempted to convey the apparently indiscernible fact that it had been quite a while since I had touched anything, the orderly would grab the food tray and rush back to his other duties. Although breaking one's neck is not a weight-loss program that I would recommend, it certainly turned out to be effective for me.

The one sound I dreaded most was the buzzing of a mosquito near my ear. In my most gracious tone of voice, I would kindly invite the insect to take blood from anywhere below my neck that he wished, just as the medical staff did. But as far as I could tell, not a single mosquito took me up on my generous offer. Instead the mosquitoes would attack my head, the only place where I had any feeling. How could they have known how much those unattended itches tormented me!

On the twenty-fourth day after the accident, I was transferred by gurney to Rehabilitation Hospital of the Pacific in Honolulu. My rehabilitation began in earnest, and I eagerly participated. The day after I arrived, I had my first shower in almost four weeks. (As a clean-and-tidy kind of guy, I don't want anything to get in the way of my monthly shower.)

Since I had yet to successfully sit up in a wheelchair, when they sat me up to shower me, I fainted. When I regained consciousness, they placed a girdle around me and put support hose on my legs to keep me from passing out again. They also exchanged my old neck brace for a waterproof one. Then they took me to the shower, and one of the therapists placed a bar of soap in my hand.

"Okay, wash up," she said as the soap fell to the floor. It would have been funny had she been joking.

I didn't have a clue what to say, so I just stated the obvious. "Umm...I'm paralyzed."

"Can't you do anything?" she said.

"Well, I can do this."

She stared at me for a moment and then said, "What? You're not doing anything."

"Exactly," I said.

The showering caused a lot of dizziness and head pain, and it was embarrassing to be bathed by a female, but that didn't matter. Any kind of shower at that point was more than welcome.

Best of all, the last bit of sand from Magic Sands Beach finally washed out of my hair. I had already discovered why that beach was called Magic Sands. Sand from that beach seems to reproduce more prolifically than rabbits. For more than three weeks, anytime someone lifted my head, a pile of sand had to be swept away. Ellen and David had spent hours scratching my head and removing the sand without making much headway. Now at last I was sand free.

My first few therapy sessions were little more than evaluations of what I could feel. In other words, they were really brief.

"So the goal of therapy will be to help me regain more function?" I said.

"Oh no," the occupational therapist said. "Your therapy sessions are geared to help you keep what functions you have."

"Keep what I have? But I don't have anything."

She smiled and proceeded to gently jab me with various sharp objects and dull instruments. On the right side of my body I felt nothing. But on the left, I was sporadically beginning to feel vague sensations on my arm and the bottom of my foot.

"Apparently," she said, "the part of your spinal cord that controls the right side of your body is one hundred percent severed. That's the bad news. But the good news is better than we could have expected. It looks like the part of the cord that controls the left side of your body is only partially severed, so it's possible you can gain back some very limited function on your left side. Were you right- or left-handed?"

"Right-handed. Even before my injury, the function of my left hand was limited."

"Don't worry," she said. "We'll teach you to be a lefty, although there still won't be a lot that you'll be able to do."

One day, after an intensive physical therapy session, a member of the medical staff explained that I would need to deal with the fact that I would probably never walk again. My spinal cord was irretrievably damaged at the C3 and C4 level.

"This is an injury as severe as that of the actor Christopher Reeve, well-known for his role as Superman," she said. "If Mr. Reeve—a world-class athlete, who has invested a lot of hard work, the best of cutting-edge medicine, and millions of dollars in an attempt to recover from his spinal cord injury—if he's still confined to a wheelchair, you'll need to face the fact that you will be too. There is no known cure for a spinal cord injury."

I replied, "That may be so, but I've seen a lot of miracles in my lifetime, and thousands of people around the world are praying for me. If God wants me to walk again, I will walk again."

When I was wheeled back to my room, Ellen noticed that I seemed depressed. "What's wrong?" she asked.

"She said I would never walk again."

"Honey, you have thousands of people around the world who are praying for you, and we have seen so many miracles before. If God wants you to walk again, you will definitely walk again," she said, with no shred of doubt in her voice. I learned later that on that day, when Ellen walked through the door of the tiny apartment she shared with David, her head hung low in despair.

"Mom," David said, "what's the matter?"

"They said that your dad would never walk again."

"But Mom, we have thousands of people around the world praying for Dad, and with all the miracles we've seen before, there's no question that if God wants Dad to walk again, he will walk again." I wonder who David went to for encouragement.

Once a week I attended an hour-long instructional class, along with a twenty-year-old Hawaiian man who had an injury similar to mine. The classes were informative, but we would leave them feeling depressed after hearing about all the many things we could never do again. We learned that bones and muscles can regenerate, but nerves cannot, especially those around the spinal cord. Once the central nervous system is damaged, a person must live with the resulting impairment for the rest of his or her life.

A few weeks earlier I had asked my first therapist, Pekka, whether there was any possibility that I would get some of my feeling or mobility back.

"Maybe," she had said. "Once the swelling from your injury and surgery has subsided, you'll be able to assess how much of your disability is permanent."

From then on, I had held on to that hope. But now, in rehab, I mentioned this to a nurse, who said, "That's true that some feeling can return after the swelling goes down, but when was your operation?"

"It's been only seven weeks."

"Oh, I'm sorry, Mr. Sanborn. If your operation was seven weeks ago, the residual swelling would definitely be resolved by now. I'm afraid that you presently have all the feeling that you will ever get back."

I appreciated that the medical staff seemed so *delighted* to share with me from their vast storehouses of medical understanding, but delighted wouldn't exactly be the word I would use to describe how I felt at receiving these golden nuggets of knowledge. Each of the physiological dissertations generally boiled down to one thing: I was going to spend the rest of my life in a wheelchair.

At one of our weekly instructional classes, I noticed that the handsome, young Hawaiian man seemed unusually depressed. When a nurse wheeled me back to my room, I asked if she knew why.

"The poor guy just learned that his fiancée has called off their marriage," she said.

"That's terrible," I said.

"I know, but it's the normal response. Your relationship with your wife is the exception. The divorce rate for patients with spinal cord injuries is over ninety percent."

That disturbed me more than I let on, but I reminded myself that I, for one, had no cause for alarm with my amazing wife who had put up with me in the toughest of times.

One day, the attending physician brought an orthopedic resident into my room and began instructing the resident. "This is a spinal cord syndrome patient. See how the shoulders have dramatically atrophied?"

When the doctors left, Ellen came into the room. "Are you okay, honey?" she said.

"I know what atrophy means," I said. "My body is wasting away."

Ellen laughed. "The only thing that is atrophying on your body is your stomach. You are looking fitter, younger, and more handsome every day."

"Ah, yes," I said. "What a burden it is to be such a hunk."

Ellen smiled and kissed me.

The hospital's psychologist, Dr. Hughes, interviewed me once a week. In our first session, she asked if I'd had any thoughts of suicide or self-destruction. I told her that as a servant of Jesus I would never entertain such thoughts. "I know that even if I never walk again, God will give me the ability to be content. I would rather be serving God in this wheelchair than running without Him. But Dr. Hughes, may I ask you a question?"

"Of course," she said.

"Why would you ask a quadriplegic such a question? I mean, even if I wanted to kill myself, what could I do about it? Hold my breath?"

Dr. Hughes burst into laughter. I suspect that she later passed my oh-so-witty remark on to the nurses, because, one day, a nurse came in and saw me holding my breath.

She ran to my bed, pressed the emergency button, and grabbed my hand. "What are you doing?"

"Don't worry," I said. "I'm not trying to kill myself. I'm just trying to see how long I can hold my breath. I can't seem to hold it for more than fourteen seconds."

"With your injury," she said, "it's a miracle that you can breathe on your own at all."

"But immediately after breaking my neck, I held my breath for more than a hundred and ten seconds."

She said nothing, but she gave me a look that clearly said, "In your dreams."

Apparently, by counting to 110 Mississippi, I had not only managed to keep calm in the midst of the accident but also unwittingly provided the opportunity for God to give me another sign of His miraculous intervention. Michelle had explained that the nerves C-3, C-4, and C-5 (which were directly impacted by my injury) are absolutely essential for breathing. She had told me that while in medical school, she had learned a mnemonic that goes like this: "C-Three, C-Four, and C-Five keep the diaphragm alive." That's why, from the time the ambulance arrived, I had been hooked up to oxygen tanks. But in the half-hour wait prior to the ambulance arrival, I had been able to breathe freely. Awareness of that little miracle gave me a hope for more miracles to come.

And the miracles did indeed continue to come. Each day, I was able to move more and more. By February 1999, to the astonishment of the medical staff, I was able to move both my legs and even support my weight when transferring from my bed to the wheelchair. I could stand for only a second or two, though, and could not pivot my body to sit down in the wheelchair.

An occupational therapist said, "This is amazing. I think that in time you may even be able to walk a little. I've heard about this, but I've never actually seen it. I think you're what we in the medical profession refer to as a 'walking quad.'"

"A walking quad?" I said. "What's that?"

"Someone who should be a quadriplegic and has little use of his or her arms and no ability to feel but for some unknown reason can walk with assistance."

"Well, I serve a God who can heal completely," I said. "If what I've got already is a miracle, then God can miraculously restore the rest of my body."

Later, when I was wheeled back to my room, Ellen took one look at me and said, "What's bothering you, Art?"

"I was told today that the most I can hope for is to be a walking quadriplegic."

"Oh, honey," she said, "remember that Dr. Robinson said that anything is possible. And look, here are e-mails from dozens of countries around the world. Thousands of people are praying for you. You inspire everyone with your courage and perseverance. You just do the possible and have faith in God for the impossible."

My chief physical therapist, Jennifer, spent a lot of time helping me to get from the wheelchair to the therapy bench. At first I would fling myself onto the bench from my wheelchair.

"I know it's hard," she said, "but try to focus on moving slowly with more control."

"Flinging is easier," I said. "Braking myself is hard to do."

"You can say that again. Don't worry. We'll work on building up your strength so that you can make your transfers with control and with minimal assistance."

Several days later, Jennifer said that I had gained enough strength to try to learn to walk with assistance. Under her supervision, I stood up. My legs supported me enough to sustain my standing for several minutes.

I had not seen the world from this perspective in a couple of months, and I felt like a giant. At five feet six inches, I had always complained about being short. But now, as I peered over my neck brace to drink in the panoramic view of the grey tile floor, I became very grateful to God that I was not any taller.

Wow, I thought, *that is a long way to fall.* I've never had much fear of heights before, but way up in this stratosphere, a whole five and a half feet above the ground, I had to fight off the vertigo. Still unable to feel my body, I naturally wanted to look down to see where my feet were, but my therapists advised me against doing so. This would have been strenuously difficult for me to do anyway, since I still wore a large neck brace.

In therapy I had to use my full concentration to put one foot down, shift my weight, pick up the other foot, then put that one down. Every time I tried this, I placed my feet in the wrong positions. I would have plummeted to the floor if my therapists, Lavonne and Jennifer, had not been holding me up.

"I know you'll find this hard to believe," I told them, "but before the accident, I could actually walk and chew gum at the same time." My favorite therapy was the daily pool exercise. Ellen would join in, helping the therapist to move me through the water. At the end of one session, Ellen turned to me and said, "May I have this dance?" She positioned her feet under mine and put her arms firmly around me. We slowly waltzed through the water as her singing resonated above it.

My doctor recommended that I take an excursion out of the rehab building as soon as I was able. To take me out for even just a few hours, Ellen and David had to first become certified in every area of my care, but they managed to do so with apparent ease. I was about to see the real world for the first time in two months.

I had really looked forward to getting out of the hospital, but I had not anticipated just how hard it would be. David drove us to a beautiful Honolulu beach. How surreal it was to be outside and see the ocean for the first time since my accident. Everything appeared different from how I had ever seen it before. The outside world, this echo of my lifelong past, now seemed almost alien. I wondered what kind of new life I was entering.

It hadn't occurred to me that people would become so uncomfortable when they looked at me. The people who passed by either looked quickly away and pretended they didn't see me or stared at me as if I was from the circus. It was also unnerving to be lifted up and down the stairs in the wheelchair, though Ellen and David managed it like pros.

The next day I asked Jennifer to teach me how to get from the wheelchair to the floor. "I want to be able to lie on the sand at the beach next weekend," I said.

Jennifer worked with me all week, but I just could not get onto the floor without falling. And once on the floor, I tried with all my might to get back into my wheelchair but, again, without success. Would I be dependent on caregivers for the rest of my life? Ellen and my kids had so much to give to the world. Would they feel obliged to spend all their time caring for me? What kind of life would that be for them?

During my last two weekends at rehab, David and Ellen sprang me twice from the hospital. It got easier each time. In the meantime Dr. Hughes had asked me if I would like to teach a session of her sociology class at the university. She had learned that I had lectured around the world on cultures from a Christian perspective. Having lived more than twenty years outside of the United States (primarily in Libya, England, Thailand, Malaysia, and Singapore), I've developed a sincere love and respect for the uniqueness of the many cultures God has made. (Our grown children also love cultural diversity. Not only have they all spent several of their adult years overseas, but also our son Sean married an Australian, and our daughter, Michelle, married a Korean-American.)

So on my last Friday in Hawaii, I had the attention of Dr. Hughes's class for an hour. My time with that class illuminated a positive aspect of my quadriplegia. I'm sure that as a white, Anglo-Saxon, Protestant minister, I've often been perceived in America as a walking gene-code of political incorrectness. But now, thanks to my wheelchair, I noticed that people were more open to what I had to say. I could speak freely about how Jesus created the beautiful diversity of cultures without my Christian perspective being immediately assaulted.

Now that I was wheelchair-bound, I was for the first time in my life politically correct. It almost seemed as though God had given me too much. Throughout my life, I'd had all the benefits disproportionately granted to white men in this society, and now I had the advantage of the growing favor granted to those on the fringes of society. The best of both worlds.

Now that Ellen and David had become certified caregivers, the doctor agreed to release me from the rehabilitation hospital. After nine long weeks, I would finally be returning to our house in Florida. Going back to Asia was still out of the question for now, but I was confident that it would be only a matter of time before I could return there as well.

I was also growing more independent. My left hand could now reach my chin. From my chin, I could walk my index and middle fingers up to any place on my head that itched. This was such a luxury after two months of enduring every little itch in agony. The first time I was able to scratch my head, I thought I must be in heaven.

"God," I half seriously prayed, "if this is all I get back, it's enough."

With minimal assistance, I could also feed myself, using my left hand propped to a support device. My perception was greatly impaired, though. Like a toddler, I made a huge mess, with only one in five spoonfuls actually landing in my mouth. I told Ellen, "I don't think we should invite the queen over for tea anytime soon."

I had lost thirty pounds since my injury, but even though my body looked thinner, I had the strangest sensation that I weighed a ton and must look like the Pillsbury doughboy with arms and hands as bulky as Popeye's. But when I looked down at my body, I saw just how atrophied it had become. When I tried to move, I felt like I was encased in wet cement. However, I was grateful that my arms and legs could move at all, contrary to the experts' predictions.

My mother-in-law, Liz, called to tell us that our friends the Saltsmans and the Baloghs had added wheelchair ramps to our house in Florida. Also, she had found a secondhand, above-ground pool that she, Sean and his wife, Anne, and some friends were installing for me. Sean and Anne had come to live in Florida for a few months to attend a Frontier Missions School with YWAM and were assisting Liz in making our house handicap-accessible.

While David and Ellen finished packing for the flight back to Florida, a number of the hospital staff came to say good-bye and to wish me luck. Tony, a strong Hawaiian therapist, asked what my plans were, now that I would be mostly wheelchair-bound for the rest of my life.

"First, I'm going to write a book," I said.

"How are you going to write a book without being able to type?" he said.

"My son Sean has installed a program in our computer that will type out whatever I say into a microphone."

"Excellent," Tony said. "What will your book be about?"

"The first chapter is going to be about my accident and my experiences in the hospitals here. In the following chapters, up to the last chapter, I'll recount many of the miracles that God has performed in my life."

"You said, 'up to the last chapter.' What will the last chapter be about?" one of the nurses asked.

"My miraculous healing from quadriplegia. I plan to write it as soon as I beat my sons in basketball."

"Could you beat your sons in basketball before your injury?" Tony asked.

"It would have taken a miracle," I said. "Then, after beating them in basketball, I'm going back to Asia. I'll plan to stop here on my way and challenge each of you guys to a one-on-one basketball game—one year from now, in March of 2000."

One of the guys rolled his eyes and said, "Oh man, am I scared."

Tony said, "Art, considering who your Coach is, maybe we'd better start practicing. You're gonna defy the odds, bro."

It took me a few months in the comfort of my home in Florida to finish the first chapters of the book. A lot happened during that time, but you'll read more about that in the last chapter, which I knew at the time I wouldn't be writing until I was out the wheelchair.

Some people might have seen that as a pipe dream, but I had seen God perform many brain-baffling miracles in my lifetime. I had always known that with Him, nothing is impossible—even restoring a destroyed spinal cord. Deep within me, I was convinced that God was not finished with me yet. I knew that the One who had so faithfully led us in the past is the same One who holds our future. Plus, with all that God had done for me, I was already a living miracle. And if it was His will, I would soon be a walking miracle.

TWO

Once Upon a Time

MY FATHER worked for the Central Intelligence Agency (CIA). When I was ten, we moved to Tripoli, Libya, for three years. I had some wonderful times with the Arab community there. Once, I actually got lost in the Sahara. But that's another story. Other than in Libya, I spent most of my growing-up years in Washington, D.C., and northern Virginia.

We were a fairly typical American middle-class family attending a traditional Methodist church. Although I believed that Jesus was the Savior of the world, I hesitated to make Him Lord of my life. I thought that Christians didn't have any fun, and I wanted to live by my own rules.

I served as a navy reservist during college for two years, then went on active duty in 1965. On July 8, 1967, after a three-year courtship, Ellen and I married and moved to London, England. Ellen had studied at the London Arts School, and our marriage faced its first hurdle when she was cast in the original London production of *Hair*.

Everything that *Hair* represented—orgies, drugs, and rebellion—was magnified behind the scenes. We yearned for a solution to the constant barrage of temptations and offenses that came with her new job. We found our solace one evening when I was sharing with Ellen about Jesus. That night, Ellen gave her heart to Christ. She was the first person I ever led to the Lord, and I was so convicted by my own words that I became the second person I ever led to the Lord.

Through a clerical error, Ellen ended up losing her UK work permit before *Hair* opened. (We both eventually saw this as a blessing in disguise.) Soon after that, in 1969, we discovered we had a baby on the way. We moved back to Virginia, where I began working in hospital administration while Ellen continued to sing professionally. Over the next four years, we were blessed with three delightful little miracles: Sean, Michelle, and David. Though finances were always tight, we were a pretty happy family.

Ellen and I diligently read our Bibles and devotional books and were quite active in church ministry, but we both secretly wrestled with unconfessed sin. We longed to be free to experience the kind of victorious Christian life we had heard about.

In 1974, God intervened. He brought Ellen and me to a place where we were forced to be totally open with each other. As we revealed to each other all of our failures, frustrations, and sins, even things that had taken place before we had met, we wept in heartbroken repentance.

This time of openness and brokenness lasted for two weeks. The Bible says, "Confess your trespasses to one another, and pray for one another, that you may be healed" (James 5:16). We learned through bitter experience that to know true freedom, we had to confess not only to the Lord but also to each other, not to be humiliated but to be healed—and changed.

I had assumed that if Ellen truly knew who I was, she would stop loving me. Ironically, Ellen had thought that I would stop loving her if I knew everything about her. We were now so grateful that we hadn't waited any longer to discover the joys of true, deeply honest intimacy. Areas that had once been our greatest vulnerabilities now became strengths. As we learned to keep short accounts with each other, we discovered that the temptations drastically diminished. At the end of those soul-purging fourteen days, we experienced the greatest joy and freedom we had ever known. It was then that the Lord birthed in our hearts the desire to become overseas missionaries.

One Sunday morning, a missionary from Africa came to speak at our church. His gripping stories and passion for God stirred our hearts. That day, Ellen and I told our pastor that we had decided to answer the call for missions, and he joyfully announced the news to the congregation.

We began to pay off all of our debts and to learn all we could about other countries and mission groups. We joined the missions committee at our church, and before long, I became the committee's chairman. We assumed that God would lead us to the right place within a year or two.

One evening, we talked and prayed with our three preschool-aged children about what we should look for in a mission organization. Our children were really too young to fully understand the issues, but we wanted to ensure that we made all important decisions as a family, since these decisions would directly affect all of us.

That evening, we felt that the Lord gave us three criteria to guide us in choosing a mission agency to join. First, the agency would uphold that all the gifts and powers of the Holy Spirit are still operational today, just as in the book of Acts. Second, it would not require us to send our young children away to boarding school, as we believed that the children were an integral part of the missionary team. Third, it would have a vision to expand, to reach out to more and more people with the love of Jesus. Simple enough, we thought. But as we began to receive information from various mission agencies, we could not find a single one we qualified for that met all three criteria.

One mission agency wrote to us, "We would love to have you join our mission, but you must first sign a contract that you will not minister in the gifts of the Holy Spirit, either publicly or privately, while you are a member of our mission."

Though we knew we could not sign this mission's contract, we remembered that it had not been long since we, too, had been skeptical about the active work of the Holy Spirit. A few years earlier, we had asked my mother if we could borrow her car while ours was being serviced. She had said we could on one condition: Ellen and I had to attend a healing service with her.

My mother had been a Christian since the early 1960s and often went to these healing services, where she said she had witnessed miraculous healings. I had seen only the counterfeits and was not too keen on seeing yet another one. But Ellen and I knew that Mom had the right motive, so we found ourselves in church on a Saturday afternoon.

The evangelist spoke for about forty-five minutes. At the end of his sermon, he instructed all those who wanted to be healed to line up for prayer. The people in the queue looked fairly healthy to me. I guessed that they probably suffered from backaches or similar complaints, making the effectiveness of the preacher's healing prayer the equivalent of a placebo.

Then I saw a woman with visibly inflamed and swollen knees who required the assistance of a walker. I decided that if this woman was healed, I would believe that the age of miracles hadn't passed.

When it was her turn, the evangelist laid his hand on her forehead and shouted, "Be healed!" He then turned to the next person in line as the woman reached for her walker. At that, the evangelist turned and grabbed the woman's walker, twisted it up, and said, "Woman, where is your faith? I told you that you were healed."

The evangelist told the people to raise their eyes toward heaven and thank God for His healing power. As others looked at the ceiling, I watched the crippled woman tearfully limp out of the building. At that moment I hardened my heart and decided that all healing evangelists were con artists.

Then God arranged certain events to change my heart. In May 1973, we began attending a new church, Halpine Baptist. The senior pastor, Richard Kline, believed that God moves as actively today as He did in biblical times. Pastor Kline told of many testimonies about miraculous healings and gave others the opportunity to testify how God had healed them from life-threatening diseases. Some even brought their physicians to the church to confirm the testimonies. I was genuinely impacted by these stories, but I still doubted, until the day we almost lost our one-year-old son, David.

Having three preschool-aged children really kept us on our toes. It sometimes felt like a full-time job just keeping them alive. One of our safety precautions was a wooden gate that blocked the entrance to the long, steep stairway that led to our basement recreation room. One evening, David somehow unlatched the gate and tumbled headfirst down the stairs. He landed at the bottom with a crash against the concrete wall.

Ellen and I heard the crash, followed by a thump that sounded all too much like a tender head hitting the floor. We raced down the stairs, our hearts throbbing in our throats. When we reached little David, he was unconscious. His face was turning purple, and a large, swollen knot rose on his forehead.

I grabbed a mirror near the steps and placed it under David's nostrils. No breath fogged up the glass. I placed my thumb on his wrist. No pulse.

My heart sank. I said to Ellen, "Call Dr. Cohen and tell him to meet us at the emergency room right away."

Ellen was already sprinting up the stairs. Sean, our four-year-old son who had been playing in the basement, yanked on my trousers.

"Sean, what is it?" I said. "Can't you see that your brother is hurt?"

"Daddy," Sean said, "when you've got a little hurt, it's good to go to a doctor. But when you've got a big hurt, you gotta go to Jesus."

His words pierced my heart. I looked at the clock. The seconds were spinning by. I didn't know what else to do, but I certainly did not seem to have the same level of faith as my four-year-old.

"You're right, son. Would you pray?"

"Dear Jesus, please heal my baby brother. Amen."

Like a sprinter at the starting line, I waited for that "Amen" to begin my mad dash to the car. But David gasped and started to breathe again. My heart leapt, and so did my eyes, as I watched the lump on David's head shrink and vanish and the ominous, bluish-gray color of his skin give way to a warm, pinkish hue.

Having worked around hospitals for many years, I knew that when someone experiences a trauma like this, the body goes into shock and loses its appetite. What happened next, I believe, was God's way of keeping me from rationalizing away this miracle.

David opened his eyes and said, "Daddy, I'm hungry."

Now David has never been especially interested in food. To this day, he says that if he doesn't remind himself, he seriously sometimes forgets to eat for an entire day. But that day, beaming like a prince in his high chair, he happily ate anything we put in his bowl. Ellen and I watched in amazement and relief.

The phone rang. It was Dr. Cohen. "I'm at the hospital," he said. "Why aren't you here?"

"I'm so sorry," I said. In the chaos, we had forgotten to call our wonderful doctor, who had interrupted his busy schedule to rush to the hospital. "I feel terrible that we put you to all this trouble. But um…we actually ended up taking David to another Jewish doctor…named Jesus."

We now had no question in our minds that the Holy Spirit is just as actively involved in the lives of His servants today as He was two thousand years ago. And there was no way we were going to the mission field without drawing upon His power. We faced even more difficulties, though, in finding a mission agency that would agree to the criterion that our children not be sent away to boarding school.

In the mid-1970s, most of the mission groups we investigated required their members to send their children to boarding schools if there was not an international school nearby. Many organizations felt that this was best for the children. Some groups argued that the care of the children took away from the mother's involvement in mission work. Several mission groups required that the children leave home at the age of five, while others allowed children to wait until they were going into high school. We have seen that this separation can be unimaginably heartrending. Although some teens thrive in a dorm environment, especially if they have a choice in the matter, we have seen many other boarded missionary kids with shipwrecked faiths.

When we eventually became missionaries in Asia, we found that our children were our greatest assets, just as we had expected. When I arrived in remote villages, my round eyes, pale skin, and big nose invariably attracted a crowd. The villagers would graciously listen to my teaching and allow me to pray for them, but they still doubted my motives. When Ellen came with me, the people would be somewhat more open, but when we brought our children, the walls of resistance came tumbling down. The people could see how important our family was to us, and that was absolutely crucial in their cultures. Plus, well-behaved children from other cultures seem to melt even the hardest of hearts.

Our criterion that the mission agency have a vision to expand was also important to us because without the Lord's leading, we would be compelled to set safe goals that we could achieve in our own strength. We wanted to trust God to do the impossible through us, accomplishing things for which only He could receive the credit.

From 1974 to 1977, we regularly received offers from mission organizations, but none of the offers fulfilled all three of the criteria that God had given us. People at church began to ask us if we had changed our minds about becoming missionaries.

In September of 1975, Sean started kindergarten at a local public school in Rockville, Maryland. During the first couple of weeks, his classes lasted for just two hours. Since I used our only car to drive to work in Washington, D.C., Ellen had to walk Sean to school, accompanied by his four-year-old-sister, Michelle, and two-year-old-brother, David. Since it took thirty minutes to walk each way, the school's principal granted Ellen permission to stay on the school grounds during Sean's classes.

Many of the neighborhood children attending this school knew Ellen because she had led a children's Good News Club during the summer. Now, after school, these children asked Ellen to lead them in the songs she had taught them, and she was happy to do so. Each day, more and more kids would gather around her to join in the singing. Ellen noticed that some of the teachers glared at her angrily, and she wondered what she had done to offend them.

On Thursday of that first week, one of the kids said, "I love that 'Shadrach, Meshach, and Abednego' song. Where does that story come from? Is it true?"

Ellen explained that it was based on a historical event recorded in the book of Daniel in the Bible. To her astonishment, a large number of the children said that they had never heard of the Bible and asked where they could find one. She promised that she would give a Bible to any of them who were seriously interested in reading it.

That evening, when I came home from work, Ellen said we needed to purchase thirteen children's Bibles. The following day, she sat with the children in the playground and handed out the Bibles to the thirteen children who had requested them. She was jolted out of her gift giving by the sound of some women yelling. When she turned to see where the voices were coming from, she saw a mob of teachers marching toward her, accompanied by a uniformed policeman.

The policeman grabbed Ellen's arm and pulled her to her feet. "Come with me, ma'am," he said.

What in the world was this all about? Ellen said, "One moment, sir, I—"

"Lady, I said 'now.'" At that, he began dragging her toward the school building.

Children cried as teachers yanked the new Bibles from their little hands. Sean, Michelle, and David trembled with wide- and teary-eyed alarm, and they ran as fast as their little legs could go to keep up with the officer, who hauled Ellen into the principal's office.

As soon as they entered the office, the principal said, "I want this woman arrested. Take her to jail now."

Ellen fought back the tears. "I didn't realize I was breaking any law," she said.

"Ma'am," the policeman said. "You have just committed a federal offense."

The principal said, "I want her to serve as an example to prevent anyone in the future from polluting my school with religion."

"Please," Ellen said. "I'm so sorry. I didn't know I was doing anything wrong."

The principal glared at her. "Not good enough."

"Look, lady," the policeman said. "If you promise not to do this again, I'll let you off with just a warning this time. But if I ever catch you so much as talking to any kids other than your own on the school grounds, I will arrest you."

Ellen agreed to the terms, gathered our three frightened children into her arms, and rushed home. When I came home and heard the story, I was furious, but I didn't know what to do about it. I told some friends what had happened, but they, too, were at a loss about what to do.

On the following Monday, Sean pleaded with Ellen not to make him go to school. Before this, he had always been excited about going to school, but now he feared that he might be arrested if he talked about Jesus. He had always been the kind of kid who was ready to boldly go where no kid had gone before, but now he was beginning to turn inward. Something had to be done, so Ellen volunteered as a parent helper in Sean's class. Michelle and David would quietly busy themselves in the corner of the classroom with crayons and crepe paper.

We were stunned by the school's hypocrisy. Sean's teacher began each day by reading daily horoscopes to her class. She taught Sean that he was an Aquarius and that the stars, not God, controlled his destiny. Another teacher required students to memorize verses from the Qur'an (the holy book of Islam). One day, the principal even invited a Buddhist monk to talk about his religion with all of the kids in the school.

The school consistently tolerated and supported pretty much any religious system other than Christianity. We began to look around for a new school and found one that our children could attend the following year, Washington Christian School (WCS), in Silver Spring, Maryland. Unfortunately, with our current finances we wouldn't be able to afford the tuition. For both Sean and Michelle to attend, we would need $1,836.

After a great deal of number crunching, we determined that with several sacrifices, we could do it. We just had to pray that our old, rusty car would break down a little less often and that our house would hold together without needing any costly repairs.

Unexpectedly, the very day we enrolled our children at WCS, my boss gave me a pay raise. The annual amount of the raise came out to $1,836.56.

Now all we had to do was to figure out what extravagance we would buy with that extra fifty-six cents.

Any Time Now

T H E years passed as we waited for our imminent departure. Our children continued at WCS, and each year, we would explain to their teachers that we might be leaving before the year's end. We had prepared our spirits, but the Lord did not seem to be opening any doors.

Every night we prayed together as a family, "Dear God, please send us to the mission field." From the age of six onward, Sean would add, "And when we go into missions, please send us to Hawaii first."

The first time Sean said that prayer, Ellen and I laughed and gently explained to him that God would probably not send us to Hawaii, but rather, to Asia, Africa, or South America. But Sean continued to pray that prayer regularly.

I was now working at George Washington University Medical Center as an administrator, and Ellen continued to wear many hats of responsibility as a full-time mom, voice teacher, and professional singer. She got the chance to open for Ella Fitzgerald, Sarah Vaughn, Gene Krupa, and many other well-known musicians. She sang for the Presidential

Press Club during Jimmy Carter's presidency. With her jazz combo, the Midnight Sun, she performed at a number of respectable venues in the Washington, D.C., area.

One evening in 1978, while singing with her band, she met the vice president of Word Records. Not long after that, Word offered Ellen a recording contract. This was her dream come true, but after struggling in prayer about it, she turned the offer down. The contract would have dictated that she continue to live in the United States, and she decided that our missionary calling was more important. She has never regretted that decision.

One wintry evening in February 1979, I sat in my favorite cushy chair next to a cozy, warm fire, listening to soft, relaxing music. A tremendous sense of well-being engulfed me. My life had become so comfortable. Why would I want to disrupt this lifestyle by accepting the uncertainties of foreign missions? Perhaps the reason God had stirred our hearts for missions was not so that we would go, but rather so that we would support others who wanted to go. We were now doing well enough financially to donate a considerable amount to several missionaries.

I called Ellen and the kids together to discuss this new proposal. We prayed, asking God for guidance. After a brief time of waiting on God, I asked each of them what they felt God was saying. The response was unanimous. We all believed that God did indeed want us to go to the mission field.

"But when are we going?" I asked. "Will it be soon or when the kids reach high school or college age?" For the past four years, it had been so difficult to keep a stance of readiness without having any idea of when we might actually leave.

Again, we prayed and asked God to direct us on this issue of His timing. I handed each family member a piece of paper and asked them all to write the date they felt God had told them. The children were still so young, but even little David knew his numbers well, so I instructed them to draw three columns.

"In the first column," I said, "write a number from one to thirty-one. In the second column write a number from one to twelve. In the third column write a number that's higher than 1979. For instance, 2020 happens to be a higher number than 1979. That wouldn't be such a bad time to go."

After praying and waiting for God to speak to us, we privately wrote down the numbers on our pieces of paper. We then passed the papers to Ellen, who unfolded each piece of paper one by one. The same numbers appeared on all five pieces of paper: "1–1–1980."

When I told our pastor that we would be leaving for the mission field by January 1, 1980, he put us in touch with the Christian Service Corps, which sent out our resumes to mission agencies all over the world. By May of 1979, we were receiving offers weekly. We prayed over each offer, but none met all three of our basic criteria.

In September, I gave my three months' notice of resignation to my boss at the medical center. To my surprise, my non-Christian coworkers granted me a new level of respect for this. When my boss offered to double my salary if I agreed to stay, I thought, *Man, I should've threatened to quit years ago.*

One distinguished psychiatrist, who habitually punctuated his sentences with the profane use of Jesus' name, said that out of respect for me, he would stop dishonoring the name of my Lord.

Some of our Christian friends, however, accused us of acting irresponsibly. "Charity begins at home," they would say. "If you want to reach out to the lost, you should first focus on those in need in the United States."

My own father told me, "Son, if you and Ellen want to travel to the ends of the earth, as adults, that's your prerogative. But you have no right to take my grandchildren away from me and have them starve to death in some far-off country."

My father grew more and more agitated as we continued to pursue our plans. My mom, feeling the weight of his unhappiness, planned to talk to me after lunch one Sunday. But we had a schedule conflict that day and had to postpone our visit.

On Monday, Mom listened to a sermon by a well-known radio pastor, whose main text was taken from Mark 3:21, 31–35. The pastor spoke of how Jesus' mother and brothers were waiting to see Him. Based on other scriptural references, it appears that they were embarrassed about Jesus' activities and wanted Him to stop and return home. When someone told Jesus that His mother and brothers had demanded that He go out and talk with them, He said, "[W]hoever does the will of God is My brother and My sister and mother."

The message hit home with my mom. "God," she prayed, "are You telling me to keep my hands off?" She immediately knew the answer to her question and decided not to try to dissuade us from our decision to go.

The same Sunday that my mother had planned to try to deter us, a respected leader in our church pulled me aside and said, "I feel that as an older brother in the Lord, I need to admonish you. You must be aware that every young church is enamored with missionaries for a while. It might even put you in the budget for a season. But eventually, every church runs into budget problems, and the first item it cuts is the missionary budget. What will you do then while living somewhere out there in a jungle? Becoming a missionary is one of the most irresponsible things you could ever do. Think about your wife and your three young children. You must be practical. Drop this foolhardy idea."

In November, we told the children that we needed to pare down our belongings to fill only two suitcases each. By now we had a lot of stuff—bicycles, toys, stereos, furniture, televisions, cars—and we had to give it all away before the end of December.

We wondered how the kids would deal with giving up their belongings. Four Christmases earlier, we had gone into deep credit card debt to buy all the toys on the kids' Christmas lists. That Christmas had been a disaster. The children acted selfishly and ungratefully, and we were deeply grieved. We knew we had spoiled them and determined to never again go overboard. Since that time, the children's attitudes had improved significantly, but we had no idea just how much.

In early December of 1979, Ellen needed to buy a birthday gift for one of Michelle's friends. She took our three kids and two of their friends to Toys"R"Us in search of an inexpensive toy. Christmas shoppers crowded the store, their carts filled to the brim with hundreds of dollars' worth of games and toys. After several minutes of pressing through the crowds, Ellen managed to find an appropriate little toy and then led the kids to the checkout line.

Sean perked up at the sight of a large pile of empty boxes. "Wow, Mom! Do you think the manager would let us have some of those large boxes for us to make a fort?"

"Go and ask."

The queue had hardly moved by the time the kids came racing back.

"Mom, you'll never believe it. He said we could take as many as we want."

Ellen noticed that her little tribe had attracted the attention of the other shoppers. She turned her voice up one notch. "Kids, what would you think if you woke up on Christmas morning, and the only thing you found under the Christmas tree was a pile of empty boxes?"

"Wow!"

"Yeah!"

"That would be so cool!"

The kids ran to gather up the boxes. Ellen smiled sympathetically at the shoppers around her, who stared helplessly at their carts full of merchandise.

Nearly every day, I would return home from work to find that something else had been given away: our cars, our televisions, our comfortable king-size bed, my favorite chair. One day, I went to play our stereo, but it too was gone. Ellen had given it to a widow who had never owned a stereo but had been praying for one. For Ellen and the kids, the more they gave, the more they wanted to give.

I had a difficult time hiding my disappointment. I had thought that I had been the master of my belongings. Now I realized that my belongings had been the masters of me. Our children, by contrast, thought this was the best Christmas ever.

Now unencumbered by multiple earthly possessions, we felt ready to go anywhere. On December 6, 1979, we had a family meeting. I said that since I would soon be out of a job and someone else would be living in our house, we had to determine which mission we would join. The most likely candidate was a mission in Mexico that believed in the miraculous workings of the Holy Spirit and did not require us to send our children away to boarding school. The mission had an orphanage, and we had always loved working with kids. I would be administrating the mission's twelve-bed hospital facility. Twelve beds sounded so manageable.

Although learning new languages has always been difficult for me, Spanish seemed to be one of the least intimidating languages to learn, even though I had to take beginning Spanish twice in high school. In university, I took beginning Hebrew and barely passed. In fact, I think the only reason the teacher passed me was so that she would not have to see me in her class again. I assumed that I could only hope to learn a new language if it was at least Latin-based.

Our one concern with this mission organization was that it didn't meet our third criterion, vision for growth. It was in the process of downsizing. This, however, was becoming less important to us as our deadline drew near.

The next day, despite some misgivings, I drove to the Christian Service Corps headquarters in Washington, D.C., to talk to the director. I was just about to tell him my decision when a long-distance phone call interrupted us.

I overheard the director say, "You need a qualified health care administrator? Well, yes, I do know of one. He has nine years of experience. As a matter of fact, our agency has existed for twenty years, and in that time, we've had doctors, nurses, plumbers, electricians, all kinds of professions, but we've had only one hospital administrator, and he just walked into my office. Would you like to speak with him?"

He handed me the phone.

The voice on the other end introduced himself as Colonel Vic Lipsey. "I represent a mission organization called Youth With A Mission, Vic said. "Have you ever heard of us?"

"No," I said. "I'm afraid I haven't."

"Perhaps you've heard us called YWAM," he said.

"No, I've never heard of Why-Wam either."

Vic explained that YWAM was looking for a health care administrator to join its mission right away. It had just purchased a large ship, christened the *Anastasis* (meaning "Resurrection"), which it planned to partially convert into a hospital vessel for mercy ministries.

The United Nations had approached YWAM with an offer to pay for the refurbishment of the ship if YWAM would agree to transport groups of Hmong tribal people from Thai refugee camps to Guyana. Additionally, the Guyana government had offered to donate land to the Hmong people. The land had previously been owned by the cult leader Jim Jones. By killing all his followers along with himself, Jones had cast a dark shadow on the worldwide perception of Guyana, through no fault of the country itself. The government hoped that this humanitarian act toward the Hmong refugees would improve the country's international reputation.

YWAM had readily agreed to transport the refugees, but the United Nations had some stipulations before it would invest any money. First of all, it required YWAM to secure a qualified health care administrator.

Vic now asked me, "Would you be interested in joining us?"

I had a few questions of my own. "What's your policy on reaching the lost? Do you allow your workers to say that Jesus is the reason for their charity? Do you have a vision for growth, to reach more and more people with the Good News about Jesus?"

"Yes," he replied. "Our goal is to reach the whole world for Christ in this generation."

Okay, that's a bit much, but it certainly fulfills requirement number one.

"Also, I have a family. Does Youth With A Mission allow children to minister alongside their parents?"

Again his answer floored me. "Absolutely. As a matter of fact, we have a group called the King's Kids, which is designed specifically to release children into ministry. They have already had a powerful impact on thousands of people around the world."

Okay. Criterion number two: check.

I moved on to question number three: "Does Youth With A Mission believe in the power and guidance of the Holy Spirit in the lives of Christ's followers today?"

"Of course. If we are walking in God's will, whenever a need arises, God will supply. In fact, we're praying for the Holy Spirit to miraculously enable us to understand the Hmong people in their own language, since we don't have enough time to study their language. And we believe that the Holy Spirit will bring both emotional and physical healing to these poor, hurting people as we reach out to them with our prayers and our physical resources."

Wow! That has to be either the most absurd or the greatest faith-filled answer that I've ever heard.

"What kind of hospital will you have on board?" I asked. "Will you have a surgical ward?"

"We'll have everything, including operating rooms and fifty intensive care beds."

Now the credibility gap was seriously widening. They did have vision, but way more than I could handle. I didn't know of a single hospital in the entire world that had fifty intensive care beds, and those are hospitals that are located on solid ground. How could they possibly do this on water?

Before saying goodbye, I promised Vic that I would pray about sending my resume to him. That evening, when I related this telephone conversation to Ellen and the kids, they all became very excited.

Ellen said, "Let's pray and ask God if this is the mission for us."

"No way," I said. "I mean, not just yet, anyway. First, I need to investigate and make sure this is a legitimate Christian mission and not a cult."

Over the next few days, I called all over for information about Youth With A Mission. I could not find anyone who had ever heard of it. Finally, I asked my mother. She said that Loren Cunningham, the founder of YWAM, had once appeared as a guest preacher on *The 700 Club*. My mother had been so impressed that she had ordered an audio-cassette of his sermon.

A lightning bolt had recently started a fire in my parents' house. It had destroyed most of my mom's tapes, among other things. My mother still managed to find the Cunningham tape and gave it to me on the off chance that it still worked. I stifled a laugh as I looked at this deformed and blackened object that vaguely resembled an audiocassette.

Couldn't hurt to at least give it a try.

That Sunday, after putting the kids to bed, Ellen and I put the cassette in our tape recorder. To our surprise, the tape played flawlessly. Listening to the heart of Loren's words, we became convinced that this was a man who was totally sold out to God with an enormous capacity for servanthood, humility, and leadership. We listened to the tape again and again until four o'clock in the morning.

That day I dragged myself to work, and Ellen went to her Monday-morning prayer meeting. At the meeting, she expressed her excitement about Loren Cunningham's vision for YWAM, and the other women asked if they could listen to the tape. Ellen called me that afternoon to tell me what had happened next.

"Art," she said, "the tape wouldn't play. We thought at first that it must be a faulty machine, so we put the tape into another tape recorder, and then another. And when I got home, I tried it in our tape recorder again, and it still wouldn't work, no matter what I did. Honey, I think this is a sign from God."

Ellen's excitement would have normally captivated me, and her amazing testimony should have strengthened my faith. Instead, uncertainty and apprehension gripped my heart. If destroyed cassettes could mysteriously work for a single moment in time, how could one feel secure about any natural law?

That night, Ellen and the children wanted to pray about joining YWAM, but I was still hesitant. The following day, Ellen called me at work and told me she sensed that I was really struggling with fear.

"Don't be ridiculous," I lied.

"Are you sure?" she said.

"Of course. I'm fine."

"Good, because I mailed your resume to YWAM this morning."

"Oh. Uh…okay…" I had indicated to Vic Lipsey that I might send my resume, so I couldn't argue with what Ellen had done. But I definitely felt less than enthusiastic.

"Art," Ellen said, "why don't you call Colonel Lipsey and ask for more details about what would be expected of you if we did join YWAM. I'm sure you'd feel better after speaking with him."

I knew she was probably right, so I called him immediately. "Vic," I asked him, "if we did join YWAM and I became the hospital administrator on your ship, what would my job entail?"

"As the administrator, you would be responsible for everything," he said.

How I dislike vague words, especially the word *everything*. Needless to say, his answer did little to abate my fears.

"As an example," I said, "let's suppose that you did have at least one ICU bed and something went wrong with the life-supporting equipment in the middle of the ocean. Would I need to help repair it?"

"Yes, pray and improvise."

After that answer, I became more determined than ever not to join YWAM. I was sure that I could not possibly fulfill its expectations.

Over the next week, I received numerous phone calls from friends who, just weeks before, had never heard of YWAM. Now, it seemed that everyone had information to tell me about this mission group. YWAM had unwittingly launched an invasion against my little comfort zone. Scores of local churches had begun preparing for an upcoming "March for Jesus" at the nation's Capitol steps, and YWAM was the primary coordinator. The very next Sunday, December 16, a team of YWAMers spoke at our church.

"Honey," Ellen said after the Sunday service. "I think we know now that YWAM is legit. This is a good mission. Don't you think we should pray and ask God if this is the mission for us?"

"I know you and the kids believe that God is directing us toward YWAM," I said, "but I…I just don't know."

On Thursday, December 20, my good friend Dean Curry invited me to come to a prayer meeting during the lunch hour in his office at the U.S. Information Service. Just before the prayer time started, a guy stood up and said, "God has a message for someone in this room, and it's this: God isn't looking for men and women who will step out only in their own abilities and talents, because then they would receive the glory. Instead, God is looking for those who will step out in faith and do what God asks, regardless of their own small abilities. Then, when God's tasks are accomplished, He will receive all the glory."

That message hit me like a ton of bricks. I knew that God was speaking to me. After the meeting, I told God that if He wanted us to join YWAM, we would. As soon as I returned to my office, my secretary said that I had a long-distance phone call on hold. I picked up the phone and heard Vic Lipsey's voice on the other end. Vic said that they had reviewed and approved my resume and had forwarded it on to the United Nations, who had also approved it.

"So what have you decided?" Vic asked. "Will you join us?"

"If you had called any earlier, I probably would have said no, but now… What would we need to do to get started?"

"First, you and Ellen must complete a six-month DTS."

"What's a DTS?"

"Oh, I'm sorry. That's a Discipleship Training School. We have schools in hundreds of locations worldwide, but I would recommend that you train here in Kailua-Kona, Hawaii, where Loren Cunningham has his home base. The next school starts on January 3, but we'd like you to come a couple of days early."

"So you'd like us to arrive in Hawaii on January 1, 1980? Somehow I thought that might be the date you would suggest," I said, smiling at God's sense of humor. I told him that we would pray about it first thing and let him know our decision.

When I hung up the phone, I recalled Sean's prayer: "Dear Lord, when You send us to the mission field, please send us to Hawaii first."

FOUR

God Is Leading

EVEN though I still felt nervous about taking my young family away from the security of a home and weekly paycheck, I knew without a doubt that God was leading us. The Christian Service Corps had sent out a number of letters on our behalf asking for financial support, but we had received only a few firm commitments. We were grateful that we had at least a small sum stored up in our savings account. Our children were now ages six to nine, and I wondered how we would educate them overseas. As I look back, I am amazed at the courage God gave us to take such a huge step of faith.

We had already committed to attend a training course with the Christian Service Corps for the months of January and February, so we wouldn't be going to Hawaii just yet. On January 1, 1980, we moved into a temporary, two-bedroom apartment in Washington, D.C. As I locked the front door of our house in Maryland for the last time, my head spun with a mixture of nostalgia, trepidation, and excitement.

Had I known the journey that lay ahead of us, I'm not sure whether I would have been filled with more courage or more fear. I might have turned right around and said, "Okay, everybody, back in the house. We're not going anywhere."

On the other hand, if that prescient knowledge of the future had been accompanied by the same sense of peace and joy with which God has saturated our journey, I would not have just walked to the car. I would have sprinted, yelling, "Come on, you guys. What are we waiting for? Let's go!"

Just a few weeks later, one event especially served to fuel both our faith and our holy fear of God.

The Christian Service Corps required us to actively share the Good News about Jesus as part of our preparation. Talking with total strangers was not easy for me, but over time, I learned to enjoy it. Union Station in Washington, D.C., was an ideal place for witnessing, since many passengers arrived in the morning and had to wait the entire day to catch their connecting trains. During that long, boring waiting period, people were usually pretty grateful that we took the time to talk with them. We had the opportunity to counsel quite a few lonely and hurting people.

One afternoon at Union Station, we spotted a policeman standing in a corner.

Ellen said, "Art, we should go over and talk with him."

My mind thumbed through various arguments I could use to talk her out of it. "I don't know," I said.

"I really think we should."

I was hesitant, but I went along with her. It turned out that he appreciated the chance to break up the monotony of his job, and we seemed to really hit it off—until we mentioned that we were Christians.

"I grew up in a Christian home," the policeman said. "My family members are strong Christians, but I can't trust in God anymore. I'm not saying I'm an atheist. It's just that if God does exist, He's an unjust God."

"Why?" I asked.

"Just look at all the innocent people who suffer in this messed-up world," he said.

"Has something happened to you personally to make you feel this way?" I asked.

"Yes, as a matter of fact. When I grew up, I married the woman of my dreams, and we had a beautiful little girl. My life was wonderful. Then God pulled the rug out from under me. When our little girl was only three, my wife ran off with my best friend and took my daughter with her." His eyes grew red with restrained tears.

"I'm so sorry to hear that," I said. "I can imagine that this experience was unbearably painful. But I believe that God has been in pain along with you. God hates divorce. He hates it when relationships are damaged or destroyed. It's your ex-wife who deserves the blame, not God."

"Maybe," he whispered.

Then Ellen asked, "Did something else happen to cause you to feel that God is unjust?"

The man took a deep breath and then smirked. "Yeah. In the summer of 1963, when I graduated from high school, I decided to hike the Appalachian Trail with two of my friends. These two guys were total opposites. One of the guys planned to serve God as a missionary or pastor. As we hiked, he talked a lot about God's love and creativity. I thought to myself, 'Man. God's going to bless this guy. Maybe if I stay close to him, I'll get some of that blessing.' The second guy was really fun, but he took the Lord's name in vain a lot and would ridicule the other guy's faith. He'd say things like, 'You want to be a pastor? Pastors are people who aren't smart enough to get a real job. A missionary? You want to be a missionary? Missionaries are responsible for most of the problems in this world.' This guy joked and criticized; he took nothing seriously. I thought, 'This guy better be careful or he'll get struck by lightning.'"

The man then lowered his voice and said, "But God is not just. The first guy and I got drafted into the army and were sent to fight the war in Vietnam. One day, he saw a Vietnamese child crying and went to help. The kid was booby-trapped with a bomb, and in a matter of seconds, they were both dead. As for the second guy, the one I thought God would curse, I hear he's now some big shot at a hospital here in Washington, D.C. Go figure. He's apparently doing just great. You call that justice?"

His story sounded strangely familiar, and I began to feel extremely uncomfortable. My heart was pounding, not with excitement but with conviction.

After a few moments of internal wrestling, I managed to get the words out. "Are you…Fred?"

Taken aback, he paused, then looked more closely at my bearded face. "Wait a minute. You're not Art Sanborn, are you?"

You see, I was the blasphemous young man in the story that he had just told. I was the one he assumed would be struck down by lightning.

We both fidgeted a little. He had not meant to embarrass me, of course. I reflected on that hike so many years ago. I had just been joking around and having fun. I had had no idea that my careless words would be taken so seriously and leave such an impact. My thoughtless behavior had given cause for this man's broken relationship with God. I felt deeply ashamed, knowing that I had also grieved my heavenly Father.

I awkwardly told Fred that I was now a Christian embarking on overseas missionary service with my family, and I asked him to forgive me. I knew that this was the beginning of a long-awaited healing in his heart.

I needed this lesson on the power of words before becoming a missionary. I needed to remember that, just as God had created the universe with words, our words could be either constructive or destructive, bringing healing or pain. I was also awestruck that God loved us so much that He had arranged this divine appointment.

On March 9, 1980, the Sunday before we planned to travel to Hawaii, the elders and pastors of our church commissioned us, anointed us with oil, and gave us several words of encouragement. One of the men said something which at the time seemed strange but which later proved to be remarkably on target.

He said, "The door you plan to go through will close, and another door will open. This new door is the one I have commissioned you to go through. Right now you think you know God's destiny for you, but God's destiny for you will be revealed in His perfect timing."

A few days later, we had a tearful farewell from friends and family at the same train station where we had met Fred. We traveled by train from Washington, D.C., to San Francisco with three young kids and the ten suitcases that contained all of our remaining possessions. This was a bit overwhelming, but the kids proved to be real troopers. The subsequent long flight to Kona, Hawaii, only served to fuel their enthusiasm.

Since Loren Cunningham was out of town, Vic Lipsey met us when we arrived at the YWAM campus on March 14. Vic explained that they planned for us to board the *Anastasis* as soon as we had completed the three-month lecture phase of our DTS. When we told our DTS director, David Gustaveson, he said, "But the three-month outreach after the lecture phase is not optional. Who told you that you could skip that portion of your DTS?"

"A person with some influence in this mission," I said. "Loren Cunningham."

"Well," Dave said with a glint in his eye. "It is true that Loren has some influence in our mission, but I get my orders from God regarding this DTS. I'll talk it over with Loren and let you know."

Dave did not feel right about bending the rules for anyone, and Loren agreed that the outreach would be a helpful experience for us. The ship would just have to wait.

The primary purpose of the DTS lecture phase was to teach us to understand God's heart and character. The topic of intercessory prayer was taught by a wonderful New Zealander named Joy Dawson. Instead of just praying for our personal concerns and desires, Joy instructed us to ask God what He wanted us to pray for. This was a new but refreshing concept for us. We did not know then how crucial this lesson would be for us in our upcoming outreach.

We formed small groups of four to six people and went through the steps that Joy outlined for us. First, we thanked God in advance for revealing His heart to us, and we declared our submission to Jesus as our Lord. Second, we invited the Holy Spirit to convict us of any unconfessed sins and asked forgiveness. Third, under the authority of Jesus, we commanded all demonic voices in the spiritual realm to be silent. Fourth, we requested the Lord's help in quieting our own inner voices and imaginations. Lastly, we waited in expectation for God to speak to us.

During these prayer sessions, God would speak through that "still, small voice," giving us Bible verses, countries, pictures, people groups, or individuals for whom we would then spend time praying for God's peace, blessing, and protection.

In one of our first experiences in intercessory prayer, I led our small group. After going through all of the steps and then waiting a few minutes in silence, I asked, "Does anyone need more time?"

Everyone appeared to be ready, so I asked each of them to say what they felt God wanted us to pray for.

The first person said, "I got a vision of a young man on drugs, slumped down in an alley. I believe we're supposed to pray for his deliverance from addiction."

The second person said, "I think we are to pray for the YWAM coffeehouse ministry in Honolulu that reaches out to the prostitutes and street people around the bars and slum area of Hotel Street."

Ellen spoke next. "I know this will sound strange, but I saw the word *Keefe* in big red letters." She turned to an Indonesian student and asked, "Is that an Indonesian word, Joel?"

"Sorry," he said. "I've never heard that word before."

"That's okay, Ellen," I said. "Hey, we're all just learning this new way of listening to God's voice, so it's only natural that we'll sometimes make mistakes."

It was now my turn, so I gave the scripture verse that had come to my mind, 2 Peter 3:9: "[God] is longsuffering toward us, not willing that any should perish but that all should come to repentance."

I said, "Let's pray for this drug addict, that he would be ministered to by the people in the YWAM coffeehouse in Honolulu. Let's pray that he'll repent and be set free in Jesus. Then let's thank the Lord for telling us what He wanted us to pray."

The following Monday afternoon, Ellen was sorting mail in the school office. A letter addressed to a Reverend Mr. Dennis Keefe caught her eye. Keefe? Turning to Dave Gustaveson, she said, "Dave, who is this Reverend Mr. Keefe?"

"He was a student in our last DTS," Dave said. "He's on outreach in Honolulu now. As a matter of fact, I was just about to call his team. You can talk to him if you'd like."

"Absolutely," Ellen said.

A few minutes later, Dave handed Ellen the telephone. After brief introductions, Ellen said, "The reason I wanted to talk to you is that God gave me your name during our intercessory prayer time last Friday. Did anything special happen in your ministry over the weekend?"

"As a matter of fact, yes," Mr. Keefe said. "I was on my way to work at the YWAM coffeehouse, and there was a young guy sitting on the ground outside the entrance. He had just spent all of his money getting high on drugs, but when he passed our coffeehouse, he sobered right up. When he saw me, he said, 'I don't understand what's happening, but I know that somehow you people are behind it.'"

Mr. Keefe had then told the guy about God's love for him. The guy was so impacted that he repented and asked Jesus to be Lord of his life. The next day, he attended church for the first time in his life.

"I believe he really was delivered from his drug addiction and that he's on the way to getting his life straightened out. So tell me, what were you guys praying about?" Mr. Keefe asked.

Ellen told him how his story lined up exactly with what the Holy Spirit had directed us to pray. After hanging up, she ran to tell us how God had answered our prayers. "And the man who led the drug addict to the Lord?" She winked at me. "His name is Keefe."

FIVE

Tragedy Strikes

A F T E R completing the lecture phase, we went on an outreach to Honolulu. Despite our lack of experience in this realm, Ellen and I found ourselves leading a team of thirty-one, including the children. We all shared a large house on Kapiolani Boulevard and began taking on a great deal of ministry, including the coffeehouse, Bible studies, and church work.

The youngest member of our team was nineteen. Frank had grown up in a Christian family but had been rebellious during his earlier teen years. As far as we could tell, the only reason he even enrolled in the DTS was to appease his parents. During the DTS, though, Frank had a genuine encounter with God. He wasted no time in writing several letters asking forgiveness of people whom he had hurt.

During a group worship time on the morning of June 24, 1980, Frank cried out to God, "O Lord, never let me be tempted to return to my old lifestyle. Take me home to be with You first." Later, we would all be reminded of Frank's prayer.

Frank's dramatic lifestyle changes made him one of those people whom everyone enjoyed being around. Frank still loved listening to his heavy metal Christian rock music, however, with the volume on full blast. His roommates, being older and more mellow, asked him to please listen to his music elsewhere. After lunch on the third day of our outreach, Frank went looking for a spot to relax and listen to his music, boom box in hand. That evening, we began to worry when Frank didn't return for supper. Someone suggested that since Frank would be leading a group of teenagers in a Bible study that night, perhaps he had decided to fast in preparation. By six-thirty there still was no sign of him, so I appointed another person to lead the study, and the rest of us dispersed to attend to our various responsibilities.

It seemed out of character for Frank to be out so long without at least communicating his whereabouts. By ten o'clock everyone had returned, and we still had no word from Frank. Ellen and I were extremely worried, so we called the team together to pray for him. I asked each teammate what he or she sensed God was saying. Here's what the team said:

"I believe Frank's lying somewhere, and he's hurting."

"I got the phrase 'neck and swelling.'"

"I sense that Frank is in pain across his chest."

"It's hard to breathe. It's hard for him to breathe."

One student suggested, "Let's look for Frank in the local bars. He used to drink a lot before his conversion."

In my heart, I didn't want to believe that, but I suggested that we look for him near bars, alleys, and secluded areas. If Frank really was in danger, we had to find him as soon as possible. The mothers with young children stayed home to telephone the hospitals while the rest of us went out in groups of two or three. We searched most of the night without success.

In the early hours of the morning, I called the police to report Frank as a missing person. Then I drove to the airport to pick up Loren Cunningham, who was stopping in Honolulu to pick up a visa for his trip to Chiang Mai, Thailand. The timing was such an incredible blessing. I was desperate for any advice Loren might have for us.

When I told Loren what had happened, I was surprised to discover that he knew a lot about Frank's history. Loren wondered, as some of my fellow students had, if perhaps Frank had returned to some of his old habits.

"I know that's possible," I said, "but he had such a true heart conversion, and his behavior has reflected it ever since. I just can't believe that he would go back to his old lifestyle." I then told Loren about the prayer that Frank had prayed the day before.

Loren set aside some time to encourage and pray with our team. We were blown away, once again, by the wisdom and compassion of this man of God. Afterward, I took him back to the airport so that he could continue his trip to Asia.

Feeling rejuvenated, I returned home, only to find a police officer waiting for me. "I think we may have found your friend," he said. "Could you come with me?" I didn't have a clue where he was taking me until we pulled up in front of a building with a large sign that read "City Morgue."

"Come with me," he said.

Dazed and numb, I followed him. Once inside, I heard the chilling words, "Can you identify this body?"

The police officer pulled out a drawer from a refrigerated cabinet and turned back the sheet. It all seemed so unreal. How could a mortuary freezer suddenly become so swelteringly hot? So hot it was hard to breathe. And the fluorescent lighting was playing tricks on my eyes. That couldn't really be Frank's lifeless body I was looking at.

The police officer explained that Frank had been killed while sunbathing on the lawn of a nearby high school. He said that the school's maintenance man had accidentally run over Frank with his jeep.

My mind started to spin wildly until the words from Moses' song in Deuteronomy 32:3–4 pierced through the blindness of my thoughts. "Ascribe greatness to our God. He is the Rock, His work is perfect, for all His ways are justice."

Tears streaming down my face, I allowed the police officer to guide me back to his car. Staring blankly out the car window, I wondered who could possibly help us walk through this tragedy, since Loren and almost all of the leaders of YWAM Hawaii were away at an international leadership meeting in Thailand.

Back in our office, I began calling around to find out whether any YWAM leaders had stayed back from the international meeting. I learned that Peter Jordan, the director of the Kona Crossroads DTS, had remained on campus. Peter offered to help in any way he could. The first thing he did was to call Frank's parents, sparing me the heartrending chore of telling them that their only son was dead.

During the ensuing hours, the police were kind and helpful. However, by the next day, their attitudes had changed. They appeared to have turned against us and began treating us as though we were the ones who had committed a crime. They began harassing us for having thirty-one people living together in one house. They accused us of being a hippie drug commune. They then notified us that we were violating local zoning laws and I would therefore have to meet with the housing commissioner.

I spent much of the next three weeks filling out government forms and presenting them to various city government officials in meetings that dragged on for hours. In the midst of this chaotic nightmare, we strove to keep the team's morale up and to continue ministry.

Two days after I had identified Frank's body, the phone woke me up in the middle of the night. I peered through the blur of my eyes to see the clock. It was 3:30 AM. My hand searched for the phone and picked up the receiver. Frank's father, a prominent lawyer, was calling from Indiana, and he was irate. (It occurred to me that it was 8:30 AM in Indiana, and he probably wasn't aware of the time difference.)

"You lied to me," he said. "I'm not going to see my son again." His voice faltered. "When I first heard about Frank's death, I struggled but was able to accept it, because I thought my son was with the Lord… that…that I would see him again someday in heaven. In the midst of everything, this thought brought me comfort, but now…now I find out that you're a bunch of hippies and that my son died from drugs."

"That is absolutely not true, sir," I said.

"Well, I have today's newspaper in my hands. It implies that you are a cult and that Frank died from drugs."

I couldn't believe what I was hearing. Why would a newspaper nearly five thousand miles away print such a thing? It didn't make any sense. I had to get my thoughts together so that I could respond calmly and reasonably. Frank's father deserved at least that much.

"Sir," I said, "what you read in your local paper is a lie. We are not a hippie commune, and we do not do drugs. We are a group of Christians who are sharing the love of Jesus. Frank did give his life to the Lord. I am absolutely convinced that he is in heaven and that you will see him again. The paper is wrong. You must believe me."

At the end of our conversation, Frank's father was still distraught. For the rest of the night, turmoil arrested my thoughts and sent them spinning, keeping sleep at bay. First thing in the morning, I marched into the coroner's office in Honolulu and demanded to see the autopsy report on Frank. The coroner claimed that because of some further testing, the report would not be available for at least thirty days. I realized that he must have been looking for some sign of drugs in Frank's system.

Having worked in hospitals for years, I knew what had to be done. I called Frank's father to tell him that we would arrange for Frank's body to be sent home, and I pleaded with him to have an independent autopsy performed there. I breathed a prayer of gratitude when a few days later we received word that the autopsy completed in Frank's hometown revealed absolutely no alcohol or other drugs in Frank's body. The report cited the real reason for Frank's death: Frank had drowned in his own blood as the result of a heavy vehicle driven over his neck.

Frank's father graciously sought my forgiveness and asked if he could come to Hawaii to meet the team and investigate further. Greatly relieved, I welcomed him to do so. He arrived in Honolulu the following week, accompanied by one of his daughters, and we did everything we could to assist him. Through his investigations, he managed to piece together all the evidence. The following account is based on what I recall of his analysis:

On Monday, the day before his death, Frank had gone to the local high school to ask the custodian if YWAM could use the swimming pool. Frank felt it was a reasonable request, but the man refused permission. The two of them evidently had a rather heated exchange. When Frank returned to the YWAM house later that day, he was clearly a little disappointed but in good spirits otherwise.

The following day, with his music blaring, Frank was sunbathing on the lawn of the high school. The custodian apparently recognized him and decided to drive close to his head to give him a good scare. The custodian swore that he had not meant to hurt Frank but that his vehicle had hit a rock, throwing the jeep off balance. As a result, one of the wheels ran over Frank's neck. As the panic-stricken custodian sped away from the scene, Frank somehow managed to rise and stumble to a nearby house, where he apparently banged on the door before losing consciousness.

When the residents of the house returned home, they called the police. During that first critical hour, Frank might have been saved, but evidently no one sent for an ambulance, assuming that he was already dead. Instead, the police officers took photographs and performed investigative work. It appears as though the police turned against the YWAM team to cover up their own mistakes and protect the custodian, who, as a local, was "one of their own."

Once the whole story had been exposed, the police once again went out of their way to be helpful and kind. Frank's father asserted that he would not press charges and that he was not out for revenge. He simply wanted the truth. He went to talk with the custodian to extend forgiveness, but the man was too frightened to speak with him. We were all deeply touched by Frank's father's gesture.

During the next two weeks, Frank's family arrived and inspired us all. In the midst of their grief, they went out with us to minister to the poor, the drug addicts, the alcoholics, the homeless, and the prostitutes. In the following days as they ministered, they were often asked, "What do you know about pain and suffering? You obviously have everything you could possibly want." Their answers naturally dumbfounded the hearers. As a result, Frank's family were able to communicate that the true reason for their peace was Jesus.

We heard the most amazing account from one of Frank's sisters. On the day that Frank died, most of the family had been at a piano recital. Upon returning home, this sister had looked out of the car window. Thousands of miles away from Hawaii, she saw Frank at his bedroom window, warmly smiling and waving at her.

"Mom!" she said. "Frank's home. I just saw him in the window."

"It can't be, honey," her mother said. "Frank is still in Hawaii."

Undaunted, the girl sprinted up the stairs to Frank's room. She was baffled to find that he wasn't there. Later, when they learned of Frank's death, they calculated the time that they had arrived home from the recital, taking into account the difference in time zones. It was precisely the time that Frank had died.

SIX

Outreach in Honolulu

WE NOW understood at least one of the reasons why we had to wait five years before going into missions. I can't imagine how we would have dealt with these things had we been less mature and less dependent on God. We might even have returned home after the outreach. Despite all the difficulties and all that our team went through with Frank's tragedy, more than eighty people turned their lives over to God during our ninety-day outreach.

One of those people was an alcoholic who had been living on the streets for seven years. Ellen led him to the Lord and then brought him to me to disciple. I must admit that I felt inadequate to assist someone with problems as severe as his. "John" was in his mid-forties. He was half Samoan and half Native American. Before he came to live on the streets, he had been a merchant marine. He had been happily married and had a beautiful daughter. His life rolled along enjoyably until a crew member on his ship began antagonizing him.

This crew member fought John with increased intensity until John's hatred for this man consumed John's thoughts. One day, their ship was caught in a terrible storm. As the rest of the sailors fought to secure those things that could be in danger of washing away, these two men had another clash. When a huge wave turned their vessel completely sideways, the other man lost his balance and John shoved him overboard.

The man was declared lost at sea. Since John was considered mild-mannered, no one ever suspected him of this murderous act. John was free from his enemy, but now guilt became his tormenter. He couldn't shake the sight of his victim's face, that look of terror the moment that the man had fallen to his death.

John started drinking heavily in an attempt to forget, and he soon lost his job. His wife tried to help, but after two years, she gave up hope and moved to the US mainland with their daughter. Since that time, John had lived in a constantly inebriated state. At long last, after that seven-year stupor, he was now ready to deal honestly with the past.

I spent many hours with John. I explained that because of Jesus' sacrifice on the cross, we can be free of guilt, that His sacrifice has the power to cleanse our consciences completely. However, we must also accept the consequences of our actions. I urged John to report to the authorities what had happened. It would then be up to the law to decide what to do with this information. John took my advice and bravely confessed his actions to the police. I never heard the final ruling, but I do know that the authorities ultimately decided not to incarcerate him.

Immediately after making his commitment to Jesus, John stayed sober for two weeks. During that period, he underwent withdrawal and delirium tremens, but it was not nearly as severe as expected, considering the length of time that he had been intoxicated. Then, just as he seemed to be conquering his addiction, he succumbed to drinking again. This started a cycle in which he would achieve sobriety for one or two weeks only to once again fall off the wagon. I was beginning to wonder whether he was a lost cause.

One day he asked me, "Art, do you think God would help me be reunited with my wife and daughter?"

"Well," I said, "we know that God can do anything."

As I prayed with John for his wife and daughter, his eyes filled with tears, and I felt renewed compassion for him. Philosophically, I believed that all things are possible with God, but I'm embarrassed to admit that I didn't have much hope. For one thing, John had absolutely no idea where his wife was now living, and after seven years, it was pretty likely that by now she had remarried.

Another reason I wrestled with doubt was because of our experience with another homeless alcoholic that Ellen and I had met many times on Hotel Street (the red light district of Honolulu at the time). Christopher was an exceptionally intelligent man from Portugal. Because of his lifestyle, he had poor circulation that caused the skin on his legs to rot, giving off a terrible odor that, combined with the lingering stench of urine, made us feel nauseous.

Christopher told us that he had met Christians like us about five years earlier. They had been very kind. They put him through a detox program, gave him a room in their home, and helped him find a job. When it appeared that he had conquered his alcohol problem, he was invited to speak at churches and Christian fellowships. He would testify about how he had been an incurable alcoholic and how Jesus had delivered him from the demon of liquor.

"What happened?" I asked. "Why are you back on the streets?"

His answer was astonishing. "I guess I just missed my life on the streets."

Apparently, after living a productive life for a couple of years, Christopher had decided to go back to the bottle. He lost his job and then began stealing money from the people who had taken him in. His friends tried for a while to help him work through his addiction but eventually gave up and told him he would have to leave. At first, they would visit him on the streets, but it had now been a couple of years since he had last seen them.

"Don't you miss being sober and living a productive life?" I asked.

"Sometimes." He shrugged his shoulders.

"If you'd like some help to get off the streets again, we'd be willing to assist you," I said.

"It's no use. This is where I belong, and this is where I will die," he responded.

After our experience with Christopher, one can imagine how skeptical I was regarding John's chances at renewed happiness. But eight days before the end of our outreach, John ran up to me on the street.

"Art, thank you, thank you! How can I ever repay you?" With his enormous arms, he wrapped me in a big bear hug. "It was your prayers that brought my wife and daughter back to me."

"Wha...? Are you serious?"

"Yes. I was just walking down the street one day, and suddenly, there she was. She was amazed to see me sober, and I was able to tell her that I hadn't had a drop in twenty-one days. It was the first time she'd returned to Hawaii in all these years. She was here to visit an old friend when we ran into each other. When I told her that I had given my life to Jesus almost three months ago, she said that she had become a Christian over five years ago and had been praying for me ever since. Art, she never filed our divorce papers. We're still legally married, and—can you believe it—she's willing to give me another chance." His voice broke off at the end as he struggled to hold back the tears.

"Wow," I said. "That's incredible. What a miraculous answer to prayer."

I looked at John, so full of hope, and could hardly comprehend that he was the same man. As I hugged him, I also embraced a deeper realization of God's power. I knew that John's journey would not be easy, but I also knew that we were both serving a God who could accomplish anything.

Another guy we met during this time, Brian, was a transsexual. A couple of the girls on our team had spent a lot of time with him, and after ten weeks, Brian submitted his life to God. When the girls brought him to me, I thought he was a woman. I soon learned that he had been born a male but in addition to taking estrogen pills, he had begun a series of operations to become female. I had never met anyone like this before, and I felt ill-equipped to counsel him.

"I'm happy to do what I can to help you," I said, "but I'll be in Honolulu for only another two weeks. You really need someone who can mentor you over a long period of time."

As we sat talking in the coffeehouse, Brian began inundating me with questions. "But tell me," he said, "will God restore my body back to the way it was before my operations? Should I ask God to help me to be drawn toward women, or, since I'm attracted to men, should I complete the sex-change operations? Can I marry and father children and live a normal life? Will God ever forgive me for mutilating my body?"

I took a deep breath, and before Brian could think up another avalanche of challenging questions, I said, "There's no question that God can and will forgive you. I don't know whether God will restore you to your old body or give you an attraction for women, because sometimes we have to live with the consequences of our choices and actions."

As we talked, I did my best to be helpful, but I knew that I was way out of my league. It's difficult balancing nonlegalistic love and unhesitating truth.

"Does God hate homosexuals?" Brian asked.

"Absolutely not," I said. "God doesn't hate homosexuals. God is the very definition of love. He makes it very clear that He hates sin, but He loves the sinner. And we are all sinners. It's true that the Bible says, 'neither fornicators, nor idolaters, nor adulterers, nor homosexuals, nor sodomites...will inherit the kingdom of God' (1 Corinthians 6:9–10). However, many heaven-bound people—even some of the great men and women of the Bible—have been guilty of practicing one or more of these sins, but they repented, turned their lives around, and were forgiven."

"That's me," Brian said. "I was guilty, but I've told Jesus how sorry I am, and I know He's forgiven me. I've changed. I'm not the same as I was."

"That's wonderful, Brian. Do you mind my asking why you started having sex-change operations in the first place?"

"My psychiatrist told me that emotionally I'm a woman trapped in a male body, so changing my sex would benefit my mental and emotional health."

"I'm so sorry," I said. "You know, I'm not a trained psychiatrist, but while I was working at a hospital in D.C., I was privy to research—from Harvard, I think it was. In their study, one hundred percent of those having sex-change operations showed no emotional or mental health improvement, and a large percentage actually got worse, just as you, yourself, have experienced. You really need a professional counselor who is Christian and can guide you through all of this. Also, we need to find you a good church that will accept and love you just as you are."

My heart broke as I realized what a tall order that would be. Would people be able to get beyond their human hang-ups and see this guy the way Christ saw him, with absolute acceptance?

Over the next ten days, we met and spoke with several pastors, but most felt, as I did, that they were unqualified to adequately counsel Brian. Others said that their congregations would have a hard time receiving a man who had been surgically altered to look so much like a woman. This man desperately needed the healing touch of acceptance and loving guidance from a caring church family, and I was getting increasingly concerned that we would leave without finding such a church.

In the last few days of our outreach, Dave Gustaveson visited our team, along with his DTS assistant, Paul Hillhouse.

Paul asked me, "Have you located a church that's willing to disciple Brian yet?"

I sighed. "No, but we're still looking and praying."

"I told a friend of mine, Pastor Cohen, about this guy," Paul said. "He has a real heart for people with special needs and said he'd love to disciple him. The only problem is that he lives on the island of Kauai. Do you think Brian would be willing to move away from Honolulu?"

"I'll ask him," I said.

Brian seemed keen on the idea and said he had a Christian grandmother who lived in Kauai. When we contacted her, she told us that she had been praying for him all his life and would be absolutely delighted to have her grandson live with her. He didn't waste any time in moving to Kauai. The church there heartily embraced him, as did his grandmother. We were overjoyed at how God had answered a grandmother's prayers.

Meanwhile, my parents had uncharacteristically surprised us with a visit. My dad joined me on my daily rounds. After a few days, he asked, "Son, do you think it's wise to have my grandchildren working alongside you and Ellen when you minister in the red-light district?"

"Dad, I can understand your concern," I said, "but actually, we purposely want to expose them to the terrible consequences of immorality, abusing alcohol, and using drugs. And we want them, even at their tender ages, to experience the joy of reaching out to the untouchables of society, to see that helping others does make a difference. And you wouldn't believe what a difference it makes to these people when they receive a hug or even just a smile from one of our kids. The kids are quite the little missionaries."

While conversing, we came upon Christopher, my Portuguese friend, lying in the gutter. He was in terrible distress. His legs, which were usually a light purplish color, had darkened considerably. The lower parts of his legs had become almost black.

"Please," Christopher whispered, "take me to a hospital."

With great difficulty, we managed to lay him in the backseat of my dad's rental car. As Dad started the car, I told him the fastest route to the nearest hospital.

"No," Christopher said. "I'm a veteran. Take me to Tripler, the military hospital."

We drove to Tripler, as requested, and delivered Christopher into the capable hands of the emergency personnel. The next day, we returned to Tripler to check in on him. Even though he looked pale and his legs were wrapped in gauze, he was in great spirits. He and my father engaged in a very witty and entertaining conversation. After about an hour, I explained that we had to go, but before we left, I prayed for him, asking God to heal his legs.

As Dad and I said our good-byes, Christopher grabbed each of our right hands. He tearfully thanked us for rescuing him. Then he said, "The doctors have told me that if I don't change my lifestyle, I will lose my legs and possibly my life. I want you to know that, with God's help, I'll start living right, starting today."

As we took the elevator down to the ground floor, my dad mumbled, "I need to get out of here before you make a missionary out of me."

I knew this was my dad's way of saying that I finally had his approval.

One hot and muggy Friday morning, in the closing weeks of the outreach, we almost had a mutiny on our hands. Ellen and I had just returned from picking up free eggs for the team when one of the older team members met us at our front door.

"We've all discussed it and decided that we will not minister today as scheduled," he said. "We're all going to the zoo instead. You can come or not. It makes no difference to us."

A few days earlier, our team had spent all day at the beach. The sizzling Hawaiian sun had left us with sunburns and depleted energy levels. Now it was Friday, and we were facing our two busiest days of the week, Saturday and Sunday.

"Look," I said. "I know everyone's tired, including me, but let's take some time to ask God about it."

"As I said, do whatever you want. The rest of us are going to the zoo."

Ellen and I met with our faithful assistant leaders, Diane and Matt. To be honest, part of me hoped that God would, indeed, direct us to cancel our ministry obligations for that day.

Praying in the way we had learned in our DTS, we received two scriptures. My heart sank as I read the first: "If anyone will not work, neither shall he eat" (2 Thessalonians 3:10). The second reference was a little more encouraging but was still clearly directing us to press on: "Strengthen the weak hands, and make firm the feeble knees" (Isaiah 35:3).

I repeated these verses to the rest of the team and said, "Guys, we believe we're to go out as scheduled. We've already obligated ourselves, and we think it would be irresponsible to cancel at such a late hour. I'm giving you the choice, but we'd sure appreciate your help."

The whole team reluctantly agreed, with the exception of the man who had originally confronted us. That man took his family to the zoo.

After a routine day of ministry, we piled into the vans in the evening. I scanned the weary faces of our team members and wondered how we could possibly accomplish anything while so fatigued. They all chose their assignments, leaving Ellen and me to serve at the coffeehouse ministry. Words could not express how grateful I was to be near such a ready supply of caffeine.

Even the caffeine didn't seem to help, however. I was about to resort to propping my eyelids open with toothpicks when a young man walked in. He had a wild haircut that was dyed a sort of purplish red. He said that during the past few weeks he had talked with other members of our team, who had told him how they had found hope for their lives through Jesus.

He said to me, "They told me that there is a Creator God who is all love."

With all the strength I could muster, I managed to nod my head and say, "Uh-huh."

"But Adam and Eve betrayed God and gave the authority that God had given them to Satan," he said.

Again I nodded.

"Then Satan brought pain, disease, and death into the world."

"Uh-huh."

"But Jesus, who is the one and only true Son of God, came and did lots of miracles. He was killed but came back to life and defeated Satan, and if I accept Him, He will forgive me and change me."

I couldn't believe what I was hearing. This man had done all his own research, and I didn't have to say a thing. I just nodded, said "uh-huh" a few times, and watched this man lead himself to the Lord.

By the time we closed the coffeehouse that night and picked up the other team members from their various locations, we had all been transformed. Fifty-seven people had committed their lives to God (which was more than double the amount of commitments during the other eighty-nine days of the outreach combined). Our Indonesian team member, Agus, had talked to a group of dancers from Bali, and twenty-eight of them, all Hindus, wanted to accept Jesus as their Savior.

Our team, now alert, awake, and laughing, talked late into the night, relating the astounding things that God had done. We had witnessed God moving in ways that we had not seen in any other day of the outreach, before or after.

As for the family that went to the zoo? It rained, and they ended up exhausted, soaking wet, and miserably sick. I truly felt bad for them. The rest of us spent the remainder of the outreach ministering with more energy than we could have thought possible. We had given to God what little energy we had left, and He had filled us with a strength that was way beyond our means.

Besides, who needs a zoo when you're living with thirty other crazy Christian missionaries?

SEVEN

Secret Agent Man

AS OUR Honolulu outreach came to a close, we learned that the leaders of the repressed Hmong people had turned down the invitation to resettle in Guyana. Having escaped from socialist dictators, the Hmong said they had no desire to end up in yet another socialist country. They would rather remain in the Thai refugee camps until they could find permanent homes. Understandably, the United Nations had to rescind its offer to refurbish the *Anastasis*, since it would not be using the ship after all.

Now the *Anastasis* would have to be dry-docked in Greece for at least a year while YWAM raised the funds needed for repairs and remodeling. That meant it would be a while before YWAM would need me to serve as the ship's hospital administrator. Ellen and I accepted Dave Gustaveson's offer to staff the next two DTS sessions. Even though we were a little disappointed about the delay in our original plans, we looked forward to working with Dave.

Returning to Kailua-Kona, we once again moved our whole family into just one room at a place called King's Mansion, where we came to know and appreciate YWAM even more. Dave was an outstanding leader, though his schedule demanded that he travel quite often, leaving either me or John Davidson in charge. Dave explained that this was one of his methods for training leaders. "I have the gift of leaving," he would joke.

We continued to be stretched and challenged and had a number of terrific students who went on to become pillars in our mission (dear friends like Ron and Judy Smith, Bob and Kathy Fitts, and Mark Nakatsukasa). Our three children attended the local Christian school.

Our days were full, but not always with work. I'll never forget the day we decided to take our kids to a remote beach. The scenery was just as breathtaking as we had been told. The crystal clear water, which washed onto a beach unspoiled by civilization, provided a perfect setting for snorkeling.

We were so overwhelmed by the dazzling incandescent rainbows of life swimming beneath the ocean that we lost track of time. When we noticed that the sun was nearing the horizon, we gathered our belongings and began our trek back up the mountain. In those days, the trek to this beautiful tropical bay, called Captain Cook Cove, was little more than a footpath. The multimile trek down to the cove had not been that difficult, but the hike back was steep, rocky, and strenuous. Worst of all, we had neglected to pack enough drinking water, though we had packed a lunch.

Less than a mile up, seven-year-old David said, "Daddy, I'm so tired. I can't walk anymore. Would you carry me?"

"Sure, son," I said and lifted him onto my back.

A few minutes later, eight-year-old Michelle said, "I'm so tired and thirsty, I can't walk another step."

Balancing David on my back, I lifted Michelle into my arms.

Not much later, ten-year-old Sean said, "I'm exhausted, Dad. Think you could carry me, too?"

I looked pleadingly at Ellen, who said, "Don't look at me. I was hoping you could carry me as well."

At this point, I stopped and said, "Kids, I'm exhausted too. We need to pray for God's help."

I tried to hide my fear as we prayed together. I was scared that our young children might suffer heatstroke and dehydration, and I was angry at myself for putting them in such a dangerous position. After we prayed, I encouraged everyone to just put one foot in front of the other and do the best he or she could.

We resumed our slow trek up the side of the mountain when, seemingly out of nowhere, a beat-up pickup truck, driven by an elderly, distinguished-looking Hawaiian gentleman appeared. The man was strong and broad-shouldered with black-gray hair. We were stunned that a vehicle could have approached us from the trail behind us, since the trail seemed quite impassable for anything more than a dirt bike.

The man said, "Hey, would you like a ride?"

"Yes, please," we all replied.

Ellen and the kids jumped into the back of the truck, and I sat with the driver in the front cab. As we drove, the man asked me questions about my relationship with Christ.

"Have you given your life to Jesus?"

"Yes, sir," I answered.

"How did you meet Him?"

To the obvious delight of the old gentleman, I spent the rest of the ride sharing my testimony.

When we arrived at the main road, the man asked, "Do you want me to drop you off at King's Mansion?"

"No, thanks. If you could just drop us here at the gas station, we can buy some drinks. Then we'll be able to walk the last few yards home."

After thanking the man profusely, I handed out money to Ellen and the kids to buy some drinks from the soda machine. I then turned back to watch the man drive away. Thanks to him, we would actually be home before sunset. As I whispered a prayer of gratitude for this man who had been such an angel of relief to us, I noticed that the truck had no license plate.

That's odd, I thought.

Suddenly, without turning, the truck just seemed to evaporate. I didn't even remember blinking, but somehow, the truck had vanished. I stared down the long, empty stretch of road before me. Were my eyes just playing tricks on me, or had we just encountered a truck and driver that were unrestricted by natural limitations?

"Did you see that?" The question came blaring in full stereo as Sean and I spoke simultaneously.

"Hey, where did the driver go?" Ellen asked.

"That's what I mean," Sean said. "You saw it, too, right?"

"Yeah," I said. "I mean, it's not what I saw so much as what I didn't see. He just seemed to vanish into thin air."

It certainly could have been some intense optical illusion, but we couldn't escape the alternate notion that we had just been rescued by an angel. As incredible as it sounded, we had no more logical explanation for such an illogical incident. After all, angels don't need license plates.

Joe and Colleen Harbison, the directors of YWAM Thailand, came to help staff the next DTS with us. As we met together weekly to pray for Thailand, a special love was birthed in our hearts for both the Thai people and the Harbisons. We offered to work and minister with the couple in Thailand until the ship needed us.

The Harbisons didn't wait for us to ask twice. They excitedly began prepping us, teaching us about the Thai culture and language, and telling us about the work that we'd be involved in. The leadership of the *Anastasis* also recommended that we go ahead to Thailand. They anticipated that the ship would someday minister in Asia and felt it would be beneficial for us to become familiar with an Asian language and culture.

We began preparations for our March 1981 departure, anticipating that we would stay in Thailand for only one or two years. Once again, we each had to give away anything that would not fit into two suitcases.

Just before leaving Hawaii, we heard the disconcerting news that President Reagan had been shot, though not fatally. I must admit I was grateful that I no longer served as an administrator at George Washington University Hospital, where former friends and colleagues of mine were now attending to the president. I could imagine the chaos that would accompany such an event, especially amid the disruptive clamor of the press.

En route to Asia, we heard more unsettling news on the radio: "Fighting in Bangkok, as rebel forces try to overthrow Prime Minister Prem's government..."

"How can we go to Thailand in the middle of a war?" I asked Joe.

"Don't worry, Art," he said. "Coups d'etat are fairly routine in Thailand, but as long as King Bhumibol reigns, things should stay stable."

Thankfully, the coup was over by the time we arrived in Thailand. On our way there, however, Joe and I stepped into a hornet's nest of our own during an extended stopover in Hong Kong.

While in Hong Kong, we learned of a ministry that recruited Westerners to hand deliver Chinese Bibles into mainland China. Even though taking Bibles into China was not officially illegal, customs officials generally confiscated these precious books. The authorities would then issue a receipt so that the foreigners could get their Bibles back when they left China.

Recently, though, the authorities had arrested and imprisoned an Asian woman for the possession of several Bibles. Our alarmed friends wondered whether this was a change in policy or just an isolated case. They decided that the safest way to find out was to send the Bibles with Americans, since China was in the process of trying to obtain a preferred trade status with the US government.

Joe and I readily volunteered to be God's smugglers. Joe demonstrated his obvious experience in Bible smuggling by carefully wrapping each Bible to look like a gift and then placing it in the bottom of his suitcase beneath his carefully folded clothes.

I followed Joe's example and gift wrapped each pocket-sized book. But then I got a little carried away. Wanting to make this trip as productive as possible, I stuffed my suitcase to the brim with Bibles, leaving just a thin layer of clothes at the top. Then I donned some baggy clothes that I had found in a giveaway bin, which gave me plenty of room to tape several more books to my body. I taped six books across my chest and stomach and four books on each leg. A string held up three books in each sleeve of my raincoat. I casually draped the raincoat over my arm, since it was too warm to wear it.

I thought I was well disguised, but when we boarded the train to Mainland China, Joe took one look at me and said, "Y'know, maybe we should split up until we've made it through customs." Since this sounded like the way trained spies would do it, I eagerly agreed. I had grown up watching James Bond movies, and now I felt like a double-0 agent for God.

At the border, I breezed through immigration, but customs would likely be a different story. I surveyed the room, looking for a customs officer who would not intimidate me. I decided that I would avoid all female and young officers, since I had learned that women and younger men generally had to work harder to gain recognition. I looked for a relaxed, middle-aged man, a family man who saw more to life than his job.

I spotted such an agent and parked myself at the end of his line. There was only one problem. All the other customs agents had small queues, but this line had attracted roughly twenty customers. I wondered what *they* were smuggling.

I gazed around the room. A large-boned female agent with a stern face caught my eye and motioned me over to her line. My heart skipped a beat, and I pretended that I hadn't seen her. To my dismay, she sent two police officers to escort me. One of the officers reached down to pick up my suitcase, but I quickly grabbed it.

"That's all right," I said. "I can get it. I mean it's really not that heavy."

I realized that I shouldn't have said anything, though, when I began to feel my face turning bright red, veins popping out of my neck in the strain to carry my overstuffed suitcase. The police officer eyed me suspiciously while I struggled to repress the grunts that came with each breath.

As I approached the customs agent, I told myself, *You can do this. Just be cool and calm. Pretend that you are Bond, James Bond.* The agent gave me a cold stare and then started bombarding me with questions. "You have television? How about VCR? Tape recorder? You got computer equipment? Watches? Cameras? Jewelry? Radio? Electrical appliances?"

I answered each question with a simple, "No ma'am," bracing myself for that inevitable question: "You have books? Bibles?" I knew I would have no choice but to be honest if the question came. All the agent had to do was unzip the suitcase to discover the truth, not to mention that lying would hardly be an effective way to honor God.

Man, it is so hot in here.

I began to tremble slightly. My body refused to cooperate with my commands to stay cool. Before long, trembling gave way to shaking, and light perspiration gave way to profuse sweating. As the sweat poured down, my clothing started to cling to my body, revealing the imprint of the Bibles on my chest. The tape on my legs became wet and pulled away from my skin, just barely hanging on to the leg hair. Instead of emulating James Bond, I was more like one of the Three Stooges. I knew the customs agent saw "guilt" written all over my face.

"Dear God," I silently prayed, "I need to get these Bibles into the hands of my Christian brothers and sisters, but I'm completely inept. There's no way these Bibles will get through customs unless You step in with a miracle. God, please help me."

Just then a high-ranking official in an observation room shouted down to my customs agent. He spoke what sounded like Cantonese and held his right hand to his ear in the universal sign of the telephone.

The customs agent dismissed him with a wave of her hand. She was obviously more interested in the suspicious stooge in front of her. The official then shouted out something that sounded like a name, and all at once, the woman's demeanor changed. The woman softened, and her snarl turned into a shy, love-struck grin. Until she looked back at me. She glared at me for a moment and then said, "Go on through."

I reached down to pick up my bag just slowly enough to see her turn and pick up the phone. Undoubtedly, the caller was someone very special to her. I was amazed at how quickly God had answered my prayer. They had not even opened my suitcase.

I shuffled out of there as fast as I could without attracting more attention. Just as I was about to reach the stairs that would lead to my escape, the Bibles taped to my leg began falling out. I discreetly picked up the fallen Bibles and stuffed them into my pockets. I wiped away the sweat that had begun blurring my eyes and rushed up to meet Joe at the top of the stairs.

"Your slip is showing," Joe said.

What an absurd thing to say to a man.

Joe pointed to my raincoat. There, boldly dangling back and forth by a string from my coat sleeve, was a Bible. I stuffed the book back into the sleeve.

"Art," Joe said, "look what's happening in the line that you originally chose."

That customs official was thoroughly examining every suitcase, and he had officers frisking every single person.

"Thank you, Lord," I prayed.

Western tourists were required to enter China as a part of a tour and stay with the tour guide at all times, so we now headed straight for our tour bus.

As we boarded the bus, I whispered, "Well, Joe, here we are in China. What do we do next?"

Joe whispered back, "Our contact person will meet us in the men's room at the art museum."

Joe and I found seats toward the back of the bus. As soon as it seemed safe to do so, I took the Bibles from my chest, legs, and coat and crammed them into our two suitcases. My already-baggy pants and shirt now looked even sloppier.

Our guide stood up and announced a change in plans. She said that because it had taken the group longer than usual to get through customs, we had to skip the first scheduled stop, the art museum.

Joe spoke up. "But we came to Mainland China just to see this museum."

"We have to go there," I said.

"So sorry. No time," our guide said.

We refused to take no for an answer, so she ordered us off the bus, pointed north, and said, "You walk. Art museum only two kilometer that way."

Lugging our suitcases down the road, we breathed a sigh of relief when we at last sighted the museum. We bypassed the exhibits and went directly to the men's room. Then the waiting began. Ten, twenty, thirty minutes passed with no sign of our contact person.

Super-spies that we were, we still attracted enough attention. It was hard to avert the puzzled stares of those who passed in and out of the restroom. I guess for some strange reason, they weren't accustomed to people admiring the bathroom mirrors and wall tiles with the same level of fascination devoted to the other exhibits in the museum.

A full hour passed before it occurred to us that in a large museum like this there might be more than one men's room. Brilliant deduction, I know. I offered to go find out. I exited the room and casually sidled up to the information desk. I cleared my throat to get the attention of the woman behind the desk.

"Excuse me," I said. "Could you tell me how many men's restrooms there are in this museum?"

"Enough," the woman said.

"But how many exactly is enough?" I felt stupid asking this question but could not think of a more suave approach.

"Why you wanna know how many restroom in museum?" she said.

"Well, I see one over there in the corner." I pointed to the restroom I had just left. "Is there another one?"

Looking at me as if I needed a mental ward instead of a men's room, the woman pointed out another restroom outside the building. I thanked her for her assistance and then went to get Joe. As inconspicuously as possible, we carried our ridiculously heavy bags to the outside restroom. To our joy and relief, we met two Chinese men there with suitcases similar to ours. Joe confirmed that they were our contacts.

"Why so late?" one of them said.

We tried to explain, but the language barrier kept us from communicating fully. At any rate, the men made it clear that they were very grateful for the Bibles, which Joe and I were relieved to hand over. We transferred all the books to their bags, and they headed out. We then realized that our previously bulging suitcases now looked conspicuously emaciated. We filled the suitcases with toilet paper and paper towels and, pretending that our bags required a sufficient amount of exertion, made our way out of the museum.

About an hour later, we reached the hotel where we had arranged to rendezvous with the rest of the tour group for lunch. Joe and I carefully but honestly fielded questions about our vocations. In this 100-degree weather, my ridiculous choice of clothing garnered a lot of stares.

Despite everything, we had accomplished our mission. And I learned that God doesn't need a James Bond or an Indiana Jones to get His work done. With God, even a stooge can do the impossible.

EIGHT

Smuggler's Paradise

W H E N we landed in sizzling, humid Bangkok, we experienced a new dimension to the word hot. In America, we threw around clever hyperbole to describe heat, but here such figures of speech became gross understatements. The pavement was hot enough to melt your shoes if you were not careful to keep moving. We were relieved to learn that April was the hottest month of the year, which gave us hope that the weather would eventually get better.

To our surprise, the crowded, dusty streets showed no sign of the military fighting that we had seen on the news just days before. The unsuccessful coup d'etat had ended, leaving no noticeable imprint that it had ever even happened.

After ten days, we traveled to Chiang Mai. Flying over the city for the first time, our whole family had the uncanny sense of being home. How extraordinary, considering the fact that Thailand was such an exotic country. Nothing was familiar—the language, the food, the holidays, the culture—yet all of us concluded upon arrival, "We're home."

The Thai people were true to their reputation. This was certainly the land of smiles, and we fell in love with these precious people almost immediately. We also hit it off with the rest of the little YWAM team: Julie, Judy, and Mike.

We had arrived in Chiang Mai just in time for Easter. Not wanting to disappoint our kids, Ellen and I combed the city for any kind of familiar candies or chocolates to fill their Easter baskets, but to no avail. We realized once again what a challenge it would be to foster traditions and make memories for our young family.

A little disheartened, we ended up filling the kids' Easter baskets with fruit, wondering how our children would respond to these non-traditional offerings. The next morning, if the kids were at all disappointed, they definitely didn't show it.

"We didn't expect to get Easter baskets at all," Sean said, and Michelle and David wholeheartedly agreed. What an inexpressible joy to see our children so grateful for the simplest of things.

Church that morning was definitely a change of pace for all of us. We sat through a three-hour service in a language that we couldn't understand. There was no denying the sentiment of the words, though. These were our brothers and sisters declaring the praises of God in their own uniquely Thai way. Despite the language barrier, we found that we still thoroughly enjoyed the service. Ellen was even moved to the point of tears.

We were also pleased at how valiantly our kids endured the long, unintelligible proceedings without a peep of complaining. After church, God rewarded them with an unexpected blessing. The Dunhams, whom we had only just met, graciously invited us to join their family for an Easter egg hunt, giving our kids the opportunity to release all of their pent-up energy in their favorite Easter activity.

Dan and Mary Dunham were two of the most respected missionaries in all of Thailand, and they earned a permanent place in our hearts as they welcomed us into their home and into their family. Their kids, Vangie, Darin, and Joshua, reached out to our kids as if they'd always been buddies. In the evening, we attended an English-speaking church and met dozens of missionaries from other organizations. We were so encouraged to see that we weren't alone.

Our children enrolled in the local mission school, which had just a handful of kids in each grade, and they loved it. Since we all sensed that Thailand was going to be our home much longer than we had planned, Ellen became more than a little apprehensive when she learned that the school had no classes higher than eighth grade.

"We can't send our children to boarding school," she said. "I couldn't bear it."

"Honey," I said, "Sean is only in fifth grade. We have three years to come up with a solution. Let's cross that bridge when we come to it."

Ellen took heart and trusted our kids once again into God's hands.

We met daily as a team to pray and strategize, and Ellen and I began language study. Our team juggled a variety of ministries. We ran an international preschool, hosted outreach teams, taught English classes for university students, assisted Thai pastors in discipleship, and visited prisons to help out in any way that we could. We were gradually adjusting to our new life.

In May, Joe volunteered himself and me to deliver Bibles across the border to the Chinese province of Yunnan. Several Thai ministries had banded together to collect over 3,400 Chinese Bibles at the request of seventy Chinese churches bordering Burma.

During the cultural revolution of the 1960s, the Chinese government had confiscated everything belonging to the churches, including Bibles. Then in the 1980s the churches had requested the return of their possessions, and the government amazed them all by doing just that— to a point. The government returned an average of less than one Bible per church. The churches now called on their Christian brothers and sisters in Thailand for help, and we were glad to assist.

We left Chiang Mai in three pickup trucks filled with more than a thousand Bibles per truck and drove straight to the area of Burma known as Smuggler's Paradise. There, on the banks of the treacherous Salween River, the Burmese smuggled teakwood, heroin, and precious stones into Thailand. In the opposite direction flowed opium and weapons, including M-16 and AK-47 assault rifles, mortar shells, bombs, and land mines. Khun Sah, the infamous drug warlord, controlled this area with his ruthless, well-equipped army. The national armies stayed clear.

Because the swift current of the Salween River proved perilous for the inexperienced, we commissioned local boat owners to carry our Bibles across the river. After we had piled all of the books into long, narrow boats with forceful tail motors, an Asian man wearing green army fatigues approached me. He seemed friendly, and I was curious though somewhat apprehensive of his interest in me.

"I know who are you."

He certainly had my attention. "Really? Who do you think I am?"

"You, Christian missionary. I never see white man here before, but I know only white man crazy enough to come here—Christian missionary."

I wasn't sure whether I should be disturbed or flattered by such a statement. I've learned that besides having the fruit of the spirit, craziness is one of the highest pinnacles a person can reach. If Solomon had asked for craziness instead of wisdom, I wonder whether God might have said, "It's not quite as noble a request as wisdom, but almost as useful."

I smiled at the man. "You are absolutely right. I am a Christian missionary."

He grinned, no doubt pleased with his cunning detective work. "I now say who I am. I commander of this territory, and I welcome you. Stay. Teach my people about your God."

Wow. That was the last thing I expected to hear. "That is a very gracious invitation. Let me ask the others."

I asked the leader of our expedition if we could stay at Smuggler's Paradise for a day or two longer to fulfill the commander's request. He explained that staying longer could jeopardize the whole operation. We were on a strict time schedule.

I relayed his answer to the commander. "But," I said, "I will try to return as soon as I can."

He nodded. "Okay. Oh, when you come, you bring Western invention?"

"You mean the Bible?"

"No, no, no. Not Bible. Invention."

"I'm sorry. I don't know what you mean. What invention?"

"You know. You put up big white sheet. With people on it." He leaned slightly forward and raised his eyebrows. "You know?"

A sheet with people on it? "Oh, you mean a movie projector?"

"Yes. Movie projector. You bring with you, yes?"

"I will do my best to find one. If I can, I'll bring it with me."

We said our goodbyes, and I hopped back into the truck with Joe.

As we drove back down the mountain, I called out to Joe above the roar of the truck's engine. "I meant to ask you. What happens to the Bibles when they reach the other side of the river?"

"Didn't you see all the elephants waiting on the other side?" Joe looked sideways to see my reaction.

"You mean—"

"That's right. You've heard of air mail. Well, there they have elephant mail." (Apparently they have been using "e-mail" for centuries.)

In June, Joe attended a leadership meeting in Singapore. Upon his return, he stunned us all by announcing that he and Colleen had decided to move back to America. Since he was resigning, he said he had received Loren's approval to turn the leadership of YWAM Thailand over to me. That evening we talked with heavy hearts. Joe and Colleen, in addition to being such dear friends, were good, experienced leaders, fluent in the Thai language, and well-versed in the culture. Ellen and I tried in vain to talk them out of it. Not long afterward, the Harbisons went back into missions and have played key roles in the service of a number of organizations ever since.

Not only did we feel overwhelmed with the responsibility, but also we realized that if we were to make a long-term commitment to Thai ministries, we would be unable to join the *Anastasis* ship ministry. Loren, however, had given his blessing for us to commit to this new assignment, and we were later relieved to learn that another administrator had agreed to serve the *Anastasis*. After praying long hours about the proposal and seeking feedback from our staff, we made the decision to stay in Thailand indefinitely.

We marveled at the seemingly roundabout route that God had used to so effectively bring us to our new home. Little did we know then that we would never lay eyes on the *Anastasis*.

After the Harbisons left Thailand, I visited the leaders of all the Christian ministries in Chiang Mai to ask how they viewed the role of YWAM Thailand. I was disappointed to learn that other ministries saw us as rather insignificant. But at least these visits did give me the chance to emphasize that YWAM had no desire to compete with the other ministries. We were here to serve while developing our own vision.

After much prayer and discussion, our team decided to maintain all the ministries we had but to shift our focus more to the unreached villages of the north. I reminded the team about my contact at Smuggler's Paradise, and we agreed to pursue this opportunity. An outreach team from overseas was coming, and we began making plans to visit the commander's village.

We contacted Campus Crusade in search of a Christian movie, but none were available. The Baptists said they had a movie that we could use. The movie was called *Maesariang Tii Rock,* meaning, "To Maesariang, With Love." The movie was a modern Thai version of the Good Samaritan parable. In the movie, a rich Thai man is beaten up and robbed of his money, his clothes and his four-wheel-drive truck. Then Christians from a fictitious village named Maesariang come and help the injured man.

I had hoped to obtain the movie *Jesus,* but since it was not available, this other film would have to do. We borrowed a projector, a generator, and a makeshift sheet-screen and made plans to leave before sunrise that Friday. The timing seemed perfect. The monsoon rains, which annually turned already-rutted roads into impassable mud baths, had ended just two weeks earlier.

We packed up the truck and headed out in the direction of the Thai-Burma border. As we slowly but steadily traveled up the winding dirt roads, it began to rain heavily. Driving through the downpour became increasingly difficult. The rain pummeled our truck, the road, and our bodies as we ventured out to push, shove, rock, and roll the truck toward our destination. Our original goal to arrive by evening was now an insurmountable feat. Our progress had slowed to about two kilometers per hour, and we still had about sixty kilometers to go.

As dusk approached, we decided to stop at the next village we found. I guessed that this would not be a waste of time, since these villagers would probably be among the millions in Thailand who had never heard that through Jesus they could be freed from their ever-present fear of evil spirits and witch doctors. And at the very least, who doesn't enjoy a good movie?

Before the hour was out, we arrived at the next rural community. At my request, some villagers led me to the chief's house. After introducing myself, I showed the chief the government permit that authorized me to talk about Christianity.

"We'd like to invite your whole village to come and hear us tell about our God," I said.

"Is he a good god?" the chief asked.

"Yes," I said, "the powerful and loving God who created everything."

The chief gave his permission and promised to gather all of his people together that night for our program. Seeing that our team was exhausted, disheveled, wet, and covered with mud from head to shoe, the kind chief sent us to the school headmaster, who allowed us to bed down in the school. We had just enough time to clean up, spread out our sleeping bags, and prepare a quick pot of noodles. When the chief informed us that his people were waiting for us, we scarfed down a few last bites and rushed to set up the projector and screen.

The rain had finally stopped. The entire village, about three hundred people, had come to see the weird-looking strangers who had arrived unannounced into their village that day. The people were hospitable and friendly, and as far as we could tell, none had ever heard of Jesus.

We performed skits, sang songs, and spoke from our hearts in the glare of our truck's headlights. Our audience showed an unusual level of interest and attentiveness. We ended the night by starting up the generator and showing the movie. Everyone watched intently, and when the movie was over, I shared the good news of Jesus.

The people conversed among themselves and asked us many questions. "If God has all power, what does He want with us? Why did He send you? Why would the Creator care about us?"

It had been a long day for us, and it was now inching past midnight. The five hours of pushing the truck over muddy roads was steadily taking its toll on our mortal frames. I imagine the villagers could have stayed up all night asking their questions, but they decided that the rest of their questions could wait until the next day.

The chief invited us to stay a few more days so that the people could learn more. Despite our fatigue, we were enjoying our time with these beautiful people, and we were delighted that they seemed so touched by all that they had seen and heard. We spent the next couple of days answering questions and enjoying the fellowship until the road became dry and easily passable.

As our team piled into the truck, I thanked the schoolmaster for his hospitality.

He said, "May I ask you one more question?"

"Of course," I said.

"You realize that we are just a small village of three hundred people. I was wondering, why did you go to all of that effort to make that movie just for us?"

"Actually," I said, "we borrowed the movie from another Christian mission. It was made for all the people of Thailand, not just for this village alone."

"But the movie's title is *To Maesariang With Love.*"

"Yes, that's right," I said. "*Maesariang Tii Rock.*"

"So you did make it for our village, then."

"Why do you say so?"

"Don't you know the name of our village?"

"No, I must admit that I don't."

"The name of our village," he paused for effect, "is Maesariang."

The Culture Game

L I T T L E by little, we were adjusting to the Thai culture, trying our best in every situation to pause, observe, and imitate the manners of our Thai friends. We soon discovered that we could not take any standard of etiquette for granted. For instance, growing up in America, we had learned that it's rude to reach over someone at the dinner table, so you must ask the person to pass the dish to you. In Thailand, though, we learned that it's rude to interrupt someone else's meal if you're perfectly able to lean over and reach the dish yourself.

In Thailand, when you extend an invitation for a meal, the recipient must politely refuse the first few times. Then, if you are persistent about the invitation, he or she will eventually accept. In Burma, you should ask roughly seven times before the invitation can politely be accepted. On visits back to the United States, I've found that if I persist in asking people more than a couple of times, they often get exasperated and say, "What part of *no* do you not understand?"

Language aside, even the way people greet each other differs from culture to culture, beyond even such obvious differences as bowing, or "wai-ing," versus handshaking. In America, "How are you doing?" is commonly spoken as a simple greeting, not as an actual question. The proper response, of course, is not to start listing your ailments.

In the same way, when Thais greet me with the question, "Where are you going?" they generally do not want to hear me recite my list of "Things to Do." Before we learned that the question was rhetorical, our poor Thai friends were so patient with us, smiling politely and looking so very interested as we began, "I'm on my way to the bank, and then I need to go to the grocery store, and then…"

We soon learned that "Where are you going?" is simply the accepted greeting, to which the response should be either "I'm going for business" or "I'm going for pleasure." As a matter of fact, pretty much every culture that I've studied has a rhetorical question used for greetings. The Chinese often ask, "Have you eaten?" and the appropriate response should be either a simple yes or no. They don't want a culinary dissertation. The Karen Burmese ask, "Where have you just come from?" and once again, it's simply a rhetorical question that basically means, "Hello."

We also learned that Thailand has two seasons: "hot and dry" and "hot and wet." The Thai do have what they call a "cold season," but that simply means that temperatures might dip slightly below 80 degrees Fahrenheit. We thought the moniker of "cold season" was laughable until our bodies adjusted to the Thai weather, and we found ourselves shivering and running to get our jackets when that season came around.

Since Thailand is usually hot, those who don't have electric fans traditionally rest during the hottest part of the summer afternoons. And since adjusting to a new culture is all about learning to watch and emulate the behaviors of those from the host culture, our family decided that we needed to be culturally sensitive and head for bed as soon as the sun hit the apex of the sky. Actually, we learned that this was the most practical way to deal with the heat and get through the day. We found that we could accomplish more in the long run.

One day, as we settled down for our midday rest, the howls and yelps of our neighbor's dog jolted our senses. I got up to see what was wrong, and I watched as our sweet, friendly neighbor mercilessly beat her chained dog with a stick.

I asked her, "Do you think you might be able to keep the noise down? And by the way, what exactly did the dog do to deserve such a beating?"

"Oi," she said. "In this dog's previous life, he was my uncle, and he treated me terribly when I was a little girl. Now I'm getting back at him."

The philosophy of reincarnation has permeated the beautiful Thai culture, bringing with it a host of such distortions. I believe that every culture on earth was inspired by God, but through sin and deception, each culture has been warped. It should go without saying that the Creator naturally fits into the uniqueness of every culture. Jesus doesn't want us homogenized. He desires to redeem and highlight the intrinsic beauty of every people group that truly honors Him. We have observed, however, that many of the issues that separate cultures have little or nothing to do with moral standards; they are often simply a matter of human preferences.

Recognizing these differences can save the outsider from a lot of embarrassment. Insensitivity to the culture can not only carry the price tag of personal humiliation but also impede the whole purpose of our mission, which should be to bless the people. It can erode our credibility and effectiveness, especially when we unwittingly exhibit behavior that is offensive in the eyes of our host culture, creating barriers difficult to penetrate—even for the formidable gospel of Jesus Christ. I learned my lesson in this the hard way.

As we trekked from village to village, it became increasingly clear that reaching every person in Thailand with the Good News about Jesus would not happen in our lifetime, at least not at the rate we were going. I decided that we should split our evangelism teams into smaller groups, groups of four to five, each with at least one translator. I congratulated myself on my brilliance. This new approach could accelerate our goal by years. Maybe even decades. I got the chance to try out this new strategy with the next outreach team that came to town. With the new team divisions, we were able to reach seven villages instead of just one.

When the teams returned from their trips, we gathered to hear their reports. One group of four young men reported that after only four days of sharing in their target village, two men had committed their lives to Christ. One was in his late teens and the other was in his sixties. This news of course delighted us, and all seemed well, until a few days after the team left the country.

We heard through the grapevine that the Buddhist priest in that particular village had reported to the chief that two of his people had accepted a foreign god. Under pressure, the chief had the two men brought before him. When he interrogated the men, they both confirmed that they were now Christians.

The chief commanded the older man to put his head on a chopping block in the village square. The chief then placed an ax at the back of the man's head and told him that he had a choice: either give up his foreign god or lose his life. The man acquiesced and agreed to return his allegiance to the Buddhist spirits.

When the younger man was threatened with the same fate, he declared that he would rather die knowing Jesus than live without Him. The chief decided against killing the young man but instead banished him from the village. The young man's entire life support was tied to that village: his home, family, and rice field. When the young man told us what had transpired, we rallied around him.

The next day at church, I took Pastor Boonmark aside and told him all that had happened to the young man. I was angry at the injustice, but Boonmark told me that it was my own fault. I had completely ignored proper Thai protocol. Boonmark reminded me that I had a visa and a work permit issued by the Thailand Department of Religious Affairs. Had I originally accompanied the team, I could have shown the chief my credentials and submitted my request to speak to his people. This would have demonstrated my respect for the chief's authority. But since the outreach team had completely bypassed the chief, it had inadvertently shown contempt for the chief's authority and for his responsibility in fathering his people.

"Isn't there something I can do to correct my blunder?" I asked.

"I don't think so," Boonmark said. "But maybe you can recruit the assistance of the Nai Umpur (the district governor). It's highly unlikely that he would interfere with the chief's decision, but I suppose it's worth a try."

Just as Boonmark predicted, the Nai Umpur was reluctant to get involved, but our persistence eventually wore him down. He agreed to ask the village chief to reconsider his banishment of the young man. The Nai Umpur made it clear, however, that he would not allow the chief to lose face and that the final decision in the matter would be completely up to the chief. He also made it clear that we had better be willing to lose face if we were going to make any headway.

Of course, we wholeheartedly agreed. Losing face would be a small price to pay to ensure that the young new believer would have his family and his livelihood restored to him. The leadership of our team, with heads bowed low in respect, went and sat before the chief. For what seemed like an eternity, the Nai Umpur waxed on and on about how inexcusably stupid we foolish foreigners had been. Our leadership sat quietly and nodded, accepting full blame, while the Nai Umpur passionately strove for a new world record in the number of times he could use the word *khun ngo,* meaning "stupid," in one very long, run-on sentence.

It was all more than worth it when the chief agreed to reverse his decision and allowed the young man to return home. In the years since then, that young Christian has grown into quite a leader in the village. The older man, however, has continually battled condemnation and alcoholism, hesitating to fully embrace his faith in Jesus. Reckless enthusiasm and cultural ignorance can certainly have calamitous consequences.

Early one morning, a Thai village chief knocked at our door. Ellen invited the man in and escorted him to the dining room, where I was thumbing through our financial accounts. I immediately recognized him from the year before when we had spent some time ministering in his village near the Burmese border.

Heeding his culture's rules of propriety (what I like to call The Culture Game), our conversation went something like this:

The chief asked, "How is the health of your grandparents?"

"I only have one living grandparent," I said, "my father's mother. She's currently in good health, even though, at ninety-two years old, she's very frail. How are your grandparents doing?"

"All four of my honorable grandparents have gone from the land of the living. How is the health of your father and mother?"

"I'm truly sorry to hear of the deaths of all your grandparents," I said. "My mother and father are living in America, and they communicate with us regularly. In their last correspondence, they told us that they are both in good health. I hope your parents are also in good health."

"It is good to hear that your parents are both well. My father has joined our ancestors in the afterlife. My mother lives with me, and her health is failing. Your wife appears to be doing well. Is she?"

"Oh, yes. She's tired right now, but she's enjoying good health. How is your wife doing?"

"My wife is well, thank you," he said. "How are your children?"

"All three of my children are healthy, growing, and enjoying life. How about your children? How are they doing?"

"My three boys and two girls are all very healthy, thank you. I understand you have a horse. How is his health?"

"We no longer have the horse." I struggled to restrain my Western-grown impatience to get to the point of his visit. "We returned him back to his original owner because he had proved to be very troublesome. However, the last time I saw the animal, he looked like he had gained a kilo or two. How are your pigs?"

The chief's eyes lit up when I mentioned his pigs. "My pigs are doing very well. How is your dog?"

"Our dog drives me crazy. I wish I had his energy. I am thankful, though, that he has been such a good companion for our eldest son. How are your chickens?" I was so grateful that we would soon come to the point in The Culture Game at which I would finally be able to learn the purpose of the chief's visit.

"My chickens are well, thank you. They are daily producing fat eggs for my family. How are your ducks doing?"

"One duck continues to get bigger and bigger, but the other ducks require a lot of attention. My children are very happy to attend to them, though."

After about two hours of conversing like this, we at last reached the moment I had been waiting for. "Chief," I said, "it must have taken you several hours to travel here from your village. Is there something you wanted to tell me?"

His smile vanished. "We are under a grave attack from powerful spirits."

"What kind of attack?"

"These evil spirits have made our people sick with fever. Already, fourteen have died, and many more are sick. Could you please come to our village and drive out the evil spirits?"

I could not believe what I was hearing. People were dying, and here we were spending hours talking about the health of pigs, ducks, and chickens. I had to remind myself that their cultural rules were not only valid but also important. Convincing myself at that moment, however, was not an easy task. I had to remind myself that we weren't there to change or judge the culture. We were there to introduce the people to the One who created them and their culture. Plus, we had learned so much from the Thai people and their sense of priorities (priorities that our Western culture would do well to heed).

Getting my thoughts in order, I went to the telephone and dialed World Vision. Dr. Geoff Atkinson answered in his distinguished British accent. "Hello?"

"Hello, Geoff. This is Art. I'm with a chief from a village near the Burmese border. There's been considerable fighting between the warlords in that area, and even though this village hasn't been directly involved, they're being affected. It sounds to me like a malaria epidemic. I'll put the chief on the phone so you can question him directly. If you confirm the prognosis, we will need to purchase a large quantity of chloroquine, or whatever you recommend, from the World Vision pharmacy."

After Geoff gathered the information he needed from the chief, he confirmed what I had feared. Geoff told me that if I could rush over to his office, he would have the medications ready. I did as instructed, and within five hours we were at the village handing out the life-saving medicine. To our relief, every person who received the medicine recovered. In the end, the delay caused by the two-hour pigs-and-chickens repartee had its only negative repercussion on one thing: my nerves.

When I returned home a few days later, Ellen ran out to greet me. "How did it go, Art? Did you get there in time? Were there enough drugs for all the people?"

"Honey," I said, "we'll have plenty of time for all your questions. But first, tell me, how are your grandparents?"

TEN

Followers of Christ

" W H A T were you thinking? You have seriously insulted these poor Thai people with your little skit," the missionary said in his crisp Finnish accent.

"I'm so sorry," I said. "I had no idea. What exactly about the mime was offensive?"

"Everyone on the team had their faces painted white. To do such a thing is extremely offensive in the Thai culture."

This well-respected missionary had been among the first missionaries to come to Thailand from Finland a number of decades before and had served the Thai people with zealous dedication. Of course I was more than willing to heed his counsel.

The following week, I was meeting with a group of about fifteen pastors to discuss and pray for an upcoming outdoor evangelistic service. Pastor Wanchai asked if YWAM had an outreach team that could perform a drama for the event.

"There is one team that we're hosting right now," I replied, "but the only drama they have is a mime, where they paint their faces white, and I understand that's very offensive in the Thai culture."

"What?" Wanchai said. "Where do you think you are? Finland?"

"Seriously," another pastor said, "Everyone knows that's offensive in the Finnish culture but certainly not in the Thai culture."

Not long before that, we had spent a year sheltering a young Thai woman named Thom after she had become pregnant. When her boyfriend, a soldier, died in a border clash, the woman had nowhere to go and became suicidal. It was not an easy situation. The woman didn't believe in God and felt no compulsion whatsoever to do anything to contribute toward the household chores that the rest of us shared.

When she delivered her baby, the woman explained that in the Thai culture, new mothers are not allowed to do any work or even get out of bed for three months after their babies are born. Wanting to show our respect for the culture, the entire staff rallied around her, doing all of her work and personal jobs, even walking and feeding her baby in the middle of the night.

After about six weeks of this, I said to Pastor Boonmark, "I find it so fascinating that the Thai culture doesn't allow mothers out of bed for the first three months after giving birth, that the other family members take care of the baby instead."

"Wait a minute," he said. "What culture are you talking about? Three months in bed?" He burst out laughing.

I had learned another valuable lesson. Not only could I offend people with my ignorance of their culture, but also I could be quite easily misled and manipulated. I thus came to an important conclusion that seems to have held true in my years of observation and experience since then: generally speaking, the best evangelists are those who have traveled the farthest, but the best pastors are those who are homegrown.

One day, a new Christian friend, Khun Noy, came to our door.

"Achaan," he asked me (using the Thai word for "teacher"), "now that I am Christian, you will please take on the responsibility of feeding my family from now on, yes?"

Did I hear right? I was not yet fluent in Thai. I repeated his question to make sure that I had understood.

He nodded. "Yes, that's right."

Khun Noy had responded to a challenge given by one of our outreach teams while he was visiting a relative in another town. When he returned to his home village, he announced that he had turned his life over to the Creator God. Then the persecution began. The elders decided that an example should be made of anyone who turned his back on the Buddhist spirits. They recited the popular catchphrase "To be Thai is to be Buddhist" and proceeded to confiscate Khun Noy's family's rice field.

In desperation, Khun Noy had now come to us for help. I assured him that we would do what we could to provide for his family, but I also explained that God doesn't want us to rely on middlemen. I advised him to allow God time to answer his prayer, and then to give God the credit for the provision. Khun Noy seemed satisfied with this answer and asked if we could come to his village to speak about Christ.

A week later, Pastor Boonmark and I went to talk to the chief of Khun Noy's village. The pastor reminded the chief that the King of Thailand openly protected Christianity as well as other religions. The chief agreed that we could come, on the condition that we could find a large enough facility with a covering, since it was now monsoon season. Thankfully, the village schoolmaster offered us the use of the school.

When I prayed about who should give the message, I felt confident that God had chosen Gwen Bergquist, the assistant leader of a visiting outreach team. I knew that unmarried females under the age of thirty are generally not taken seriously in this culture, but I also knew that Gwen was an extraordinary woman of God and had it in her to really connect with the people.

After the songs and dramas, Gwen presented a clear, concise, and anointed message. She filled two glasses with pure spring water. She then passed the glasses around for the people to quench their thirst. When they had emptied the glasses, she put a spoonful of dirt into one glass and then added a little water. She offered the glass of thick, muddy water to the people to drink. Naturally, they all declined her offer.

Gwen said, "I'll add more water, like adding merit to your karma."

She offered the now half-full glass to the villagers. Again they refused to drink from the glass.

"No problem," she said. "The glass just needs more merit."

She filled the glass to the brim with water. She invited the villagers to drink from the glass, and again they abstained.

"Why do you reject this water that I've offered you?" she asked. "Look, I've filled the glass with clean water."

"But the dirt is still in the glass," one of them replied.

"Exactly," Gwen said. "It's the same way with our souls. All of us have sinned; therefore, we all have dirt in our human vessels. The Lord, being a holy God, cannot accept us into His kingdom until our vessels are clean. Merit cannot make us clean. Merit only dilutes the dirt in the water. It doesn't take care of the core problem—the filth, the sin in each of us.

"Therefore, God sent His Son, Jesus, to die on our behalf, to receive the penalty for our sin, so that by His sacrifice, we can be made clean. When we accept Jesus as Lord and Savior, He totally cleanses our human vessel so that we can stand before God forgiven, totally clean of all sin. Then, once we are clean, He can fill us with his water of eternal life."

Gwen then offered the people the opportunity to respond, but no one budged.

A week later, we returned to the village with another team and found out that two families had decided to become followers of Jesus. Khun Noy was elated. He also told us the good news that the village elders had decided to let him return, allowing him full rights to his rice field.

In our next visit to that village, we arranged to have a meeting in Khun Noy's home. Khun Noy's family lived in a typical bamboo house on stilts, with a thatched roof. That day, three more families made decisions to follow Jesus.

Week after week, we returned to teach and pray for the people. By November, eleven families were regularly gathering to worship Jesus. Khun Noy said it was time for them to have a full-time pastor and offered the position to me.

As I prayed about it, I was reminded that I was not yet fluent in either the Thai language or the culture. I also remembered how my cultural cluelessness had made it so easy for me to be misled and manipulated in the past.

I turned down Khun Noy's offer, but I encouraged him to visit me for weekly Bible lessons. He could then go back and teach his people what he had learned. So Khun Noy became their pastor. With the help of some outreach teams, we helped his people build a Thai-style *sala* that would serve as a church building. With a good roof and concrete floor, the sala was large enough to hold most of the village, and since a sala has no walls, it could hold overflow when necessary.

A few years later, Gwen joined Thai ministries full-time and became one of our dearest friends. I remember telling her before she moved to Thailand how I had never forgotten the compelling message she had given using the glass of water and dirt. She thanked me for my encouraging words but told me how terrible she had felt about failing both God and that poor, needy village when no one responded to her message.

"But, Gwen," I said, "didn't you know that after we left, two families discussed the matter and decided to become followers of Christ?"

"Really?" she said.

"And that's not all. That village has been transformed. The others in the village saw the difference God had made in these two families—how they were no longer tormented by evil spirits, how they were now free to adopt basic practices of sanitation and first aid that protect them from sickness and disease. As a result, many of the others have also committed their lives to Christ. Now more than thirty families come together for worship."

"I had no idea," Gwen said.

I could definitely relate to how she felt. The needs to be met were continuously overwhelming, and I had often wondered whether we were really making much of a difference. Our loving Lord, though, would frequently encourage us in surprising ways.

I remember once, on the way to a remote village, we stopped to eat lunch at a noodle shop. When the waitress came to get my order, I began to talk to her about Jesus.

"Oh yes," she said. "I know Jesus. I'm a Christian."

"How wonderful," I said. "How did you come to hear about Him?"

"But…" she said, "you were the one who told me about the Lord."

Encounters like that happened just enough to show us that we were having at least some impact.

Our first visit home to the States had been arranged by the Christian Service Corps for April 1982. Arriving in Washington, D.C., we saw snow for the first time in over two years. Expecting warm, spring weather, we didn't have any clothes appropriate for a cold, windy climate.

The weather was not the only thing for which we were unprepared. The American culture now seemed rather foreign to us. We had been through so many adventures and had changed so much since leaving the States. The children seemed content enough to be back in their old school for our three months in the United States, but they missed their home in Thailand. We had grown to love the Thais and their beautiful country.

Our schedule was packed with speaking engagements at churches, schools, and prayer meetings. Usually, I would speak, Ellen would sing and show slides, and the kids, if not in school, would perform skits. It was exhausting but exhilarating to have the chance to affirm to our Christian brothers and sisters that God was still in the miracle-working business.

Near the end of our furlough, our family went for complete physical examinations. To our delight, all three of our children were in the top ninety percent of physical fitness for their age groups. I showed the results to my father, who was visibly relieved. On a number of occasions, he also mentioned how impressed he was at their maturity. We were comforted to know that this time we would return to the mission field with his approval.

Our home church had been supporting us with a financial stipend and, even more important, with their prayers. Now I learned that they had budgeted five thousand dollars for us to use to reenter American life, since they did not expect us to return to the mission field. When we assured our pastor that we were quite fulfilled as missionaries, he asked us to submit a budget proposal. A week after submitting our budget, I met with the associate pastor, Jim Isom, who told me that they had rejected our proposal.

"Jim," I said, "I don't know what else I can possibly cut from our budget."

"We don't want you to cut your budget." he said. "We want to increase it to cover all reasonable expenses, including funds for ministry. You shouldn't have to live on such a poverty-level income."

Shortly before our trip back to Chiang Mai, Pastor Kline gave our family the privilege of conducting an entire Sunday-evening service.

Before the service, Pastor Kline said that the church had decided to give us the evening's offering.

"How much do you need to cover the five airfares back to Thailand," he asked.

When I told him the total was $3,389.23, he apologetically explained that the Sunday-evening offering was usually only six to eight hundred dollars at most.

After the service, the elders counted the offering. Without adding a penny to it, it came to exactly $3,389.23.

ELEVEN

Beloved Cuisine

IN JULY of 1982, we returned to Thailand. We were all so glad to be back home. I must admit that one of the things I was most looking forward to the opportunity to reach out with God's love to the Thai chefs.

Thai cuisine ranks among the world's finest, and one of the fringe benefits of serving in Thailand has been allowing our hosts to minister to our taste buds. That said, certain dishes did take some getting used to. And of course, it is very important to eat the food that is set before you, because one of the surest ways of offending someone's personal and cultural pride is to refuse the person's beloved cuisine.

Once, in the province of Chiang Rai, a sweet, elderly woman told me that her family so appreciated our ministry to them and they wanted to show their gratitude by treating me to a special breakfast. Anytime someone wants to bless my stomach, I'm happy to oblige, so I graciously accepted her invitation. At the time I didn't really understand why it was only me whom they wanted to bless. I realize now that it was God's mercy toward my team members.

At seven o'clock the next morning, I arrived at the door of the thatched-roof hut. The elderly woman greeted me with a big smile and bragged that she had been up since three o'clock preparing this meal. I wondered what kind of food would take that long to make. When she placed the dish before me, I realized that it was not the cooking that took so long. It was the catching. There before me was a plate overflowing with fried crickets.

"I've never had the opportunity of eating crickets before, so I'm not sure how…" I didn't know what else to say.

"You are in for a treat, then."

I forced a smile and nodded.

Clearly overjoyed that God had bestowed upon her the matchless honor of introducing me to this delicacy, she said, "Just pull off the hind legs and pop them into your mouth, like this." She demonstrated and then gave me the thumbs-up sign, watching eagerly for my first bite.

I smiled and followed her instructions. The face of the bug was still completely intact. Dead as it was, I could not avoid the feeling that it was not any happier about the situation than I was.

An inner dialogue began with the little creature. *Sorry, buddy, but I sincerely believe this is going to hurt me almost as much as it hurt you.*

I began to chew, and my taste buds perked up. *Hey, this stuff is pretty good.* My intellect stepped in. *I don't care how good it is. Bugs are not welcome in this body.*

Seeing the hopeful look on my hostess's face, I struggled to conceal the battle of the senses that raged within me. How could I disregard her labor of love? While I was trying to think of a gracious way to get out of eating the meal, I recalled the time that I first learned how true love really does conquer all. Even taste buds.

Back in the late 1960s, when Ellen and I were newlyweds living in England, Ellen had asked me, "What meal would you love to have, something that you don't ordinarily get."

"Hmm," I recall saying. "When I was about thirteen, my Aunt Elsie prepared a meal of smoked eels, and they were delicious. She was a gourmet cook. She's passed away now, but maybe we could find a seafood restaurant that serves eel."

The next day, before I returned home from work, Ellen slipped off to the fish market. Donning a very upper-crust English accent, she asked the fishmonger, "Pardon me, but do you sell eel?"

"Yup. Roight there in front of you, luv," he replied in his thick cockney accent.

"Sorry," she said, "but I see every sort of fish except eel."

Without comment, the man stepped around the counter, reached into a bucket, and pulled out a live eel. When Ellen recoiled, he said, "Would ya loike for me to cut it up for you, luv?"

"Yes, please." She was already beginning to have misgivings.

When Ellen arrived home, she took her package to the kitchen and untied it. The diced eel was still flailing about. Undaunted, Ellen opened her cookbook and began searching for any recipe involving eel. She found no such recipe, but since the eel was seafood, she decided to just fry it up using a shrimp recipe.

When I arrived home, Ellen had the table beautifully set with candles and our best dishes. Then she brought out my surprise meal. I invited her to join me, but she refused. This special treat was all for me.

Eel skin is thick and rubbery, and you could probably play basketball with it. I strained my jaw in an effort to chew this thick piece of rubber and succeeded only in straining out the fishy oils. That gave me an idea. I wondered if I should just slide the eel underneath my lip, like a thick piece of chewing tobacco, and commence spitting. Somehow, though, I couldn't see that going over too well with my doe-eyed bride.

I suddenly discovered that there was an upside to the thickness of the skin. A bone broke through, digging into the roof of my mouth. I realized that the skin had been a blessing in disguise, faithfully protecting my tender mouth from the sharp bones that filled the flesh of the eel. I faked the most delighted of smiles for my beloved bride and mused, *So this is what true love is.*

Now, years later, as I munched on crickets, I got the feeling that God was asking me, "If you could eat that eel for the love of your bride, couldn't you eat these crickets for the love of your Lord?"

One at a time, I gulped the creatures down while my hostess gazed on in delight. Since that time, I've learned to actually enjoy crickets, grasshoppers, beetles, and termites, but I do hope I'll never have to eat another eel.

A fellow missionary told me that he once avoided eating his crickets by sneaking them into his handkerchief and then stuffing them into his pocket. After breakfast, the chief invited him to speak to the assembly. The missionary did so with passion—with such passion, in fact, that when he began to perspire, he instinctively reached for his handkerchief, inadvertently raining crickets on his audience.

When eating in a hut on stilts, we have our favorite methods for disposing of unwanted delicacies. Here is one of them: As soon as the hosts are not looking, we slip the food through the cracks of the floorboards. The pigs and dogs often hang out below, and they become happy accomplices, completely disposing of the evidence.

This technique can be hazardous, though, especially when there is more than one animal under the house. If the animals start barking and fighting over the food, the hostess just might excuse herself to find out what all the ruckus is about. I'm speaking from personal experience. After all these years, I still can't think of an honest response to the question, "How do you suppose part of our meal ended up underneath the house?"

Sean once bought a bag of boiled crickets as a joke gift for Michelle's birthday. When Michelle unwrapped the gift, Sean giddily imagined the disgusted contortions that her face would soon adopt. To his dismay, Michelle smiled the most innocent of smiles and said, "Oh, I love these. Thank you, Sean." She then proceeded to eat the entire bag. The rest of us watched with a mix of astonishment and delight. "Not as good as *fried* crickets," she said, "but still quite tasty."

Our friends the Bemos invited us to assist them with their work in their village, Baan MePo. Many of the villagers, including the chief, had become Christians and decided that their cash crop, opium, was dishonoring to God. They wanted to switch to a different cash crop.

The United Nations, the US Drug Enforcement Agency, and the King of Thailand had joined forces in a program to help opium-growing villages replace opium with alternative crops. The agencies had not been successful in convincing the opium-growing villages to make the change. Not wanting to appear ungrateful, the villages had accepted the alternate crops. But without a change in mindset, they hadn't been willing to clear away their opium crops to devote their resources to the care of the new crops. Consequently, the new crops all died.

When the people of Baan MePo volunteered to participate in this program, they were given a few dozen peach trees (the remaining few dregs of the failed intergovernmental project). After they had planted the young trees, the people of Baan MePo resolved to destroy the opium plants right away, even though they know that it would take a few years before these peach trees would bear fruit and they did not know how they would survive until then.

The people said that opium made slaves of men, women, and children and was therefore dishonoring to God, so the opium needed to go—now. They said that Jesus was a big enough God to feed them and their families until their first crop of peaches came in. Their faith was so rock solid that they decided not to wait until their first crop came in before they thanked Jesus. They would celebrate their Thanksgiving feast now, in full confidence that God would provide.

The villagers were right. God did provide. And once their first peach harvest came in, the villagers began making far more money than they had ever dreamed of making from their opium. Moreover, they no longer lived in submission to the opium warlords, and their children were no longer exposed to the lure of opium addiction.

For their Thanksgiving feast, the villagers invited me and some other friends to come and teach from the Bible and then to share in a villagewide Thanksgiving meal at the end of a week of feasting on God's Word. Because our daughter, Michelle, was sick, Ellen stayed with her in Chiang Mai while I took Sean and David with me to the village. When all the teaching had concluded, we sat down with the elders of the village to partake of the Thanksgiving meal.

"What do you think they eat for Thanksgiving?" Sean asked me. "I haven't seen any turkeys around here, so they'll probably serve chicken, right?"

I said, "I don't have a clue, son, but they've said it will be something very special. So we'll just have to wait and see."

Now, there are many connotations of the word *special,* probably too many. This meal took that word to a whole new level for me.

The suspense was soon over. The boys each received a bowl of rice adorned with generous portions of pig skin—thick pig skin with pure, greasy fat and the hair bristles still sticking out.

In unison, Sean and David said, "Dad, do we have to eat this?"

"Come on, guys," I said. "You don't want to offend them. You'll be fine. Just stick the fat into your mouth and swallow. I'm sure it'll just slide right down."

The boys, troopers that they are, did as I asked. As they ate, though, they struggled unsuccessfully to keep their faces from revealing how their stomachs felt about this meal.

"Careful, guys. You'd better not let the hosts see you making those faces."

Then I was served my meal. And here's where that word *special* really comes in. They served me an extra large bowl of rice along with chunks of pig fat that simply served as a garnish for the pig's stomach and other innards. There's no mystery why gluttonous people are called pigs, but to describe that stomach before me as large would really not do it justice. I was looking around to see the crane that they must have used to lift this thing off the stove.

A more righteous man would have prayed, "Dear God, bless this food and let it—please let it—be nourishing to my body." But as soon as my eyes told my body what might be coming into my mouth, all kinds of signals started streaming into my brain. My stomach in particular said, *There's only room in this body for one stomach. If you think it'll offend them to not eat the food, just see how they'll react when I send it right back out again.* So I prayed, *Dear Heavenly Father, how can I get out of having to eat this without offending my hosts?*

I noticed that all the other men at our table had been served meat—nice, appetizing, Atkins-friendly portions of pork. I asked the chief why my boys and I had been so uniquely honored with our servings of pig fat and innards.

"You're our guests," he said. "We wouldn't think of giving you what the others are getting. We want to bless you by giving you the very best."

I breathed another prayer. Just then, a thought came to me. I immediately arose and began transferring my food to the dishes of the chief and each of the elders. Before I knew it, my bowl was nearly empty.

"Achaan," the chief said to me, "you've given away all of your blessing."

"I know," I said. "You see, God has sent me here not to be blessed but to be a blessing, not to receive but to give."

The chief and the elders began whispering to each other, "What a selfless, holy man Achaan Art is."

David said, "Hey, Dad, how come we had to eat our meal, but you didn't have to eat yours?"

"Sorry, guys," I replied. "You just asked the wrong father."

Missionaries and Other Wild Animals

O U R region had no English-speaking preschools available, so we started one as a way of reaching out to the expatriate community. One day, an affluent South American woman who had just moved to Thailand with her diplomat husband came to inquire about enrolling her daughter in our preschool. During the interview, the woman made it very clear that she had an intense fear of snakes. Since snakes are very prolific in Thailand, she wanted a guarantee from Ellen that our new property did not have a snake problem.

Ellen said truthfully, "So far, we've had no trouble with snakes. Our children have pet ducks, and we have been told that ducks eat baby snakes."

All at once, the woman's elegant composure shifted to panic. Ellen turned around to see what had caused such an extreme reaction. There, standing outside the glass doors, was our twelve-year-old son Sean holding a six-foot cobra by the neck. At Sean's side was his faithful German shepherd, Duke. Duke's tongue dangled out the side of his mouth as he panted and wagged his tail wildly in excitement.

"Hey, Mom," Sean said. "Look what Duke and I caught. Isn't this cool?"

By the time Ellen turned back to her guest, the woman had already made significant strides for the door.

Wow, Ellen thought. *She's fast. Even if we have snakes, I can't imagine we have any fast enough to catch her.*

Two weeks later, the woman came back. I'm sure it had something to do with the fact that there was no other English-speaking preschool for hundreds of miles.

Growing up in Asia, our children were deprived of a number of American luxuries, such as the abundance of team sports, advanced classes, and television. On the other hand, they had, in addition to snake hunting, a number of activities that the average American kid is not generally privy to. For example, at a cost of barely five dollars per person, we could rent horses for the whole morning from the Thai border-patrol police. How many kids get to take equestrian classes from a real cavalry? A couple of Saturdays a month, we would head down to the cavalry headquarters to learn to ride English saddle.

One day, the stallion that Michelle was riding became upset that all the other horses had left the ring and he had been left behind. After fighting against the reins, he tried to jump the fence. He tripped on the rail and tumbled headlong to the ground. Michelle landed on her left elbow, which shattered. She had to undergo a delicate, eight-hour operation to reconstruct the bone. As soon as her arm was out of the cast, she not only wanted to get back into the saddle right away but also resolved to become a doctor when she grew up.

Once her arm had healed, she asked me, "Daddy, can we buy a horse?"

I said, "As much as I'd love to, honey, I really don't think we could ever afford it. But pray and ask the Lord. He can do the impossible."

Michelle started praying for a horse. About a month later, our Thai language tutor told us that her in-laws had a white pony for sale at an exceptionally cheap price.

"How cheap?" I asked.

"Only twelve hundred baht, (US$48)" she said.

"That's pretty cheap, all right. That would be a dream come true for Michelle, but I don't know. Even if we could afford the initial purchase, I'm not sure we could afford the maintenance."

"We'll loan him to you for thirty days. During this trial period, you can experience how easy and inexpensive it is to take care of a horse in Thailand."

This seemed reasonable, so on the following Saturday, the tutor's in-laws delivered the pony to our home. The pony was a little over a year old, only about twelve hands tall, and one of the scrawniest ponies I'd ever seen. It would take a while before anyone could ride him.

We had about half an acre of grass on our property, and Sean had converted the old wooden shed into a one-horse barn for the pony. As our family gathered at the barn to feed and groom our latest addition, Duke came sprinting around the corner. No doubt spurred on by the excitement of meeting a fresh, furry friend, Duke had somehow managed to break free of the rope that tied him to the back of the house.

The pony took one look at Duke, reared up, shot out of his makeshift stable, and cantered down our long, narrow driveway toward the main road. Running behind him was our oh-so-beloved mutt, followed by Sean, Michelle, David, Ellen, and me. All of us were running as fast as our little human legs could carry us.

When the pony reached the open gate, he darted to the left and galloped down the road. Hot on his trail, Duke must have mistaken the horse's scent for something similar (which, with Duke, could have meant anything from a cockroach to a motorcycle), because when he reached the gate, the olfactory-gifted canine turned right.

I told Sean to go after his pet while the rest of us ran after the pony. A full hour later, we found the pony and wearily walked him home. We assured ourselves that we had nipped this little problem in the bud. Thank goodness we now knew what to do to keep this from becoming a daily routine. Or so we thought.

We had underestimated the superpowers that possessed Duke each time that he was struck with the sudden need to express his affection for his newfound friend. And we underestimated the potency of the adrenaline rush that would then overcome the pony toward his new-found foe.

Neither the reinforced chain that held Duke nor the reinforced sta-ble that held the pony was sufficient to keep the exact same episode from replaying the following day. The neighbors didn't seem to mind the rerun, though, and watched in delight. Over the next ten days, our family became very physically fit, as the same scenario occurred almost daily. I'm sure we did a lot to reinforce the sense of dignity and respect that epitomizes the Thais' views of missionaries.

To halt the insanity, we at last found chains strong enough to keep Duke secure. We were considering investing in a good old-fashioned ball and chain for Duke when we made an appointment for a local veteri-narian to give our prized steed a thorough medical checkup.

The vet arrived after lunch on a Saturday, and Sean locked Duke inside the house to make sure he would not interrupt the examination. I fetched the pony from the stable, and the veterinarian conducted a few preliminary inspections. He then asked Ellen to hold the pony's head still. Ellen encircled the pony's neck with her arms and held on tight while David held onto the reins.

Meanwhile, back at the ranch, one of our staff saw Duke in the house and said, "How did you get in here?" She held the door open for him, and he shot out of the starting gate. We all turned to see a blind-ing ball of fur blitzing toward us. As Duke approached, the pony's ears flared, his head jerked up, and in a flash, he broke free of the reins in David's hands. Ellen bravely hung on to the pony's neck as the animal bucked and thrashed about. She held on tight, but after about thirty yards of skidding through the gravel driveway, she finally had to let go.

I decided that I would wait to join the search-and-rescue team (or more appropriately, perhaps, the lynch mob) until I had first attended to my poor, wounded wife. As I laid Ellen on the couch, she said, "I'll be fine, honey. You'd better go help the kids find the pony."

I ran to meet the kids at the end of the driveway, where we split up into four directions, exploring all the surrounding areas for what we had assumed would be a fairly conspicuous pet in our urban neighborhood.

Later that day we all returned home, worn-out and empty-handed. Duke, on the other hand, returned triumphantly after a successful three-hour hunt for a shoe. He proudly displayed his trophy, as if confident that we would all be reassured to know that the day's labor had not been in vain.

For the next three days we spent all our spare time looking for the pony, but he had seemingly vanished. Privately, I was almost hoping that he had been stolen.

In the midst of all of this, we were preparing to direct the first ever DTS in Thailand. Our four Thai students had arrived, and we were still expecting a young American bachelor, a Nepalese pastor with his wife and two children, and a Korean pastor with his wife and four daughters. The night before the school officially started, we invited a number of pastors and other church leaders over for dinner. After dinner, we would hold our school dedication ceremony.

Halfway through the dinner, two men knocked on our door. Our dynamic worship leader, Virapon, answered the door and then hurried back to me and whispered that the two men urgently needed to see me. I excused myself from the party and went out to greet them.

"Are you the owner of a small, white pony?" one of the men asked.

"Yes," I said, "but he's disappeared."

"We know where your pony is."

"You do?" I said, with a mixture of relief and apprehension.

"Come. We'll take you there."

"Just a minute," I said. I rushed back into the house and told Ellen, "I have to go, but I'll be right back."

"Art, you can't leave now," Ellen said. "You're the master of ceremonies, and the main speaker."

"But those men at the front door are going to show me where the pony is."

"Okay, but please hurry back."

The two men led me to the major intersection of Hatsadisawee Road and Hueykeow. There, in front of the city's library, in the middle of the king's garden, stood our wayward colt, feasting on a gourmet smorgasbord of exotic flowers. In fact, he was so caught up in the delight of these delicacies that we had no problem rounding him up. Once I had the pony's reins securely in my hands, I asked the two-man rescue team, "How much do I owe you for your help?"

"You don't owe us anything," the duo's official speaker said. "We're glad to help."

"But what about the damage done to the king's garden?" I asked.

"Don't worry about it. Just take the animal away."

Despite their insistence that they didn't expect any recompense, I pulled out my wallet and gave each man a small gift. I then returned home with our galloping gourmet. After the pony had settled into his stable, I ran into the house, sweating like a horse—and smelling like one, too.

"Art, you're just in time to deliver your message," Ellen said.

I have often wondered what went though the minds of those students and church leaders as I addressed them that night smelling like an all-American cowboy.

We hated to break our daughter's heart, but as much as she wanted a horse, she realized that it just wasn't working out. The next day the owners came and retrieved their pony. The veterinarian bill arrived a little later.

The first two weeks of our DTS went quite smoothly. Then classes were suspended for Songkran, the Thai New Year, which is celebrated annually on April 13. Since Songkran falls right in the middle of the hottest, driest time of the year, tradition dictates that younger people should sprinkle their elders with a little water for refreshment and blessing. Over the years the holiday has morphed into a full-on, nationwide, three-day water fight.

During Songkran, it's almost impossible to leave your home without getting soaked. Trucks are loaded with tanks of water and snipers of all ages giddily tossing water at the other vehicles and at pedestrians. Others stand alongside the road, aiming their buckets and water pistols at the passing cars and trucks.

No one is exempt. Anyone is fair game. Buddhist monks are even doused with water when they venture out at dawn to make their rounds asking for food. Police officers, while directing traffic, cover their guns with plastic bags as a protection from all the drive-by water shooters.

Many of the city's activities come to a halt while the water fights play-
fully rage on. We realized that conducting classes during this holiday
would be as futile as trying to stay dry. Instead, we joined in the fun.

One day we were blessing the passersby with our water pistols and
buckets and scoops when a cop approached us. *Oh no. I must've gotten
carried away. This'll be just great for our reputation.* I could just see the
headlines: "Christian Missionaries Wreak Havoc on Thai Roadways."

The cop removed his sunglasses, looked at the water dipper in my
hand, and said, "Do you mind if I join you?"

"Not at all," I said.

"I notice that you're avoiding the motorcycles, only throwing water
on the larger vehicles," he said. "That's very wise, but I have a better idea."

For the rest of the afternoon, he would periodically step out onto
the road, blow his whistle, hold up his hand, and stop the motorcycles.
He would then nod to us, and we would "baptize" the riders. Then he
would step back to the curb and wave the motorcyclists along.

"You see," he said, "I'm responsible for their safety."

During this time, our friend Joe was having lunch with the pastor of
a large, influential church in Singapore. During their meal, the subject
of YWAM came up. Evidently, the pastor was acquainted with our mission's work in Singapore, and he asked Joe if there was a YWAM training center in Chiang Mai. Joe told him that there was indeed a local
YWAM base and that it was nearby.

As they walked out of the restaurant, Joe began describing the
quickest route to our base. At that moment, a white Volkswagen van
drove up and screeched to a halt. The van door swung open, unleashing
a torrent of water that drenched both Joe and his pastor friend. Just as
abruptly, the door slammed shut, and the van sped away.

Joe grinned and said, "That was YWAM."

That pastor never did visit us.

THIRTEEN

Spiritual Poverty

O U R Discipleship Training Schools in Thailand had the rare benefit of interspersing the lecture phase with outreach, since our targeted people groups were right on our doorstep. When our friend Pastor Wanchai spoke of his burden for the people living in the Samerng Valley, we were eager to assist him. Since approximately thirty villages were in this valley, we knew we would have more than enough ministry to keep our DTS staff and students busy.

With eight people squeezed into our Volkswagen van and ten in the old pickup truck, we weaved our way up the mountain roads of Mae Sai. Even the strongest stomachs had to fight off nausea as for more than three hours we drove up, down, and around the mountain passes toward the valley.

I diverted my attention away from my stomach and onto the stunning, panoramic view that the precarious passes provided. Every few hundred meters, the misty hues of green were interrupted by a dazzling explosion of wildflowers—deep purples, bright reds, and rich yellows—

chaperoned by a rich kaleidoscope of birds chatting away as they danced in the breezes. Surrounded by such majesty, it saddened me to realize that thousands of people in this area lived in unending fear and had been deprived of knowing the One who created all this beauty.

When we arrived in Samerng, we promptly covered Wanchai's floors with our mats, mosquito nets, and sleeping bags. Wanchai's family lived in a typical northern Thai-style teakwood house on the north side of the town. After enjoying a refreshing meal of roast chicken, sticky rice, and naam jim sauce, we began preparations for our evening program. The mayor had given us permission to hold an evangelistic program in Wanchai's front yard, and we were amazed when practically the whole town showed up for our presentation. The people's overwhelmingly enthusiastic response was more than worth the bumpy trip out there.

During the next few days, our team visited those who had indicated a desire to know more about Jesus. We also prayed for the sick, taught Bible stories, pushed trucks out of the mud, and helped repair houses and fences.

The local Buddhist abbot knew that if the townspeople turned their lives over to Jesus, they would stop paying him to ward off the evil spirits. Before the week was out, the abbot had hired a group of teenage boys to harass and drive us away. The boys began throwing rocks at our team members, causing some minor wounds and some major anxiety.

The team met together for prayer and reminded each other that Jesus said, "If they persecuted Me, they will also persecute you" (John 15:20).

I told the team a story about John Wesley. It is said that back around the height of his ministry, Wesley became concerned at the realization that he had not received any opposition in quite a while. He dismounted from his horse, knelt on the ground, and prayed, "Lord, am I out of Your will?" A man saw him praying and started throwing rocks at him, shouting, "You're that preacher fellow, aren't you? We don't want your kind around here!" Wesley jumped to his feet, his hands raised toward heaven, and said, "Thank You, Lord, for reassuring me that I am indeed in the center of Your will."

We determined to stay and continue our work. A few days later, in the dark hours of the morning, the inebriated teenage boys threw a rocklike object through our window, jarring us awake. Wanchai picked up the object to see that it was not a rock, but a bullet, with a note attached. The note read, "If you don't leave our town with your foreign god, the next bullets will not be hand thrown."

Feeling responsible for the lives of our students, we prayed and decided to leave the next morning. After breakfast, we packed our belongings and then gathered to seek the Lord for direction. After a time of worship, we prayed, "Lord, where should we go?"

Just as we started to pray, a man showed up at Wanchai's doorstep. He identified himself as Khru Idal, a Buddhist teacher who taught at an elementary school in the village of Baan Lankum, only three hours' walking distance from the town of Samerng. Khru Idal asked if our team would consider going there. The people of Baan Lankum suffered under heavy spiritual oppression, and other than our God, Khru Idal knew of nothing that might be able to deliver his village from its distressing curse.

Khru Idal said, "I was buying my food supplies here in the market when one of the merchants asked why I looked depressed. When I told him about the curse on my village, he told me about a new God, named Jesus, who has power over every curse and evil spirit. When I asked him how to contact this mighty God, he directed me here."

We realized that the Lord had answered our prayer even before we had prayed. Wanchai spent a long time talking with Khru Idal and made arrangements for us to travel to Baan Lankum as soon as possible.

As we drove to the point where we would begin walking, I said to Wanchai, "I assume this oppression that Khru Idal is talking about is poverty or sickness?"

He said, "It's a lot more than that. He told me that they recently sacrificed a ten-year-old child in his village."

"Human sacrifice? In the twentieth century? Why?"

Wanchai recounted the story that Khru ldal had told him. Just recently, one of the men in his village had gone to the forest early one morning to hunt for food for his family. When he spotted a large bird, he raised his flint rifle to his shoulder and pulled the trigger. He saw the bird fall and ran to fetch it, When he reached the place where the bird had fallen, it was nowhere to be seen. He knew that if the bird was still alive, it could not have traveled far, so he spent the rest of the day searching for his prey.

Since panthers and tigers inhabited the forest, he knew he mustn't stay in the jungle after dark. As dusk approached, he began his trek home, empty-handed. At one point, he heard the shrieking of birds behind him. He turned to see the source of the noise but saw nothing. He quickened his pace.

When he reached home, his wife was in tears. Their ten-year-old son had become violently ill. The grieving father went directly to the village maw phee (witch doctor). He offered to pay any price for the maw phee to stop the evil spirits from attacking his beloved child.

The maw phee conferred with his demons and then returned with a message for the father. "The spirits told me that you shot one of their sacred birds early this morning. Is that true?"

"I did shoot a bird. But how could I have known that it was a special bird?"

"The spirits are very angry. They have threatened to kill everyone in the village. Unless…" The maw phee looked down at the ground and sighed.

"Please," the father said. "What must I do? I'll do anything."

"The only way to appease the spirits and save our village is to pierce the heart of your son on the altar as a peace offering to the spirits, in the same manner that you pierced the heart of their beloved bird."

The father trembled and wrung his hands. He had no choice. He gave his son to the maw phee, who sacrificed the poor boy to the tyrannical spirits.

Upon hearing this story, my emotions swung between rage and heartache.

It was late afternoon by the time we arrived at Baan Lankum. Wanchai and I went directly to the chief to ask his permission for us to stay in the village and present our evangelistic program. He gave us his blessing. Our team paired off and visited every hut. We invited the people to come and learn about the all-powerful God who is stronger than demons.

That evening, no one came to our program. This was an unusual response in the "land of smiles." Their traditional hospitality had clearly been superseded by the terror that gripped their hearts. The people feared doing anything that might upset the spirits.

Khru Idal asked us to speak to the children the next day at school. The children responded readily to our message. When a number of them expressed a desire to devote their lives to Jesus, we visited each child's parents to explain the child's decision. All of the parents agreed that their children could believe what they liked, as long as this new God proved to be strong enough to protect them. However, the parents themselves were not willing to risk falling out of favor with the evil spirits who had controlled their lives for generations.

We left the village feeling hopeful. At least it was a start.

Returning to his home in Samerng, Wanchai wondered about the safety of his own family in light of the threats that had been made by the teenage boys. Because he knew that if unchecked, there was no end to what the Buddhist abbot might do, he moved his family to the other side of town and reported the evidence of the threats to the police. The police told the culprits that if any future evidence was brought against them, they would be arrested and put in jail. To our relief, the persecution finally stopped.

Over the next three years, I led many outreach teams to Baan Lankum. Each time it was the same. The children would respond, but the adults continued to distance themselves from us.

On one visit, a strange, sinewy man with wild hair wandered into the school during our presentation. The minute we started singing worship songs, he began screaming and foaming at the mouth. He threw himself down and started thrashing about the dirt floor, hissing and making loud, creepy animal noises—noises that went beyond the frequencies of a natural human voice.

A group of strong young men and I escorted him outside, and then the young men returned to the presentation, leaving me alone with the man. Summoning my courage, I grabbed the man by his shoulders. He shook and squirmed, but I managed to make eye contact.

In Thai, I said, "In the Name of Jesus, I command you, demon, to come out of this man."

The man's eyes shifted, becoming even more eerie, and his posture became defiantly rigid. A deep, otherworldly voice oozed from his lips. "Nooooo."

What? No? He's not allowed to say that. Is he allowed to say that? I mentally reviewed my *Exorcism for Dummies* checklist. Step One, I had said the Name "Jesus." Now, Step Two, it's the demon's job to say, "Oh. Right then. Guess I'll be going now."

But the demon was completely out of line. What did he mean he wasn't going? It's his duty to go. I was at a loss as to what to do next, so I just continued to demand that he leave in the Name of Jesus.

After several hours of this, one of the team members showed up and said, "Art, you look like you've been in a wrestling match."

"Yeah. I've never done this before."

"Really? I thought, since you're a missionary, you'd be an expert by now."

"I'm not," I said. "As one novice to another, would you join me in this?'

"Sure." He didn't look so sure.

The demon-possessed man began to shout louder and louder and cut open his own skin with his long, dirt-filled fingernails.

I'd had enough. Shedding all uncertainty, I said to the demon, "In the mighty Name of Jesus, the Son of the living God, who is my Lord, I command you, come out of this man."

To my astonishment, the man became stiff and then went limp. Still barely standing, he looked up. All at once, I was staring into the eyes of a completely different person—more like the eyes of a frail, wounded puppy.

"Thank you." The man's words were faint but coherent. And undeniably human. With tears in his eyes, the man took a deep breath and exhaled one word: "Free." He lowered his head and took a few more deep breaths. He looked back up at me and then at my prayer partner and thanked us again. Slowly regaining his bearings, he explained that the demon had come into him after he had angered a powerful maw phee. The demon had taken over his life.

We invited him to turn his life over to Jesus to prevent the demon from returning, but he vehemently refused.

"That would really anger the maw phee," he said.

We pointed out that he had just experienced how our God was more powerful than the maw phee's demons. But the man had made up his mind. I never heard what happened to him after that, because he left the village the next day and never returned. I struggled to understand why the demon had been able to resist for so many hours. I believe it was partially because of my unbelief, but also, it seems that an extra measure of power was unleashed when two of us joined together in prayer (see Matthew 18:19–20).

On one of our trips back to Samerng in 1987, we brought another DTS outreach team. We stopped at Pastor Wanchai's new home to ask if he wanted to accompany us to Baan Lankum. Wanchai explained that he and his wife now ran a ministry for girls who had no means of education available in their own villages. (Teenage girls with no education were often targeted by the unscrupulous flesh trade suppliers.) He had been so busy setting up a student dorm that he unfortunately would not have time to visit any of the outer villages for a while.

After a brief respite at Wanchai's house, we continued our trek to Baan Lankum. The chief once again permitted us to give a presentation, and we again visited every home to invite the people. As usual, only the children attended. I saw a young boy at the back of the room who was terribly emaciated, with sunken cheeks. His body was little more than a skeleton with a thin layer of skin. His dark, haunting eyes echoed hopelessness and despair. I had rarely seen a more frail child. We learned that the boy and his family had just moved into Baan Lankum three months earlier.

I asked Khru Idal, "What disease does this child have?"

"No disease," he replied, "just malnutrition."

I made a beeline for the child, knelt down to face him, and asked if we could pray for him. When he did not respond, Khru Idal called me aside and whispered, "I should also tell you that malnutrition isn't the only thing this poor boy is dealing with. You see, after his family moved to our village, his father brought almost all of the family's possessions to the maw phee, asking him to call on the evil spirits to restore the boy's health. The maw phee performed his chants and rituals in an attempt to summon the spirits, but in the end, the boy not only remained thin and sickly but also lost his ability to speak. He hasn't uttered a single word in six weeks."

I called together our team to pray for the boy. A young DTS student name Tuwee shocked us all by asking if she could lead the prayer. Tuwee was the shyest person I ever remember meeting. On previous occasions, she refused to speak to the group unless they all turned their heads away and promised not to look at her. I rarely saw her eyes, since she kept her head down most of the time. In the months that we had spent together as a group, I had never once heard her pray out loud, though I'm told that she would pray if only a couple of women were listening.

I gave Tuwee the go-ahead and told her that the rest of us would stand in agreement with her as she prayed for the boy. Tuwee laid her hands on the boy and began praying boldly and unflinchingly. She shed her timidity and took on the bearing of a lioness. As she prayed, the boy's mouth opened and dark spittle flowed down his chin. It was then that I saw how swollen his tongue was. As we continued in prayer, we watched his tongue miraculously shrink before our very eyes.

Tuwee then gently invited the boy to repeat after her, "Khawp koon Phra Yesu. Sundra sern Phra Jao." Thus, the first words out of the boy's mouth in six weeks were, "Thank You, Jesus. Praise the Lord."

Virapon said to me, "Achaan, I believe God wants us to take this boy to the new hospital in Samerng."

I concurred, and Khru Idal led us to the boy's parents. The boy's father flatly refused our offer.

"Is it because we are Christians?" I asked.

"No," he said. "I don't care about your religion. I just don't have any money for the hospital bill."

"Oh," I said. "I'm sorry I didn't make that clear. We will cover all the expenses, no strings attached. We just want to help the boy."

"In that case, please take him to the hospital as soon as possible. I entrust him into your care."

When we arrived at the hospital, the medical staff hooked the boy up to an intravenous feeding receptacle. The boy received round-the-clock medical treatment for three days. On the fourth day, the staff started him on solid foods and, on the fifth day, released him into Wanchai's care. Wanchai's wife is an outstanding cook, and after only one month of consuming her delicious, nourishing meals, the boy's weight skyrocketed from fifty-five pounds to seventy-eight pounds. The doctor concluded that the boy was now healthy enough to return to his village. Home at last, the boy sprinted out of our truck and into the arms of his parents.

"Thank you, thank you," they cried through their laughter and tears.

I assured them that the thanks belonged not to me but to God, who had given us both the opportunity and the means to help.

We drove back to Chiang Mai and dropped off the DTS team at the train station for their return trip to Bangkok. There at the Chiang Mai train station, my family picked up an outreach team from Halpine, our home church in Maryland. We packed them into our vehicles, and we all trucked back to Baan Lankum. I told the team that they could give a presentation for the village, but they would probably need to gear it toward children, since the adults in the village had a history of shunning our invitations.

The people of Baan Lankum proved me wrong. For the first time in the many years that we had been reaching out to them, the whole village turned up. They had seen the boy and heard about his healing. At the end of our program, we invited the people to respond to the message. I choked back the tears when the boy's father walked forward. Following his lead, the chief and each of the twenty-two village elders came forward to devote their lives to Jesus.

I could hardly sleep that night in the joy and wonder of all that had transpired. From this day forward, these people would be free from the fears that had held them captive.

We hoped that the maw phee would attend Geoff Atkinson's highly effective "Barefoot Doctor Training Program," which would enable him to retain his position as the village's medicine man. Sadly, the maw phee wanted nothing more to do with the people of his village. He wasted little time in moving out.

Meanwhile, Wanchai discipled a trustworthy young man who was accepted as the pastor of the vibrant, new congregation. This story, which began and ended with sick little boys, had a happy ending. As long as the people continue to follow Jesus wholeheartedly, there will never be another human sacrifice.

At least, not in that village.

FOURTEEN

Men in Green

THE shiny new motorbike screeched to a halt, throwing dust into the faces of my assailants. As the dust cleared, I considered the unsightly lineup of bullets crisscrossing chests, AK-47 assault rifles perched for action, and waists encumbered with hand grenadeladen belts. It would be an understatement to say that the appearance of these men was intimidating.

I saw the reflection of my shiny bike gleaming in the eyes of the ringleader. My stomach muscles knotted, and my mouth turned dry. The term joy ride obviously no longer applied to my little jaunt.

It was 1987. We were hosting a team made up of Americans, Canadians, Dutch, and Malaysians. Our destination was the Hmong village of our new friend, Khun Yuam, who had asked us to share the gospel with his people. Just the day before, the whole team had set out for the mountains in a four-wheel-drive truck and three borrowed motorbikes. Even though the roads between the cities of Chiang Mai and Pai were paved, we moved at a painfully slow pace because one of the motorbikes kept breaking down. What should have taken two hours became a four-hour journey.

In Pai, which was only the halfway point to the Hmong village, we found a place to eat and made some quick decisions about how to handle the challenge before us. The roads ahead were steep and coarsely entwined. By now, we knew that this rundown motorbike would never make it.

We decided that I would take the malfunctioning motorbike back to town and the team would continue on to the village. After lunch, I parted with the team and headed back down the mountain. Four and a half hours later, the bike slowly putted its way into Chiang Mai, where I returned it to its owner. Exhausted, but relieved to have made it back, I spent the night in Chiang Mai.

The next morning, I got up early and headed straight for Daret's Restaurant and Motorbike Rental Shop. Mr. Daret, an elder in the Chinese church, had for years demonstrated a humbling level of generosity toward missionaries. I told his son, who now ran the business, that I needed to rent a motorbike right away.

"I'm sorry," he said. "I wish I could help you, but I can't. I've rented out all the mountain motorbikes, and all I have left are the little motor scooters. Maybe if you come back tomorrow, I can help you."

"I really need something now," I said. "I have a team waiting for me. I'll try one of the other shops."

I tried every other shop I knew, without success. Wearily, I returned to Daret's for a late breakfast.

As I ate, I prayed, *Lord, please help me find a motorcycle.*

Just then, the senior Mr. Daret approached me. "Did you find a mountain bike yet?"

"No, not yet," I said.

"Well then, come. Let me show you something."

I followed him past the other diners and into a back room.

"By the way," he said, "why do you need a motorcycle anyway?"

"I'm going to a remote village in the Mae Hong Son province to share the gospel. My team is already at the village, and I need to join them."

Mr. Daret stopped in front of a large covered object and carefully pulled the canvas back, revealing a shiny, new mountain motorbike.

What a beautiful piece of craftsmanship! A dream bike. The cherry red body with black lines and shiny chrome glimmered in the dim light. *That would sure be a fun ride.*

"Will this do?" he said.

"It certainly would, but how much are you asking for the rental?" It was obviously a higher-class bike than I could afford.

"Since you need this for the work of God and for helping the Thai people, you can use it for free. Will a week be long enough?"

I protested his generosity, but when it was clear that he had no intention of changing his mind, I gratefully accepted his offer.

I shouldn't have been so surprised. How many times before had I seen the Lord's miraculous provision, His protection, His loving care, despite my flailing and failings? The Lord knew what I needed, and He had provided. It was that simple. I was thankful, too, that He had such generous and gracious servants as Mr. Daret to carry out His work.

When I mounted the motorbike, I saw that only seven kilometers were logged on the odometer. I was taking this bike on its maiden voyage. The trip back up the mountain was exhilarating. Having lost so much time, I decided to take a shorter but bumpier route. Child's play for this bike.

The rushing whip of the wind on my face was not quite enough to neutralize the blistering heat of the sun, but I didn't care. I didn't even mind the sting of the dust in my eyes. I was too absorbed in the thrill of riding this overwhelmingly smooth machine.

The landscape, speckled with teakwood, pine, and evergreen trees, reinforced the lush green of the grassy meadows. Richly painted red and white opium poppies lined the rocky roads and hillside. Snakes undoubtedly hid in the tall grass, waiting for their unfortunate prey to wander in. But on a vehicle like this, no predator could possibly mess with me. I careened down the dirt roads, flying over deep ruts carved into the red clay by torrential rains. I weaved back and forth through the hills, hugging the curves and avoiding the potholes.

After a while, it dawned on me that I should have already reached the village. I started paying more attention to the road and realized that I had no clue where I was. All these roads led to a village somewhere, though. I decided to just keep going until I found someone who could give me directions.

The heat lingered as the afternoon waned, but the air was heavy with anticipation of the evening's cool relief. With dusk drawing close, I squeezed the accelerator and took flight over the next hill. As my tires hit the earth on the down side of the hill, I looked up and slammed the brakes. The bike slid right up to the face of an insurgent roadblock.

Roughly a dozen heavily armed men stood before me, their horses laden with unmistakable bags of heroin—"white gold" on its way to payoff, to make slaves of its victims.

So here I was, alone, unarmed, and sporting a motorbike that would be the envy of any guy, let alone a drug-dealing gang whose weapons bought them anything they wanted, without regard to the cost of lives or property.

Oh, boy. These guys must be Khun Sah's men.

Khun Sah* was a notorious drug lord responsible for producing more heroin than anyone else in the world. In a few moderately safe settings, I had actually managed to share the gospel and give Bibles to some of his men. It was rumored that Khun Sah was superstitious and didn't want to hurt missionaries for fear of upsetting a formidable spiritual being.

Still, I didn't want to rely on his superstition to protect me from this motley crew. I had little doubt that they would readily shoot first and ask questions later. The men stared at me the way a hunter would at a prize buck that had just walked into the center of his target hairs.

The stench of these men forced its way into my nostrils. The men had probably been sleeping in the jungle for several days. Standing

---

*Khun Sah is half Shan and half Chinese, but his citizenship is Burmese. He had many connections in Chiang Mai, Thailand. He lived in the Shan state, a part of Burma that borders China and Thailand. In the nineteenth century, at a time when England and France were conquering much of Asia, the King of Thailand (then called Siam) gave the Shan State territory to England. "Shan" means "Siam" in the Burmese language, and the Shan refer to themselves as Thai Yai, translated "big, or older, Thai." To the French, the Siamese king gave away land that is known today as Laos. As a result of its tactically astute land concessions, the country known today as Thailand has never come under colonial rule. In this region of Thailand, though, the drug warlords have often unofficially subjugated the tribal peoples. With the exorbitant funds they receive for their drug trafficking, the warlords are able to maintain a very well-equipped arsenal of modern weapons. They often draft village men against their will, and they have killed a number of Thai and American drug enforcement officers and their wives.

barely three or four feet away from me was the man I perceived to be the leader of the gang. Dressed in an old, green uniform and streaked with dirt, he appeared to be a Burmese man in his early thirties. Long, thick, black hair was greased back over his ears and rested on his thin frame.

The man glared at me, and then his toothless smile broadened. Red beetlenut juice oozed down the sides of his mouth. I didn't need a copy of his police records to recognize that a misstep on my part could prove fatal. His cocked rifle, aimed at my head, sent a clear enough message even for someone as dimwitted as I.

"Are you alone?" he said.

As a Christian, I knew I must never lie, but I was also pretty sure that if I told these bandits I was alone, I'd be a dead man. *Dear God, what should I say?*

The words of Psalm 91:11 came to mind: "He shall give His angels charge over you, to keep you in all your ways."

With full confidence in this truth, I said, "No, I'm not alone. I am with many."

As soon as I had spoken those words, the leader's eyes diverted to something behind me. He froze in fear, and the barrel of his gun dropped to the ground. All the others looked equally spooked. Their coarse laughing instantly ceased. These grizzly warriors suddenly looked like they were auditioning to play the victims in a horror movie.

The phrase "carpe diem" (seize the day) never seemed more appropriate. I twisted the accelerator to full throttle, popped the clutch, and sped away in a cloud of dust.

Had those rebels just seen the fierce angels that I was referring to when I told them I wasn't alone? It couldn't have been any ordinary thing to have so arrested their attention. Whatever it was, it had miraculously saved my life.

If I go back, I wondered, *maybe I'll see those angels too.* Then something strangely foreign surfaced in my mind: sanity. *No way, Art, that would be stupid. Do you have a death wish?*

As I flew down that road, so full of relief, gratitude, and awe for the mighty God who had graciously spared my life, I recalled the last time that God had rescued me from the twin perils of (1) armed bandits and (2) my own cluelessness.

A few months earlier I had received a call from the American consul of Chiang Mai, Mr. Harlan Lee. Harlan had asked me to come see him in his office. He had always greatly impressed me. Harlan was an exceptionally capable diplomat who had a clear respect for the Thai people, spoke the Thai language fluently, and was one of the few government workers I'd ever met who was thrifty with the taxpayers' dollars.

The following day at his office Harlan told me that an American man had been arrested in the city of Phitsanulok, and he wanted to help the man survive his prison term, since prisoners in Thailand had to order and pay for their own food and bedding. But Harlan was concerned that if he helped the young American, it might imply that he was questioning the Thai penal system. Since YWAM was known for its prison ministry, Harlan asked if I would accompany him.

"I'd be happy to," I said.

"I'll drive you there in my limousine," he said. "I also need to visit all the northern Thai provincial governors."

The next day we left Chiang Mai and visited the governors of Lampang, Phrea, and Uttaradit. Then, on the way to Phitsanulok, we encountered a roadblock guarded by Communist bandits. As we neared the roadblock, my adrenaline began to pump—not because of fear, oddly enough, but because this was an exact reenactment of a dream I had just recently had.

In my dream, I was in a car very much like the consul's armored limousine, and we had been stopped by an identical rebel roadblock. The rebels in the dream took us captive, but I had told them, "You think that I am your hostage, but the truth is that you are my hostage. Regardless of whatever ransom my government might pay, I am not leaving until you have repented of your sins and turned your life over to God."

But this was no dream. These were real rebel forces. The consul's chauffer stepped on the gas. Our armored car pummeled through the roadblock and effortlessly deflected the rebel assault. However, I was so confident that God had given me the dream in preparation for this moment that I thoughtlessly mumbled, "Oh rats. We should've stopped and talked with them."

"Are you crazy?" Harlan said. Ordinarily, when someone asks this question, what he really means is, "You silly person, you." In this case, however, I sensed that our esteemed consul was very seriously considering how I would look in a straightjacket.

By the time we arrived in Phitsanulok, it was late. We checked into a nice, clean, cheap hotel. I spent the following morning visiting the prison and learning what the American would need to endure his sentence. The following week I made preparations to return to Phitsanulok. I packed up our old Volkswagen van with food, books, games, and other supplies I thought the American prisoner might enjoy.

Phitsanulok was about a six-hour drive from our home, and I was not able to start my trip until five o'clock in the evening. On top of that, once I got going, I was stopped by two police checkpoints, thus delaying my time of arrival by another couple of hours.

Then, just outside a village called Moo Ban Tak, I heard a loud "pop" from the Volkswagen motor, and smoke began pouring out from the rear of the van. I navigated the vehicle onto the shoulder of the road and glanced at my watch. It was now 10:30 PM, and in the pitch black of the night, I could barely perceive the silhouette of forest that stretched along the road, much less see any sign of life. I locked up the van and started walking.

About an hour passed before I finally saw the headlights of a vehicle headed in my direction. I stuck out my thumb in the international sign for "Please have mercy on my poor, weary feet," and the tour bus stopped. When I got onto the bus, I noticed that it held only three other people, including the driver.

"We're headed for the bus terminal in Tak," the driver said. "Where are you going?"

"Anywhere in Tak would be fine," I said. "How much do I owe you?"

"Don't worry about paying anything. But what in the world are you doing out in the middle of nowhere?"

"My vehicle broke down three or four kilometers up the road," I said.

When we arrived at the terminal, I thanked the kind bus driver and started looking for an inexpensive hotel. Early the next morning I asked the hotel receptionist where I could find a tow truck.

"The only tow trucks in Tak belong to the police," she said.

At the police station, I found the officer in charge of the tow trucks and told him, "My Volkswagen van broke down about twelve kilometers north of Tak, near the village of Moo Ban Tak. How much will it cost to tow my van back here?"

"It broke down near Moo Ban Tak?" the officer said. "You can forget about ever seeing that van again. That area is swarming with Communist bandits. You're very lucky to have escaped with your life. You are a very foolish man to have broken down in that area. Believe me, it would be a waste of time and money to even attempt to retrieve it. I hope your vehicle is insured for theft."

"Sir, it wasn't my intention for the vehicle to break down. But I've prayed that my God will protect it, and I'm confident that it will still be there. Please, how much will it cost me to get my van towed?"

"Okay. If you're determined to throw your money away, I'll do it for five hundred baht (about US$25 at the time). However, when you see that your van is gone, we are coming straight back to Tak. There will be no looking around for your stolen vehicle. Do you understand?"

"Agreed," I said.

We drove to where my van had broken down. To the astonishment of the officer, it was precisely where I had left it. The officer raised the van onto his tow truck, then paused to spy the terrain before jumping back into the cab of his truck where I was waiting. He turned the ignition and stepped on the accelerator.

"You are a very lucky man," he said. "I can't believe your van is still in one piece and none of your belongings were stolen. I don't know what to make of it." Then he chuckled. "The only explanation must be that your God does answer prayers. This is truly a miracle."

Once we arrived back in Tak, I went to several mechanics but found none who worked on Volkswagen engines. The mechanics repaired only Japanese-made vehicles. I was told that the van needed to go to Bangkok or Chiang Mai for repairs, and I called up Dan Dunham, who agreed to pick me up and tow the van to Chiang Mai.

While waiting for Dan to arrive, I picked up a newspaper. The front page read, "Over eight hundred Communist bandits have surrendered their weapons to government officials in exchange for farmland and a pardon from their crimes. The ceremony took place near their stronghold in Moo Ban Tak yesterday evening at six o'clock."

I stopped and read again those words: "in Moo Ban Tak yesterday evening at six o'clock." That had been only hours before my van had broken down in that exact same area. I was reminded of what the prophet Jeremiah wrote: "'For I am with you to save you and deliver you,' says the LORD. 'I will deliver you from the hand of the wicked, and I will redeem you from the grip of the terrible'" (Jeremiah 15:20–21).

When I reported these events to Harlan, I wondered whether he would ever dare to ask me on another trip.

He never did.

FIFTEEN

A Team for the City

A FEW days after Christmas, I received a long-distance phone call from international Bible teacher Dean Sherman. Dean wanted to know if he could bring his YWAM team to Chiang Mai in two weeks.

When I told Ellen, she responded with, "What? In two weeks? That's Chinese New Year. There's no way. You told him no, right?"

"Actually, I told him they could come."

"Wow." Ellen took a deep breath. "I guess we'll have to make the best of it. And it'll be so good to see Dean again. How many people are on his team?"

"Um, well, there's…seventy people."

"Seventeen? That's not too bad," she said. "Are they all young singles?"

"Uh, no, honey. Not seventeen. Seventy."

Ellen froze.

"And," I said, "they are mostly families, with babies and senior citizens. And that's not the hardest part."

"Not the hardest part?" Ellen said. "What could be harder than seventy people coming during the chaos of Chinese New Year, with only
two weeks' notice?"

"They don't have very much money," I said.

"Don't worry, honey. I'm sure we can make do. Even if they each have
as little as ten dollars a day, we just might be able to make this work."

Marveling at this courageous woman of faith that God had given
me, I almost hesitated to release the final blow. "That's the thing. They
have only two dollars each per day."

"Two dollars. Two dollars? And you told them they could come? Art,
how can we possibly take care of seventy people on two dollars a day?
Our whole staff already has plans to take time off for the holidays, and
there's no way we could possibly fit seventy more people into this house.
Then there's food, truck rental, gasoline. We're just barely breaking even
ourselves, and…Art, what could you have possibly been thinking?"

I smiled sheepishly. "Well, Jesus sent out the seventy."

"Yes," she said, without missing a beat, "but He sent them out in
groups of two. If this team wants to come in tag teams of two, they are
more than welcome, but Art, you have to call them back right now and
tell them not to come."

"Honey, please let me explain. Their situation is different from other
teams that have come here without enough finances. They had a miscommunication with the airlines. The travel agent said that all the
minors in their group would be discounted, but when they went to pay
for the tickets, they found out that only the children under the age of
twelve could receive the group's discounted rate. So now the team has
to take substantial funds out of their budgeted living expenses to pay
for all of the teenagers."

Ellen listened but said nothing.

"Remember what a blessing Dean's last team was?" I said. "And they
were completely content to just sprawl out on mattresses on the floor
of the church. Granted, this year's team is too large to fit in the church,
but I'm sure we can find a few other large rooms around town that can
house them all. Besides, Khun Noy has been asking for assistance, and
Daniel told me he could really use an outreach team at his village. I
think this team is large enough to help everyone."

"Large enough to help everyone go bankrupt you mean. This is just great. I can see the headlines now, 'Seventy Tourists Starve to Death in Thailand.'"

Thanks to the fact that Ellen usually has an endless supply of grace for my insanity, she and I rarely argue. In this case, though, we couldn't come to an agreement. There wasn't exactly much room for compromise. Either the seventy people were coming, or they weren't. I thought she was being unreasonable, and she thought I was nuts.

"Honey," I said, "I don't want to argue. If you need me, I'll be in next room praying for you."

Now, if there is one thing that a husband should never say when his wife is upset, that's it.

Stunned, Ellen started to speak, then stopped, turned around, and walked out of the room. She got in the truck and drove to the home of our dear friends, the Dunhams. Since Mary Dunham had often talked about how crazy she thought we were to host all these teams, Ellen was confident that Mary would be able to sympathize with our present situation.

Ellen poured out her heart, but to her surprise, Mary said, "You need to ask forgiveness for having a negative attitude. Let's look at the situation plainly. The team has already arranged to come, and there's nothing you can do about it now. So you'd better just get on your knees and pray."

Ellen paused momentarily to grapple with her bewilderment at Mary's response and then said, "You're right." She and Mary got on their knees and for the next three hours wept and prayed together. Ellen washed her tear-stained face and returned home with a new attitude.

I know that I had been wrong not to discuss the matter with Ellen before telling the team they could come, but Ellen was now determined to make the best of it and to support me in my decision. When we told the rest of the team, they all agreed to delay their holiday plans to help out.

Two weeks later, right on schedule, two large tour buses parked near our driveway. It's hard to put into words what it was like to see that many people with that many bags pour out onto our driveway and into our house. It was like one of those clown cars at the circus, where the car is a bottomless pit of clowns, and just when you think there's no way that any clowns could be left in the car, more just keep coming and coming and coming. I was tempted to check under the buses to see if there was some hole the people were all climbing out of.

Our meeting room was barely big enough to house all of their suitcases, let alone their bodies. Every square inch of standing room soon became a precious commodity.

We were already worn out from the preparations for the team, not to mention keeping up with all of our routine ministries. Thanks to the help of friends, we were able to find housing for the whole team. The team would be spread out all over the city, but at least everyone had a mattress and pillow. Providing them all with food, transportation, gasoline, and two weeks of meaningful ministry opportunities would take another miracle.

On that first evening, we hosted almost one hundred people for dinner, since we had also invited the local pastors and missionaries who would be assisting in the outreach. Ellen and Ruan Moon, our faithful friend and helper, had labored for several hours that day over a hot stove, preparing what they hoped would be enough rice and stir-fry for everyone.

After praying over the food, I announced, "First come, first served."

Amid the clamor of crying babies, a host of teenage boys raced to the front of the buffet line. As Ellen and Ruan Moon served, the boys grabbed their plates and began filling them. Bewildered at how grossly we had underestimated the appetite of the average American adolescent, Ellen looked down to see that the pots of rice and stir-fry were already half-empty. And that was after barely a dozen teenagers had gone through the line.

"Do we have any more food in the kitchen?" Ellen asked Ruan Moon in Thai.

"No," Ruan Moon said.

"Are any markets still open?" Ellen asked, though she already knew the answer.

"No."

"Oh, Ruan Moon. When this is over, I promise you a two-week vacation."

"No problem." Ruan Moon smiled. "This is fun."

"Fun?" Ellen said. "How can we get more food. Any ideas?"

"Let's ask God to multiply the food."

"You're right, Ruan Moon. But I'm too upset. You'll have to pray."

Ruan Moon prayed a very simple prayer, and then she and Ellen resumed serving the guests, doing their best to smile and greet each person warmly. Before they knew it, Dean, who had graciously waited until everyone else had been served, was taking his plate.

"Are you the last in line?" Ellen asked him.

"Yep. Everyone else has been served. They're sitting on the stairs, on the floor, even in the trees."

Ellen looked down at the food. There was still half a pot of rice and half a pot of stir-fry left.

Turning to Ruan Moon, Ellen asked, "Did you find more food and replace it while I wasn't looking?"

"No."

Ellen asked me, "Did you find more food somewhere?"

"No," I said, "but everyone seems to have had their fill. You and Ruan Moon did a great job."

"How is this possible?" Ellen said.

People began going back for seconds, and Ellen cross-examined our staff. No one had added anything to the pots.

"Honey," Ellen said to me, "there's no other explanation. God must have multiplied the food." She then went upstairs to the quiet of our bedroom to ask God's forgiveness for her disbelief and to thank Him for the miracle.

Somehow, the entire team ended up eating, sleeping, and traveling the countryside, ministering for two full weeks. They left the same way they had arrived, in those two large, bottomless pits that strangely resembled tour buses.

In the coming years, we would end up hosting even larger teams. Having learned my lesson, I always made it a point to first discuss the proposition with Ellen. Without fail, she welcomed every team with remarkable poise and benevolence.

One year after "The Seventy," Ellen rushed into the house and said to me, "Art, what are those tour buses doing parked outside our house?"

The truth was that the buses were not transporting an outreach team. They belonged to the wedding guests of our wealthy neighbors. I knew I was facing an important test here. Was I willing to have a good laugh at the expense of my wife's nerves? The answer to that question was, well, yes, ordinarily, maybe. But when I gazed into Ellen's eyes, which pleadingly looked up at me, I realized that some jokes were simply not worth it. So I told her the truth.

SIXTEEN

The Best Defense

THERE was no other explanation. Someone must have been stealing our gasoline. Every evening, we would fill the gas tanks of our vehicles, and every morning, we would find that the tanks had mysteriously become almost completely emptied. We couldn't find any sign of holes or leaks in the tanks. For two weeks, the team took turns watching for intruders. The guard, whom our landlord had hired, would relieve me at four o'clock in the morning, watching the vehicles until seven o'clock.

Night after night, the thief outwitted us. This was a serious problem. We were on a tight budget, and gasoline was our biggest expense. (In those days, gasoline in Thailand cost nearly three times the price of gasoline in the continental US.) I couldn't figure out how the robber was pulling it off.

One morning around five o'clock, Ellen awoke with a start. She decided to go out to the balcony to check on our vehicles.

Moments later, her voice called me out of a deep sleep. "Quick, Art, wake up. Shhhh. Come with me."

We tiptoed to the balcony and saw the guard taking a short hose out of our van's gas tank.

"Stop, thief," I shouted in Thai.

The guard quickly capped his two gas cans. Grabbing one in each hand, he ran toward his house.

"So that's why we had such a hard time catching our thief," I said.

We might have guessed, since we had previously caught the guard's wife stealing the preschool money.

"I'll confront him in the morning," I said, and we returned to bed.

First thing the next morning, I went straight to the guard's house. I told him that we knew he was the one who had been siphoning gas from our cars.

"How could you do this?" I said. "We trusted you. Haven't we always treated you and your family well?"

"I don't know who told you that I stole your gas, but it wasn't me," he said. "It must have been Thom. She hates me. I bet she was the one who told you that I was the thief."

"Thom told us nothing," I said. "She didn't have to. Ellen and I saw you clearly in the light of last night's full moon. And when we called out to you, we watched you run into your house with the containers full of gas. There's no question that you're the culprit. If you tell the truth and confess, we will give you another chance."

He started to quiver. "No sir, I'm not lying. I didn't steal your gas. Thom lied to you."

I had no choice but to ask our landlord to evict him. The landlord hesitated to believe our report, but I told her that we could not carry on with a thief in our home. After much debate, she gave in.

"Okay," she said. "I'll tell the guard he has to go, but I am not happy about it. I think it's time that you left as well. Your lease will soon be up, and you can rest assured that I will not be renewing it under any circumstance."

The landlord told the guard that he must pack his belongings and leave immediately. The guard packed up and left, but not before pouring some of the stolen gasoline into our water well.

Our gasoline bill radically declined from that day forward. I noticed, however, that our electric bill had been increasing every month. At the next team meeting, I asked that we all try to be a little more frugal in our use of the electricity.

A few days later, we were preparing to leave for a mission conference in southern Thailand, and I went to turn the electric meter off. After I shut it off, I could see that the meter was still spinning around. *That's odd.* I looked up and noticed several wires coming out of our electrical control box. The wires led right into several of our neighbors' houses. No wonder our bill had been so high. We had been paying the electric bill for most of the neighborhood. After I had called the electric company to come and resolve the problem, we all piled into the truck and headed south.

As we discussed these events on our way to the conference, we realized that we must be careful to guard against any seeds of bitterness that might threaten to take root in our hearts. Through the years, we have worked alongside other relief workers who sacrificed much in order to minister to refugees, orphans, and other desperate souls of society. Commonly, these relief workers expected gratitude in return, only to find their beneficiaries abusing their trust by stealing their cameras, watches, purses, wallets, and other personal belongings. If the relief workers gave in to feelings of resentment, those feelings could give way to attitudes that robbed them of the power to love those they were sent to serve.

But Jesus had forgiven us unconditionally, not to mention that we had already been on the receiving end of so much love from the people of Chiang Mai. We had no excuse for harboring any feelings of resentment. We arrived at the conference determined to be thankful for the privilege of ministering the love of Christ, regardless of the circumstances.

After the conference, we took our kids to their highly anticipated one-week summer camp in Pattaya while Ellen and I enjoyed a romantic getaway. Pastor Boonmark's brother-in-law, the general manager of a three-star beach resort in Pattaya, had invited us to stay at his hotel for only ten dollars a night. Ellen and I settled into our charming quarters and then went for a walk along the beach. A steady stream of cool, refreshing breezes complemented a warm, richly hued sunset. Everything was perfect, except for one little detail: the arrival of the United States naval fleet.

The battleship USS *New Jersey*, along with an assortment of various other naval vessels, had just docked in Pattaya. More than ten thousand sailors and marines poured out onto the beaches, attracting just as many Thai prostitutes. I don't know how long these men had been at sea, but they behaved as if it had been decades. The men were drinking, fighting, and performing openly lewd actions. We felt as if we had arrived in Sodom and Gomorrah.

Oh, great. I began to well up with self-pity about the ill timing of what was supposed to be a romantic getaway. About that moment, we passed a massive American sailor who was trying to gently communicate with a local woman at her fried-banana stand. This man, well over six feet tall and nearly three hundred pounds, was an intimidating figure to behold, especially in contrast to the petite Thai woman. I guessed that the woman was not even five feet tall and weighed less than a hundred pounds.

But it wasn't the man's size that caught our attention; it was the words he spoke. "Jesus loves you," he said in a deep, baritone voice.

"Mai cow jai loei, kah," the woman replied in a high, quivering voice, trying to communicate that she didn't understand anything he was saying.

Ellen and I approached the compassionate young giant and offered to translate for him. He readily accepted our invitation and told such a tender story of how Jesus had changed his life that it deeply touched us as well as the woman.

When he finished speaking, I asked him, "Are there any more guys like you on those ships?"

"Oh, yes, sir," he said. "On my ship alone, there are thirty of us who meet regularly for Bible study and prayer, but the others all decided not to come ashore."

I said, "Why don't you gather the guys and have them meet us tomorrow at the little church on Thirteenth Street?"

"Sounds great."

The next morning, we met with the thirty believers. After a time of worship, prayer, and testimonies, I asked the guys why they had originally chosen not to come ashore. They said they'd had bad experiences when coming to places like Pattaya. Lonely and so far away from the support of their loved ones, they had, at times, succumbed to temptation. They then had to deal with the guilty consciences and ill consequences that generally accompany sin.

"It's just not worth it, so we figured the best solution was just to stay on the ship."

Ellen and I had an idea. We taught the guys a few evangelistic skits and then took them straight to the center of the red-light district. There, on a street corner, we sang some worship songs and performed the skits. Then our African-American giant preached in English while I translated. We continued this for three days. By the end of our time together, seven American sailors and two Thai prostitutes had repented and given their hearts to Jesus.

As our friends were preparing to return to their departing ship, I asked them, "Over the last few days, did any of you struggle with the usual temptations?"

"Not at all," one said.

"The thought never entered our minds this time," another said. "We had such a terrific time sharing that we weren't the least bit tempted."

"Remember that," I said. "I'm sure you guys have had coaches like I had who would say, 'the best defense is a good offense.' This holds true for our spiritual battles as well. When we're on the offensive, the demons of this world will be too busy running from us to attack us."

As soon as we returned to Chiang Mai, we began searching for a new home base. Just weeks before our old lease was up, we found the perfect house on Hatsadisawee Road. The house and price were everything we had prayed for, but the location...well, that was a different story.

At one end of our street was a red-light district, home to a host of twelve-, thirteen-, and fourteen-year-old girls who had been sold into prostitution. Greedy businessmen tell the families of these girls that instead of having to grow up in a poor village, the girls will be taught a trade and will send money back home. Many struggling families believe the lie and sell their daughter to these businessmen. On the east side of the wall that circled our new ministry house were about twenty squatter families living in desperate poverty, their homes made of an assortment of cardboard, tin, and old wood.

Across the street was a Buddhist temple. The temple's high priest was a New Zealander who had a reputation for being antagonistic toward Christians. He warned me that if he ever found me or anyone else from YWAM setting foot on the temple grounds, he would call the police. His attitude contrasted with that of other high priests, who had customarily welcomed me into their temples to discuss religion with their monks.

Next to the Buddhist temple was a Muslim holy ground, little more than an open field at the center of which was a wooden post that held a loudspeaker. Five times a day, an Islamic imam would use the loudspeaker to cry out Arabic prayers.

Across the street from the Muslim property was a Buddhist cremation center. Each time the crematory was used, a deafening cannon would go off. The crematory director explained that the cannon was used to scare away the evil spirits, giving the dead person's soul easy access into the nether world on its journey to reincarnation.

I don't want to give the impression that it was all bad. We actually enjoyed living there. Though there were aspects that were unpleasant, all that cacophony also blended into a fairly desperate cry for the love of Christ.

Determined to stay on the offensive spiritually, our team began every day with prayer and worship. We asked Jesus to turn all the garbage around us into fertilizer; then He could breathe life into a beautiful garden of precious souls from our neighborhood. We would do what we could to be His hands and feet to minister to our neighbors.

We wondered whether God had taken our prayer literally when our neighboring squatters began dumping their garbage onto our property. But we realized that God was giving us a very practical way to reach out to these people with His grace. Over the next few years, we saw some major changes in our surroundings. One by one, the squatters obtained jobs and moved into better living situations. Within just a few years, only four families remained.

In no time at all, the cannon from the crematory was removed. The crematory structure remained, but it is rarely used.

At the Muslim holy ground, the loudspeaker ultimately rusted out and was removed. Rumor has it that enough money was raised to erect a mosque on the land, but a Muslim lawyer emptied the bank account and disappeared. The imam then had a little house built on the land, where he now quietly lives with his family and his cattle.

The high priest of the Buddhist temple never wavered in his contempt for us, although that did not stop the young Buddhist monks from sneaking over the temple walls to visit us. The monks were intrigued to know what it was that the high priest didn't want them to hear. They were especially intrigued by the movie *Jesus,* which we showed them on our newly acquired secondhand VCR.

The bars, cafes, and rent-by-the-hour motels of the red-light district steadily lost business and within just a few years dwindled to less than 20 percent of the district's former heyday. It remains so to this day. One bar owner of European descent told me that he had made a fortune operating bars all over Thailand but that for some mysterious reason, his bar at Hatsadisawee Road had consistently lost money. He said that the other bar owners had experienced the same problem.

"That's what happens when garbage is turned into fertilizer," I said. "Why don't you get right with God, sell all your bars, and use the money to assist these young girls in furthering their education?"

The bar owner just laughed.

SEVENTEEN

No Compromise

I WILL always be grateful for all that Joe Harbison did to familiarize me with ministry in Thailand. Joe had a policy of no compromise that even the Thai government officials seemed to appreciate. He had invited many of the immigration officers over for meals and to share his faith with them. Though none of them had accepted Christ, they all respected Joe for his concern and for his honesty about why he had come to Thailand. They knew that he loved the Thai people and that his motivation was to see them live good and fruitful lives.

When Joe introduced me to them as his colleague, I received similar respect from them. Often, in my visits to the immigration office, they would jokingly ask me how many Thais I had saved. I would reply, "Not enough."

Over the years, I found that as long as I dealt honestly with the immigration personnel, I received only favor. The officers would often tell me about foreigners who had tried to deceive them about their reasons for being in Thailand. The officers had not been fooled for a minute.

On one occasion, an officer introduced me to a tall, lanky businessman who was well groomed and spoke with a distinctly Midwestern American accent.

As soon as the businessman had departed, the officer asked me, "Do you know what kind of man that was?"

"A businessman from Chicago?" I said.

"That's what he wants us to think, but he's no businessman. He's not even American. We have confirmed that he is actually a top Russian field agent of the KGB, but he thinks he has us fooled, so we play along."

During Joe's last few months in Chiang Mai, he had told the dean of men at the University of Chiang Mai that we would be available to teach English. "We'll teach your students for free," Joe said, "but we'll maintain control of the material we use, and it will be Christian-focused."

In those days, native English speakers were rare in Thailand. The dean was keenly interested, but he offered to pay us a considerable sum of money if Joe would agree to use a secular curriculum. Joe declined. The dean said, "Well, then, put your intentions in a written, formal request for the board to review."

The dean kept calling meetings wherein he would again try to bait us with money, but Joe kept reiterating that we were not in this for the money. We were happy to equip the students with the practical tool of the English language, but we were more concerned about the students' spirits than their intellects. Joe reassured the dean that we had no intention of doing anything inappropriate like making the students memorize our Christian precepts. We simply wanted to facilitate discussions about the meaning of life. After a few months of debating the issue, the dean finally approved everything that Joe had requested.

One year later, we invited the dean over for dinner. At the closing of our meal, the dean said, "I was born a Buddhist, and I will die a Buddhist. However, this generation of students is being hit with such destructive forces—drugs, sexually transmitted diseases, Communism, and Fascism. I don't know how they will survive unless they accept your Jesus."

"I'm delighted to hear that, sir," I said, "but I'm surprised. I remember how hard you fought Joe Harbison about this issue."

"I was wrong, and I grew in my respect of Mr. Harbison when he refused to compromise," the dean said.

"If you genuinely believe that only Jesus has the power to rescue this generation," I said, "wouldn't you like to put your own life into His hands?"

Abruptly standing up, the dean smiled and said, "I think it's time for me to go now. I thank you for a delicious meal and thank you for your concern for my students, but you needn't concern yourselves with me."

We then said our goodbyes. As the dean drove away, I remembered back to the first time I had recognized the truth about Jesus. Like this man, I had originally looked to intellectual fulfillment for the answers. I had delved into the Bible, examining it from cover to cover with the sole intent of writing a thesis about all its flaws and inconsistencies. Instead, I came face-to-face with the revelation that these were indeed the words of life. But as a foolish and cocky young college student, I had decided that I would rather live life my own way.

How I now longed for the dean, and all others like him, to discover the infusion of life that fills a person who has committed him- or herself to Christ Jesus. I don't know whether the dean ever did accept Jesus, but I certainly pray that he did.

The following year, a Buddhist high school in Lam Phun requested that we present a special Christmas program. I thought it went well, but as soon as we got home, I received a telephone call from the principal.

"We asked you to come our school to tell the students in our English Club about Christmas," he said. "How dare you use that time to talk about Jesus."

"Sir," I said, "that's what Christmas is about. It's a celebration of how Jesus came to Earth to save us."

"No way, you can't fool me. I happen to know for a fact that Christmas is about Santa Claus, reindeer, and snow. It has absolutely nothing to do with Jesus."

"Sir, these things you mention are parts of folklore and traditions that are specific only to Western culture. But around the world, the foundational core of Christmas is the birth of Jesus in Bethlehem two thousand years ago."

I continued to try to reason with him, but he said that we would never be invited again. Before I could respond, he slammed down the telephone. I suppose I could have been upset, but I wasn't. I had learned from experience that we didn't need to compromise our faith in these situations. I reflected on the fruit that had resulted from Joe's legacy. Life is too short and the world is filled with too much sorrow to yield our message to compromise.

One week after my phone conversation with the high school principal, I was surprised to receive another call from him. He explained that the students in the English Club had told their fellow students how much they had enjoyed our presentation, and the school now wanted us to do a program in Thai for the whole student body. The principal told us that we could present anything about Christmas but we couldn't speak of Jesus.

"Thank you," I said, "but under those terms, I'm afraid we'll have to decline."

"If you decline," he said, "I will lose face. It would be shameful to both of us if you don't accept my offer."

"Sir, it makes no sense for us to waste the students' time talking about the peripheral trappings of Christmas without telling them what Christmas is all about."

If it had been a matter of ministering to people with food or medicine, we certainly would have helped out regardless of whether we were permitted to talk about Jesus. But we were not there to push our Western culture on the people (unless someone could convince me that their lives depended on learning about Santa Claus, reindeer, and plucky little elves).

The rest of that telephone conversation became a ridiculous unending loop. The principal would say we must come, and I would say no, not unless we were free to talk about the true meaning of Christmas. He would say we could not, and I would say that we wouldn't come. "But you must come," he would say. And round and round again we would go.

I did my best to be gracious but firm. At last, the principal consented to my terms and asked the team to come that Friday at 8:30 AM. When we arrived, we were escorted to the main auditorium, where our hostess, a head teacher, had prepared drinks and snacks for us. We went right to work, setting up our puppet theater, arranging the musical instruments, and doing sound checks while more than a thousand students filled the auditorium.

Then the principal arrived. He made a beeline for me and said, "How dare you put your puppet theater in front of our Buddha image. Remove that contraption at once." We apologized for our insensitivity and did as he asked.

The principal then addressed the students. "You were born Buddhists and you will die Buddhists. Remember that to be Thai is to be Buddhist." He then led them in a chant to Buddha. When he had finished, he informed the students that they did not have to stay and watch our presentation, as many other fun activities had been arranged.

He turned to me and said, "Remember our agreement. Don't mention anything about Jesus."

I said, "What? If you renege on your agreement, we're leaving."

"No, no, don't go. Look, won't you please talk about something else?"

"Absolutely not."

"Okay, then. Go ahead and do as you please, but do not start until I return."

About a hundred students followed him outside to participate in the other activities. Our staff, along with the remaining students, waited patiently for the principal to return. After forty-five minutes had passed, I told our hostess that we would have to leave. She begged us to wait just five more minutes while she sent a student to find the principal.

Just before the five minutes were up, the principal returned. He said, "Go ahead with your program, but you'd better not say anything about Jesus, because I'm going to tape it."

"Sir," I said, "no more games. We're going to do the program that we planned, just as you had agreed. I'm delighted to hear that you're taping our program, though. You need to hear something this important more than once."

We did our program, complete with Christmas songs, puppet shows, dramas, personal testimonies, and narration of the biblical account of the first Christmas. By the time we started, all the students who had left for the other activities had now returned. At the end of our program, we introduced a Thai pastor who had a church in that town.

Nine young men talked with the pastor afterward and told him they wanted to dedicate their lives to Jesus. All nine became members of the church and eight were baptized later that year.

Over the past twenty-five years, we have been given the opportunity to speak openly about Jesus in more than fifty public schools throughout Asia, even in Muslim nations. Only once was either Ellen or I ever threatened with imprisonment for talking about Jesus at a public school. That was at Sean's kindergarten...in the United States of America. (Refer to chapter 1 for that story.)

EIGHTEEN

Behind Enemy Lines

O N E morning, our team felt that we were to intercede for the neighboring, strife-torn country of Burma. Christian missionaries had been banned from Burma ever since 1962, when the ruthless dictator, General Ne Win, had overthrown the legally elected government of Burma and proclaimed himself head of state for life. Ne Win had suspended the constitution and parliament and abolished free enterprise and private trade.

Here's an example of just how off-kilter Ne Win was. In 1989, Ne Win's personal astrologer told him that 10 was his unlucky number and that 9 was his lucky number. Ne Win promptly released a new currency that was divisible by 9, and he declared that all currency divisible by 10 was now completely useless. He made almost no allowance for people to exchange their old currency for the new currency. In that one stroke, he effectively bankrupted a considerable portion of Burma's population.

On this particular morning, it seemed that God was urging us to reach out to Burma, at least through prayer. At the end of our prayer meeting, I looked up to see a stranger standing at our door.

"How long have you been standing there?" I asked in Thai.

"Just a few minutes," the man replied in perfect English.

"I'm so sorry. I didn't hear you knock," I said. "Please come in." I offered him a seat and handed him the customary glass of water. He introduced himself as Colonel Jimmy from the Kachin army in, of all places, Burma.

"Last week," he said, "I visited the president of the Kayah state in Burma, and he asked if I knew any Christian missionaries. I told him that I've heard of some living in Chiang Mai and that the next time I traveled there, I would try to make contact. Once I arrived here, I made inquiries at the local market and was directed here."

"That's amazing," I said. "Just this morning, God led us to pray for Burma, and here you are. I've heard that many of the Kachin people are Christians. How about you, Colonel? Are you a Christian?"

"Oh, no, not me. It is true that many of my people are Christian. As for me, I'm my own man, but I agree with Christian principles. For example, my armies have agreed to take ten percent of all the bullets and weapons we obtain and tithe it to the Nagas, our brothers in the south. They are defending their homeland against both the Burmese and Indian governments."

I didn't know whether to be impressed, concerned, or just plain humored.

"Tithing is certainly a Christian principle," I said, "though we usually tend to focus our giving more on things like food, housing, education, and health care. But tell me, why is the Kayah president asking for missionaries? Is he a Christian?"

"No. As a matter of fact, there aren't any Christians in the Kayah state that I know of. But he said he wants you to come and talk about your God."

This is a dream come true. "What language do the Kayah speak? Burmese?"

"Most of the men can speak Burmese, but their mother tongue is Karen. The Kayah state is approximately a seven-hour walk through the jungle from the border of Thailand. It's not an easy trip, but would you consider going? I could lead you there and interpret for you."

"Would we be allowed to? I mean, since General Ne Win took control, isn't it illegal for Christian missionaries to work in Burma?"

"Let me explain," he said. "The country of Burma actually comprises eight independent states: Shan, Kachin, Kayah, Karen, Mon, Rakhine, Chin Hills Special Division, and the state that is named Burma, which is the state governed by General Ne Win. Within that small state of Burma are seven divisions: Ayeyarwady, Rangoon, Magway, Sagaing, Bago, Mandalay, and Tanintharyi. But the other states are actually sovereign, independent nations under the rights declared by the Burmese constitution. Most of these nations have their own government and army, though they're not recognized by the UN. You cannot speak about your God in General Ne Win's Burmese state, but it is completely legal for you to talk with the citizens of the Kayah state. In fact, the government of the Kayah invites you to come."

"I'm very intrigued," I said. "When would you want us to go?"

"In about four weeks."

"I could be ready tomorrow. But before we can make any plans, I really need to pray about it and discuss it with the team."

The colonel and I continued to talk for some time, and my interest grew with each passing minute. Before he departed, Colonel Jimmy promised to return in two days to hear our decision.

The next morning, I presented the invitation to our team, and they were as excited as I was. Five of us decided to go, including my oldest son, Sean. An outreach team from Hong Kong was due to arrive soon, and I called them and asked if they would like to join us on our trip to the Kayah state. They responded as enthusiastically as I had expected.

When Colonel Jimmy returned, I told him that we had a team of seventeen that would accompany him into the mountains in four weeks, as he had requested. He must have anticipated my answer, because he had already worked out all the logistics of our trip. We would travel by bus to Mae Hong Son and then go by four-wheel drive to a Hmong border village. After a good night's rest, we would begin our hike into the Kayah state.

Four weeks later, in preparation for the trip, I put 110 Bibles on our dining room table—100 in the Karen language and 10 in common Burmese.

I gathered the team and said, "These people we'll be visiting have apparently never seen a Bible in their lives, so I want each of you to put as many books as you can carry into your backpacks."

Colonel Jimmy arrived at about 6:00 AM, and we started to walk out the door when I noticed that most of the Bibles were still on the table. I called everyone back and said, "Come on, guys. This could be the only chance these people will ever have to own a Bible. If you really believe that these are the words of life that we're delivering, you'll get serious about this. We're not leaving until every Bible has been packed." To the team's credit, they cleared the table in no time at all.

The bus trip lasted eight hours over bumpy and precariously steep mountain roads. When we arrived in Mae Hong Son, Colonel Jimmy walked us to a large dirt clearing, from which trucks and makeshift buses regularly transported commuters to the border areas. Since the trucks were already filling up with other passengers, we divided into three teams of six. Colonel Jimmy took the first group, Virapon led the second, and I led the third.

Barely an hour out of Mae Hong Son, my group's truck began to sputter, stop, and start again. After two hours of this, we eventually stopped at the house of one of our fellow passengers who graciously welcomed the rest of us into his home to spend the night on the floor while the driver repaired his truck.

The next morning, we set out again. We reached our destination just in time to join the other two teams for breakfast. Or so we thought.

"I figured you had car trouble and would show up eventually," Colonel Jimmy said. "I'm sorry there's no time for you to eat, but we need to leave right away."

At that, he turned and began his march into the jungle. The rest of us dashed for our backpacks and scampered after him. With so many bandits, drug traffickers, and insurgents patrolling the region, none of us dared to get too far behind the well-armed colonel.

Poor Virapon hiked those jungle trails wearing only flip-flops. I felt bad that it had not occurred to me to make sure he had brought his tennis shoes. He had to stop every twenty minutes or so to scrape off the leeches that clung to his exposed feet.

On every steep ridge that we navigated, I heard the groans from the team members: "I can't wait to get rid of these Bibles." "I'm so glad we won't have to carry these heavy books on our return trip." I determined that we would hand out the Bibles first thing when we arrived at the village.

We forged our way through the foliage, over the mountain, and through the rivers. After four hours, we stopped on the crest of a mountain range that provided a spectacular view for hundreds of miles in every direction. Colonel Jimmy began digging near a tree and pulled out two cucumbers that were as large as watermelons. Words could not do justice to the sweetness of that breakfast.

After nine hours, we arrived at the Kayah village, thankful that the last few rays of sunlight were still peeking out from the horizon. Colonel Jimmy said that this village normally had a population of barely five hundred people, but on this day, another three thousand people had traveled there to welcome us.

The elders of the village greeted us in common Burmese, which Colonel Jimmy translated into English for us. After the introductions, I handed a Bible to the mayor, who glanced at a few of the pages and then asked, "What's this?"

"Sir," I said, "this is no ordinary book. These pages contain the words of God."

"But what language is this?"

"It's...it's the Karen language," I said. "Your language, the mother tongue of the Kayah people, right?"

"No, no, this isn't our language," he said. "Oh, I know. This must be Po Karen." He handed the book back to me. "We speak Skaw Karen."

Obviously I had no idea that there was more than one Karen language. I could feel the laser-sharp glares of the team piercing through the back of my head. My mind raced for any words that might appease them: *Ha, ha. Silly me. Well, we've all had a good laugh out of this, anyway. Can't put a price on comedy, right?* I wasn't too confident that they would see the humor in their aching backs, so I turned to Colonel Jimmy and said, "How far away is the closest Po Karen village?"

"Not far," he said, "about ten kilometers."

"Will you take me there first thing tomorrow?"

"Sure."

"Also, how much would it cost to rent a horse? I need to find a home for these Bibles before the team finds a rope to lynch me."

Colonel Jimmy laughed. "I'm sure the mayor and other Kayah leaders here will at least want to keep the ten Burmese Bibles. We can pack the Po Karen Bibles on a horse that you can rent for three hundred baht, (about US$12 at the time) and I'll take you to their village right after breakfast tomorrow."

That evening, thousands of Kayah people crowded the field, and even the trees, to see our program. Our team performed some dramas, and then I got up on the platform, ready to deliver the message. Without warning, the hovering rain clouds opened up and began baptizing us, turning our meeting into a huge communal shower. Our team ran for cover, but the Kayah people stayed. I asked Colonel Jimmy if he minded getting wet.

"No, go for it," he said. "I'll stay and interpret for you as long as you want."

At the end of my message, more than three hundred drenched people came forward to accept Jesus as their Lord and Savior. We continued to minister and pray for people late into the night.

Afterward, Colonel Jimmy said to me, "You're an excellent preacher. You almost had me ready to follow Jesus."

"Almost, huh? Jimmy," I said, "this message is so simple and powerful in its truth. I must be a terrible preacher if it didn't reach your heart."

The next morning, Colonel Jimmy, Sean, and I piled the one hundred Bibles onto a pony and walked to the nearest Po Karen village. Upon our arrival, we found the chief and told him we had a gift for him. I handed him a Bible and asked, "Are you able to read the words of this book?"

He flipped through the first few pages. "Yes, of course, I can."

I breathed a sigh of relief. "If we give you this book, would you read it?"

"Sure."

"Well, then," I said, "we would be honored if you would receive this gift from us. Also, if I give you the rest of these books, would you give them out to the residents of your village?"

"Sure. I don't see why not."

Relieved, we took all the books and stacked them up in the chief's hut. A couple of hours and a few pots of tea later, we began our trek back to the other village to join the rest of our team. They had spent the day getting to know our hosts and preparing for the evening's service.

That night, the people again responded to our message with great enthusiasm. Afterward, I sat with the elders on the floor of the mayor's hut, drinking tea and talking late into the night. Impressed by their searching and intelligent questions, I asked them what had sparked their interest in Jesus.

The mayor replied, "Why wouldn't we want to know about a God who is so powerful and caring that He would protect His people from Russian MiGs?"

"I'm not sure I understand," I said.

"Surely you must know about Burma's failed attack on the Karen state?"

"No, I haven't heard anything about it. But then again, most of the outside world has no idea that all of your states are independent of the Burmese government."

A few of the elders chuckled, clearly amused at the ignorance of our Western press.

"Well," the mayor said, "President Ne Win has always wanted to overthrow the governments of the bordering states, as you probably know. Recently, the USSR discovered that the Karen state was full of precious stones and oil. So Gorbachev offered to help Ne Win annihilate the Karens, and in exchange, Ne Win agreed to give the USSR full access to the geological treasures of the land. Many of the citizens of the Karen state are Christian, so as soon as their president, General Maboo, learned that the USSR was sending six Russian MiG jets to bomb them, he called for a nationwide time of fasting and prayer. Anyone calling himself a Christian who violated this order would be put in prison. On the third day, the Russian MiGs had just begun bombing when a heavy mist came over the mountains. All six jets crashed into the mountains."

The next day, I asked Colonel Jimmy what he thought of this amazing story.

"It certainly explains why they asked me to send for you, doesn't it?" he said. "Oh, Achaan Art, I meant to ask you, did you realize that those men you talked with last night were all men of high rank in the Kayah government?"

"Really?" I said.

"Yes, you were conversing with the commanding general of the Kayah state army, the provincial governor, a government cabinet member, and the secretary of state."

I had no idea. The men had worn simple tribal dress and had introduced themselves only by telling me their names and how many children they had. Child rearing was clearly the most commendable accomplishment in their culture. When I introduced myself and told them that I had three children and that my oldest son had accompanied me on this trip, they had all nodded and smiled admiringly.

During our time in that village, the Kayah people graciously provided meals for us and gave us space inside their homes to lay our sleeping bags. They warned us that the area was infested with malaria, so during the day, we diligently sprayed ourselves with mosquito repellent, and at night, we slept under mosquito nets.

I wanted to make sure we bought a pair of hiking boots for Virapon before we started the trek back, but the only shoes available in the tiny, all-purpose town store were rubber shoes called Khun Sahdals. We resigned ourselves to the fact that they were at least better than flip-flops.

Amused that the ferocious drug warlord Khun Sah had his own line of footwear, we entertained ourselves on the hike back to the Thai border by putting together a mock advertising campaign for these shoes. The team came up with slogans like "When it comes to outracing the police, nine out of ten criminals say that they count on Khun Sahdals to keep them going," and "If you're wanted dead or alive in every free nation on earth, like me, you need to try Khun Sahdals. Their light, rubbery bounce makes it easy to run while carrying a bag of heroin in one hand and an AK-47 in the other. And just wait till you see the admiring faces of your victims when they see your stylish footwear. Khun Sahdals: because in this high-stakes world of drug running, looks really do matter."

Virapon and Jim, the team leader from Hong Kong, were the only ones who took malaria prevention medicine, so they had not been as vigilant with their mosquito nets and sprays. Upon our return, they both became dangerously ill. Though the first few blood tests were inconclusive, we insisted that the doctors again run the tests for malaria. The diagnosis finally came in: falciparum malaria. With a ready supply of medications, the doctors managed to arrest this deadly disease just in time. Losing these two outstanding men of God would have been a devastating blow.

Another close call was discovered a few hours after our return home. The press reported that South Korea's president was on a diplomatic visit to the Burmese capital of Rangoon. There in Rangoon, on the same day that we had crossed the border back into Thailand, North Korean agents had attempted to assassinate the South Korean president. They set off a bomb that killed both Burmese and South Korean government officials, but because of his tardy arrival, the primary target survived.

In an attempt to unearth the assassins, the Burmese government was now sending troops to patrol all border areas to arrest any suspicious individuals who were attempting to cross over into Thailand.

I breathed a prayer of relief and gratitude, realizing that God had delivered us home just in time to avoid that mess. Of course, I'm not saying that our little band of merry foreigners would have looked at all suspicious to the Burmese soldiers. I mean, I'm sure the soldiers would think it perfectly natural for a group of foreigners to escape a boring vacation on the French Riviera or Disneyland to go strolling around the treacherous hill country of Burma. Wouldn't they?

NINETEEN

Anna and the Short-Term Wonders

IN preparation for an upcoming outreach team, I decided to connect with Anna Capone, a Dutch missionary who worked among the Shan people. Our old Toyota pickup made it to Mae Hong Son, but from there I had to travel by sii-law (taxi-truck) to the town closest to Anna's village. I then hiked a few miles farther into the hill country until I finally reached her village.

Because the Shan people controlled territory on both sides of the Thai/Burmese border, it was hard to tell in this mountainous region whether I had crossed over the unseen border into Burma. The village certainly did reflect the personality of other Burmese villages that I had visited—until Anna's hut came into view.

At that moment, I felt as if I had been transported to Holland. Except for the bamboo structure of the house, it was almost like the kind of picturesque display you would see at the Epcot Center or the World's Fair. Manicured flower gardens with tulips in full bloom decorated the pathway leading to Anna's front door. Anna's hut even had glass windows;

that was the first and only time I think I'd ever seen such a thing in a bamboo hut. Potted flowers filled each window, and a wooden swing graced the front yard. The door swung open.

"Art," Anna said, "what in the world are you doing here? You'd better turn around and go home. This territory is much too dangerous for you."

When I told her that I wanted to bring an outreach team to her village, she said, "It's a very risky idea, but, well, we'd better go right away and ask for the chief's permission."

The chief seemed suspicious of me but agreed to consider my request. Upon leaving his compound, Anna ordered me to return to Mae Hong Son until the chief had asked the local drug warlord's permission for me to bring the team here. She told me that she would meet me at the OMF (Overseas Mission Fellowship) house when she had something to report.

The OMF house was one of the sole remaining vestiges of colonial architecture in that town. The two middle-aged women who kept residence there gave me a warm welcome. They ushered me to the veranda, where we sat down for a cup of tea. I told the women that I was staying at the local guest house but that I planned to meet Anna at their home sometime in the next few days.

"Oh, that Anna. You know, she has quite an amazing story." With the back-and-forth, tag-team storytelling that is a telltale sign of the closest friendships, the women proceeded to chronicle some of the highlights of Anna's impressive history. They told me that Anna had previously served OMF in Malaysia and later in Laos. When she was forced out of Laos by the new Communist regime, she requested to be reassigned to the Shan nation. Her mission board, however, considered it unwise for anyone to work by him- or herself, since even Jesus sent out His disciples two by two. Moreover, since the Shan were involved in drug trafficking, the board decided it would be especially unsafe for a single woman to venture there unaccompanied.

After trying in vain to find a colaborer, Anna decided that she had no choice but to resign from OMF and serve the Shan people as an independent missionary. This was an extremely bold move. The region served as home base for the most prominent opium warlords of all

Southeast Asia. These opium dealers would transfer the opium grown in other parts of Burma, northern Thailand, southern China, and western Laos into the Shan territory, where they refined it into high-grade heroin. In the early 1980s, more than 70 percent of the world's heroin was reportedly manufactured by the warlords in this region.

I later learned that Anna had recently led two young men to the Lord. Khun Sah demanded that these young men join his army, but they stood their ground. They insisted that they would never fight for the kingdom of darkness. Khun Sah warned them that if they had not changed their minds by the time he returned to the area, he would kill them and ten other randomly chosen people from their village.

Khun Sah was not bluffing, and the young men knew it. He had done it before, and he would surely do it again. Miraculously, when Khun Sah returned and saw how unbending the young men were in their convictions, he changed his mind. The general consensus in this predominantly Buddhist territory was that even Khun Sah was not foolish enough to meddle in a spiritual battle with servants of Jesus.

For three days I waited in Mae Hong Son with still no sign of Anna. On the third day, I went to the market and ordered lunch. While I was slurping up my kwey teow noodle soup, a slight Asian man dressed in well-pressed army fatigues asked if he could join me. He set his rice dish and bottle of Sprite down across from me and began conversing with me in impeccable English.

"What is your opinion concerning the politics of the US and Thailand?" he asked.

"I'm not really into politics, but..." I took the plunge. "I do love to talk about God. Do you know why you were born, the purpose for your life?"

The man held up his hands as if I had pulled a gun on him and said, "Whoa, you sound just like my sister and Dr. Anna. They're always trying to get me to give my life to Jesus."

"Well, then, they must love you and want you to live a completely fulfilled life. That can happen only when you submit to the One who created you. He longs for you to know Him."

The corners of the man's mouth slowly curled up, and the man started to chuckle. "You have no idea who I am, do you? I was sent here to check you out—by Khun Sah himself." He paused to see the effect of his words and, clearly, to see how impressed I would be to hear that my presence was known by the most infamous criminal on the continent. I was fairly nonplussed, though, which kind of surprised even me.

"You see," he continued, "I'm his right-hand man. We thought you might be an American government agent from the DEA (Drug Enforcement Agency) or the CIA. If you were, I would've had you shot and killed." He took a swig of warm Sprite and wiped his mouth. "But it's obvious that you are who you say you are. I'll grant you permission to bring your team here, but you may not travel alone. You must stay with Dr. Anna."

"Agreed," I said. "And thank you for your permission. I accept the terms. However…" I definitely was not about to let a mass-murdering drug warlord get away from this question. "Don't you have any desire to know your Creator? Surely you—"

"Look," he said, "I don't need your God. I'm probably the richest man you've ever met. I'm worth millions of dollars. And I am a graduate of Columbia University, one of the best schools in your country."

Before he had the chance to fully list his curriculum vitae, Anna showed up.

"Hello, Art," she said and then turned to the Ivy League alumnus. "Hello, my son. Today, will you stop serving the devil and start serving God?"

"Hello, Doctor Anna." The man winked at her. "I've already been accosted by your colleague here." He then switched to Dutch, speaking as effortlessly in Anna's mother tongue as he had spoken in mine. Though I could not understand the words, it was apparent that he was explaining the terms we had agreed upon. And it was pretty obvious that Anna was taking every chance in the conversation to urge him to turn from his life of crime. After several minutes, the man switched back to English, probably thinking that the change in dialect would force a change of subject. No such luck.

"Sir," I said, "you already have more money than you could possible spend in several lifetimes. If it's still not enough, you can rest assured that it will never be enough. You're probably wanted dead or alive in nearly every free country on the planet, so where can you go to spend your money? You told me that you're the richest man I've ever met, but look at how you live. You spend your life hiding out in a bamboo hut in the middle of the jungle."

The man slammed down his bottle of Sprite. "You and your God." He stood up and shoved his chair back. "I don't need anyone or anything. I am my own god."

When he left, Anna said to me, "Some people need a great deal of prayer to cut through their pride. Tell me, Art, how are you doing spiritually? Are you spending time with the Lord every day?"

"Yes. Thank you for asking, Anna. I'm doing fine."

We went from there to another Shan village, where a man whom Anna had led to the Lord was being persecuted.

When we visited his home, the man told us, "My neighbors spit into my well whenever they pass my house, and every day, my wife nags me to go back to being Buddhist. She can't understand why I choose to be different, especially since it makes so many people mad at me." He said he would be delighted to house a team that could explain to his people what Christianity was all about and why he had chosen to follow Jesus. We thanked him and promised to do our best to help.

Anna then introduced me to the chief of the village, and the three of us sat drinking Chinese tea late into the afternoon. After a couple of hours, the chief got down to business.

"I know that Khun Sah has granted you permission to bring some of your people here, and I am very pleased that you have chosen my village out of all the villages in the region. We would be honored to host you."

From the chief's house, we went to the Buddhist temple. We took our shoes off at the entrance and proceeded through the high doorway. At the far side of the room was an enormous golden idol of Buddha. Next to the idol sat the high priest, reclining in an elaborately decorated chair that resembled a throne. Young priests dressed in bright orange robes stood on either side of the chair, fanning him.

Anna asked if she could approach, and the priest nodded in approval. She warned me to stay where I was. She clasped her hands together, palm to palm, and lifted her arms straight above her head, demonstrating the highest degree of respect and honor. She then prostrated herself on the floor and began crawling on her stomach across the large bamboo floor to the feet of the high priest.

The priest hardly paid Anna any notice as she inched her way toward him. I just sat cross-legged and watched Anna's display of humility, grateful it was she and not I. After more than a minute, Anna made it to the foot of the priest's throne. She then rose to her knees, her eyes still looking downward, and asked his permission to use the temple to tell the people about her God.

The priest stared at the ceiling for a moment, then looked over at me. I knew he expected me to follow Anna's lead, but while I respected Anna's convictions in sensitivity to the culture, it would have been a compromise of my own convictions to prostrate myself before a mere man. I bowed my head in a sign of respect but then looked the priest square in the eyes. I was not about to play his little power game. At first, he was taken aback, but then he smiled, nodded at me, and looked as though he was suppressing a laugh. He looked down at Anna and said, "Very well. You may use the temple to speak about Jesus."

Anna thanked him and crawled backwards the same way she had come. She was truly being "all things to all men," giving up her own liberties, that she "might by all means save some" (1 Corinthians 9:22).

I still needed to arrange for three more weeks of ministry. I again met with the OMF women in Mae Hong Son and asked whether the outreach team could assist them in their ministry. They replied, "Short-term teams are a waste of time in spiritually oppressed areas like Mae Hong Son. This is the Siberia of Thailand. We've been working here for twenty years and have yet to see one conversion. What could you possibly accomplish in just twenty days?"

I was sorry to see how discouraged the OMF women were, but that only spurred me on all the more. "I would really like to bring the team here to serve you, to bless you in any way that we can. We can do household chores or yard work, witness to your neighbors, do whatever you need. The sky's the limit."

The women eventually agreed, but without enthusiasm. Once our ministry schedule was set, I returned home.

A few weeks later, the team arrived by train shortly after dawn. We loaded everyone onto trucks and traveled directly to Mae Sai, the northernmost town in Thailand. We set up camp on the Thai side of the Mae Kok River (the line of separation between Burma and Thailand), and we invited the townspeople to our program.

That evening we faced our loudspeakers toward the Burmese side of the river. On the Thai side, we had attracted a crowd of approximately eighty people. It was hard to see exactly how many watched from the Burmese side, but it had to have been at least double that number. At the end of the hour-and-a-half program we closed by praying for a number of the people on our side of the river.

Early the next morning, I was shaving in the cold, rushing river when I saw two of our team leaders on the opposite side of the river arguing with a woman. Because I had given strict orders that no one was to go over to the Burmese side, I leapt into the river and swam the short distance across to confront them.

"What's going on?" I asked.

"I don't know," Jim said. "We did nothing to provoke her, but she started screaming and pushing us back into the river."

I asked the woman whether she understood Thai.

"Little bit," she replied in Thai.

"Did these men do something wrong?"

"These men so crazy," she said. "Last night I watch you, so I know, you godly people. When I see your friend, no shirt, walking down road that lead to Burma soldier, I know I must do something. Burma soldier, they will shoot your friend. So I say in Thai language, 'Go back, Go back,' but they not understand me."

I turned to the two guys and said, "You need to thank this wonderful woman. She just saved your lives. Your lily-white bodies were about to be target practice for the Burmese army."

Thanks to her, we made it back to Chiang Mai alive and well.

Next we traveled to the village of Nong Kiew. Since most of the people of that village had become Christians, they had ceased growing opium and were now living by faith while they developed new crops. We had agreed to deliver some basic necessities each month until their first harvest.

For the first couple of hours of the trip, the roads to Nong Kiew were paved, but then we had to maneuver our way through deep-rutted dirt roads. The going was slow, especially since our vehicles were loaded down with fifty-pound bags of rice and cases of sardines. By the time we arrived in Nong Kiew, all of us were covered with red dirt. We promptly distributed the food and then cleaned up before holding a service that evening.

While we slept that night, the heavens unleashed a torrential downpour. The deluge made the dirt roads thick with mud, impossible to drive on. Since we couldn't leave the village as planned, our hosts graciously shared their rice and sardines with us. For the next three days, we ate nothing but rice and sardines—breakfast, lunch, and dinner, day in and day out. A well-respected physician had recommended this diet to us as both well-balanced and culturally appropriate. However, by the seventh or eighth meal, we had completely lost any pride that we'd had in providing the village with this oh-so-benevolent supply of food.

For entertainment, we cut up a cardboard box and made our own deck of playing cards. Because of the flooding, even our hosts had little to do but to talk and laugh with us. It was a great time of fellowship, but the monotonous diet finally got the best of us. Despite the rain, we decided to make a break for it.

For thirteen hours we pushed, strained, and even carried our vehicles through the mud. By dusk, we had trudged little more than halfway down the road. What normally takes less than an hour to drive had taken us the entire day. Exhausted and covered in mud, we stopped at a Lisu village and asked the chief's permission to stay the night. The Lisu are famous for their hospitality.

The chief said we could spend the night for ten baht (about US $0.40 at the time) a person. We gladly agreed and also bought bowls of fried rice for five baht each. Not surprisingly, no one complained that the rice came without sardines.

While the team arranged their sleeping bags in the main room of a large hut, I instructed them to avoid pointing their feet toward the fireplace, since the Lisu consider fire to be sacred.

The chief offered us opium, and when I said "No thanks," he offered us marijuana. When I turned that down as well, he offered us prostitutes, including his own daughter. When I again declined, he said, "I've never met foreigners like you. You Christian missionaries are very different from the trekkers who pass through our village."

The next morning we performed and prayed for the villagers. Sean even led a woman to the Lord. The chief welcomed us to stay another day for free. We thanked him but said we needed to be on our way.

To our relief, the dirt road had dried a little, and it took merely four hours to reach the paved road. Ellen had been attending to our commitments in Chiang Mai for the past several days, and when the team arrived home, she gathered our shredded, red clay–saturated clothes and threw them in the trash.

"How was the trip?" she asked.

Sean's reply pretty much summed up what was foremost on *my* mind. "Mom, I never want to eat sardines again for as long as I live."

It was now time for our visit to the Shan village that Anna had arranged. We stayed in the home of the village's only Christian, the man who had been facing such tough opposition from his wife and neighbors.

We had brought a number of Bibles in both the Shan and Wa languages, and our friend Colonel Jimmy had arranged for us to hand them out in one of Khun Sah's major camps. I could not believe how well-equipped these drug-trafficking soldiers were. They all carried modern, state-of-the-art weapons. Some of the soldiers were Shan, but most were from the feared Wa tribe. Because of the Wa's reputation as fierce fighters, people on both sides of the drug war hired the Wa as conscripts.

I was both surprised and grateful to learn of Khun Sah's orders that no one was to harm us and that we were to be given complete freedom to hand out the Bibles. As we passed out the books to the soldiers, we exhorted them to enlist in King Jesus' army.

Before we departed, I asked the camp commander, "Why would Khun Sah allow us so much freedom? Does he fear God?"

"Oh no," the commander said. "Khun Sah doesn't even believe in God. His god is heroin. But just in case he's wrong, he doesn't want to get on the bad side of your God." *But murdering people and pushing drugs is not an issue?*

When we returned to our host's home, we found Dr. Anna waiting for us. Anna had made all the arrangements for us to speak in the Buddhist temple. That night, the whole village sat close together on the temple floor. The team performed short dramas and gave personal testimonies glorifying Jesus, right in front of the big golden Buddha.

The high priest sat in the only chair in the room and, as before, was continuously fanned by the young monks. Gazing outward from his throne, he seemed intrigued throughout the service, even during the evangelistic preaching. However, when we began to pray for the people, and a few of them announced that God had healed them, he appeared uneasy.

In the days that followed, our formerly persecuted host saw a significant change take place in his village. The people no longer cursed him or spit in his well. Now they began to revere him. Even his wife started bragging to her friends that her husband was not a compromising wimp but rather "a leader of men." Five new converts made plans to meet weekly in the man's home to study the Bible under the tutelage of Dr. Anna.

We trucked to Mae Hong Son for the team's last few weeks of outreach. I left the team in the capable hands of the OMF missionaries and returned to Chiang Mai for my daughter, Michelle's, birthday. Since the school year had started, Ellen and the kids had to stay in Chiang Mai, and I was not about to let my work, no matter how important, take priority over times like this with my family.

When I returned to Mae Hong Son a couple of weeks later, I learned that the team had led nine people to the Lord. All nine young believers were being discipled by the now-revitalized and energized OMF women.

I asked the women, "Do you still think that short-term teams are a waste of time?"

"Oh, no," they said. "This team has been wonderful. They really did come to serve us. They did a great job."

I could hardly believe that these were the same women I had spoken with just a couple of months earlier. They actually looked ten years younger.

Ever since then, every time I see them they ask, "So when are you going to send us another short-term team?"

TWENTY

A Vision for Bangkok

S T E V E and Marie Goode directed YWAM Relief Services, a highly effective ministry that focused primarily on the UN refugee camps. For a few years, they had been urging us to move Thai Ministries out of Chiang Mai to their offices in Bangkok to facilitate more fluid communication between the YWAM ministries serving in Thailand.

After a few years of resisting the idea, I told them, "Very well, if you find someone who has a God-given vision for Bangkok, we would consider moving Thai Ministries to Bangkok for one or two years."

In June of 1984, an American couple on our team told us of their vision and burden for the city of Bangkok. We all prayed about it and decided to make the move.

Moving to Bangkok meant huge adjustments for our family. Our children were at home in Chiang Mai and were not thrilled about moving to Bangkok. Also, the pastors from our home church Halpine expressed their concern about the move. Every summer, Halpine had been sending outreach teams led by Pastor Jim Isom. When Jim brought the next Halpine team in the summer of 1984, he and I were able to set aside some time to discuss and pray about the transition. In the end, Jim gave his and Halpine's blessings for the move.

A few weeks before the big move, I agreed to drive three Hong Kong–bound missionaries from Chiang Mai to Bangkok International Airport. The seven-hundred-kilometer trip would also give me the opportunity to transfer some of our belongings to Bangkok. We filled the back cab of our newly acquired four-wheel-drive truck with two metal trunks, leaving enough space for two of the missionaries, their backpacks, and the little transporters that housed our three cats. The third missionary would ride in the front cab with me.

After ten hours of driving, we hit the home stretch. In the highway's left lane, countless ten-wheeler trucks crept along bumper to bumper. In the right lane, reserved for standard trucks and cars, we were clipping along at fifty kilometers per hour, not exactly autobahn speed but probably five times the pace of the traffic in the slow lane.

I was sympathizing with those traffic-locked ten-wheelers when one of them swerved out of his lane, heading straight for a collision with us. I realized I had no choice but to veer right, sending us off the highway and into the steep, sloping median that divided the north- and south-bound traffic.

We made it safely to the bottom of the ravine, but just before stopping, the truck began rolling over and over. Once it had stopped, I felt as though the sky had fallen on our heads. But then I realized, that wasn't the sky. That was the ground. We had landed upside down.

We all managed to crawl out of the truck and survey the damage. The truck's back compartment had almost completely collapsed, but in the process of rolling, the two metal lockers had shifted from horizontal to vertical positions, thus restraining the roof from fully caving in. Those lockers had protected the missionaries in the back from being crushed and killed.

As a matter of fact, before the truck was repaired, most of the people who had seen the damage found it very hard to believe that anyone could have lived through such an accident. Once again, we knew that

God had protected us. One of the missionaries in the back had broken her arm but bore the pain admirably. Other than that, she was fine, and the rest of us escaped without a scratch. However, the cats did not fare so well. One died, one ran off, and only one remained.

A few weeks later our team completed the move to Bangkok. I called a teacher who, though Buddhist, had told me that he wanted our team to talk about our God at his elementary school. I then ventured out to find the school, which was located in the largest slum area of Bangkok.

More than a million people lived in that appalling place. Navigating my way by foot through the labyrinth of shanty shacks was tricky. I eventually noticed that I was passing the same little shelters for the second and third time. I felt like a rat trapped in a maze, and the rodents that scampered around my feet appeared to feel the same way.

Since I'm a guy, I naturally hesitate to ever stop and ask for directions, but after a couple hours of circling these slums, I realized I had no choice. I stopped, closed my eyes, and asked for directions…from God. Within minutes, I saw a school. I found the principal's office and asked whether this was the Klong Toey Elementary School. The principal told me that it was not, but she readily offered me directions. I thanked her and started for the door, when she asked, "Why are you looking for that particular school?"

"I have a team of Christians who have been invited to visit the school and perform puppet shows, skits, and dramas and talk about our God," I said.

"That sounds like fun. Could you come and do that at our school? Nobody has ever done that sort of thing here before."

"Sure," I said. "We would love to come to your school. However, please understand that this isn't just for entertainment. We're going to talk about Jesus."

"Jesus? That's absolutely wonderful. Oh, please, do come."

"Oh," I said, "are you a Christian?"

"Christian? What's that?"

"A Christian is someone who believes in Jesus and follows Him."

"Oh, no, I don't even know who Jesus is. But about a year ago, an organization called World Vision visited our school and gave our students many wonderful gifts, including clothing, shoes, pencils, papers, books, toothpaste, school supplies, soap, and several other useful items. They said they did it in the name of Jesus, and then they left. The students all wanted to know who this Jesus was, but all of our staff have been quite frustrated because none of us knows who he is. We don't even know what nationality he is or how to reach him."

I smiled. "We'll be happy to remedy that and supply you with all the answers to those questions."

When I brought the team there later that week, the children and the teachers gave us their wholehearted attention. We had also invited a local pastor from a nearby church to join us. After our presentation, two teachers and four students gave their hearts to Jesus, and another ten teachers and over a hundred students said they wanted to know more. We gave them the address to the Klong Toey Evangelical Church, and many of them began attending Bible studies there.

I did manage to find the Klong Toey Elementary School and arranged for our team to visit the school. The people responded positively but not nearly as wholeheartedly as the school that I had "accidentally" stumbled upon. The Lord proved to us again that His ways are much higher than our ways. It was such an encouraging introduction to our ministry in Bangkok to dive right into the work that God was already doing in the large slum.

In Bangkok, we continued to run our Discipleship Training Schools. We usually took the students north for their outreach, basing out of Chiang Mai for those periods. Our three kids took every opportunity during their school holidays to join the outreaches. They loved involving themselves in the ministry, and they still thought of Chiang Mai as home.

It's hard to put into words just how effective our children were in ministry or how deeply it moved the rest of us to see Sean, Michelle, and David in action. They worked diligently and passionately, they understood both the language and the culture, and they had hearts full of compassion for the people they ministered to.

The people knew that our children's love was genuine. For example, Michelle was once helping a group of village women repair some broken fences. The women had been watching her closely and became convinced that her young life had clearly been touched by the Divine.

Michelle obviously had no guile or ulterior motives, and the women knew that they could expect the truth from her.

One of the women approached Michelle while the others listened intently. "Your dad claims that the most powerful God, who made the universe, came to Earth as a man and did miracles. What do you think?"

Michelle confirmed that she believed that Jesus was indeed the Son of God and the Savior of the world. That was all the women needed to hear. Simple as that was, several of the women decided right then and there that they would dedicate their lives to Jesus.

On another occasion, Sean and David were playing soccer on a dirt field with some villagers. At a break in the game, they all walked over to the trees and sat down for a short rest. The men asked my sons whether they believed the incredible claims that I had made the previous evening. "Could it really be true that the most powerful Being of the universe, the great God who made and controls everything, actually cares about and loves every human on the earth?"

Sean's and David's responses were simple and direct in affirming that not only was this true but also that anyone could have a relationship with God. The men discussed these things among themselves and concluded that everything they had heard the night before was indeed as true as their hearts had told them.

As soon as Sean had acquired his driver's license and had proven himself an uncommonly safe driver, I asked him to drive the Toyota truck during outreach, while I drove the van. One evening after ministering to a Thai village along the Laotian border, we loaded up the two vehicles and headed back to our "home base" in Chiang Kham.

It was midnight before we pulled into town. I followed Sean as he activated his turn signal and proceeded to turn from the highway onto our home street. A shrill horn broke through the silence of midnight. I turned to see a ten-wheeler barreling past me on the wrong side of the road and propelling toward an unavoidable collision with Sean.

"No!" I cried out. "Jesus, help!"

Just as it reached Sean's Toyota, the monstrous ten-wheeler inexplicably appeared on the other side of the Toyota, like some colossal phantom. It continued to careen down the highway as if to make certain that only a crash would cause it to stop or even to slow down.

As soon as we got to our home base, I jumped from the car and sprinted over to Sean and the three young men who were with him in the truck.

"Did you see…? How did…? What…what in the world just happened with that ten-wheeler?" I said.

Gampon and Chaiyot said that they had closed their eyes, clenched their teeth, and begun praying as they prepared to meet their Maker. When the shock of impact didn't hit, they opened their eyes to see the big truck on the other side of them. Sean and Virapon said that they themselves did not close their eyes. They simply concentrated on preparing themselves for certain death as they watched the ten-wheeler approach them on one side and then abruptly appear on the other side.

I had a hard time believing what my own eyes had witnessed. However He had done it, though, God had saved three dynamic future leaders of the Thai church (including Sean who would one day move back to Thailand with his wife, Anne).

Soon after that we traveled to a village near the town of Fang, along the Burmese border. The chief of this village was keen to learn about the Creator God and had asked YWAM to come and speak with his people. Upon our arrival, we learned that all the men in the village were gone.

I went to the chief's wife and said, "At your husband's request, I brought our team here to teach in your village. The chief said this would be the best time to come. Where are all the men?"

"They all left yesterday to go hunting," she said.

"But why? Didn't the chief know that we would be arriving today?"

"Well," she said, "one of the families that live on the outskirts of our village reported that an animal was eating their chickens. At first, they thought that it was probably a leopard or a panther, so they built a trap with three strings tied to a chicken. Each of the strings was connected to a rifle trigger. That way, as soon as the beast grabbed the chicken, two bullets would land in his shoulders, and one would hit him between the eyes. Everything went as planned, except the cat wasn't a leopard or panther. It was a tiger, and because it was so big, the bullets merely wounded it.

"Oh, no," I said. "A wounded tiger is far more dangerous than a hungry tiger."

"Exactly," she said. "Now it's on a rampage, killing anything unlucky enough to cross its path. So the men of the village have organized a hunt. Of course, my husband knew that you would want to join them when you arrived. Therefore, runners have been sent back to accompany you to the hunt."

"No, thank you," I replied, a little too forcefully. "I have absolutely no desire to go looking for a dangerous, wounded tiger."

Sean said, "Come on, Dad. Let's do it. That would be so cool."

"Son, I am not a hunter. I have almost no experience in this field, and I'm not going to start by hunting an enraged, man-eating tiger."

Given Sean's crazy upbringing, I guess I should have anticipated his response.

"Aw, Dad," Sean said, "we never get to do anything."

TWENTY-ONE

Adventure in India

THROUGHOUT the 1980s, I traveled to India almost every year to teach at YWAM bases, primarily in Madras and Calcutta. On my first trip to Madras, I brought along David, who was just ten years old at the time. So that we could do a little sightseeing, we arrived a few days before my week of teaching would commence.

Upon our arrival, we hailed a motorcycle-rickshaw taxi. Our little taxi approached a red light at a major intersection, but instead of applying his brakes, the driver hit the accelerator and hammered the taxi right into a four-door sedan.

David said, "We're gonna craaa…" and then blacked out at the moment of impact, his head slamming onto the pavement as he fell from the taxi.

Amid the mangled pieces of metal, both drivers and I escaped with surprisingly few bruises. Our driver had jumped out just before the crash, and I jumped out, landing right on poor David, who did not fare so well. His head was swollen and black and blue, and his right arm was shredded and bleeding profusely. He also had smaller cuts and bruises all over his body.

The drivers, totally ignoring us, began yelling at each other. I prayed frantically as I wrapped David's arm with my shirt, applying pressure to suppress the bleeding. David drifted in and out of consciousness as I put him into another taxi and asked the taxi driver to please take us to the nearest hospital.

When we reached the hospital entrance, I rushed David to the emergency room. I said to the receptionist, "My son needs to see a doctor immediately."

"Doctor is not here, sir," she said. "He is taking his lunch break."

"Aren't there any doctors at all that are still here?"

"No, only one doctor. But please to be taking a seat, sir. He will be returning in one hour only."

Still holding David firmly in my arms, I left that hospital, waved down yet another taxi, and instructed the driver to take us to a larger hospital. When we arrived, I asked the driver to wait until I was sure that a physician was available to see David.

To my relief, David was regaining consciousness. "Dad," he said, "I don't feel very well."

"I know, son. We're at the hospital now. Try to be brave."

The emergency-room doctor examined David right away. I ran outside to pay the taxi driver and to thank him for waiting. When I returned to the emergency room, a nurse told me that the doctor had already given David a tetanus shot and had taken X-rays of his injured arm and forehead.

Thankfully, the X-rays revealed no fractures. David had lost a lot of skin on his arm, though, and the doctor said that the dressing would need to be replaced every two hours to prevent infection. The doctor also wanted to observe and monitor him for neurological changes for at least twenty-four hours, and he recommended that David be admitted.

I glanced around the hospital. It was filthy. The room they were preparing was covered in dust, and the mattress had huge stains. Even the sheets looked questionable. I was grateful for the doctor's genuine concern and knew that this room was the best the hospital could offer, but my mind raced through our options.

"Daddy, do I have to stay?" David asked.

"No, son. I have a better idea."

I paid the bill and took David to the cleanest hotel I could find, the Holiday Inn. For the next forty hours, I nursed David around the clock. By Sunday afternoon, the bump on David's forehead had shrunk significantly. A scab had formed on his arm, and David's pain had become so manageable that he no longer needed to take his pain medication. Most important, David was coherent and showed no signs of neurological impairment. I felt confident that he was out of danger.

We checked out and moved to the YWAM campus, where we slept on a converted external balcony with a canopy. There was just enough room for a single bed and a mat on the floor. I wanted David to use the bed, but he insisted that he was happier sleeping on the floor.

It was captivating to see India through David's eyes. The culture is so colorful in every way. The city exploded with a symphonic mixture of sights, sounds, and smells, every bit as richly textured as a Kashmir rug. We both instantly fell in love with the people, so exuberant and bursting with personality.

Despite the fact that this country was considerably more destitute than our beloved Thailand, David thought that he had arrived in Never Never Land when he discovered that he could get chocolate there. And apples. And comic books. At the time, such things were rarities in Thailand. It delighted me once again to see how great our kids had become at accentuating the positive.

David's wounds improved daily. Everyone at the YWAM campus noticed how grateful David was to God for his swift healing. In our daily services, David was an example to us all. He worshiped God openly and unselfconsciously. Remembering myself at that age, I was grateful to God for giving me kids like this.

Our meals at the campus were pretty routine: rice with curry gravy served on banana leaves. No utensils. Some curries included vegetables, but the school did not have enough money for meat or fruit. That was enough for me, but I was glad that I had brought some peanut butter and bread to supplement David's diet.

I taught every morning and evening for the first three days but was given Thursday evening off. That evening, David and I went to a famous restaurant in downtown Madras that serves steak and baked potatoes. Steak is a rare treat in India, as Hinduism teaches that cows are superior to humans. Hindus believe the same thing about snakes and rats, but I was glad not to be fighting off any cravings for roast snake au jus or flaming, chargrilled rat burgers.

David and I ordered our steaks, and my mouth began to salivate as the breezes transported the sweet aroma of the sizzling grill to our table. My anticipation accelerated when the waiter placed David's steak in front of him. The waiter paused, holding my steak hostage for just a few more moments; then he lifted his head and sneezed all over my steak. I masked my horror as the waiter placed the plate in front of me. David, sitting with his back to the waiter, had missed this drama.

I considered my options. I could order a new dinner, but they would most likely just reheat this one and bring it back to me. Or I could simply declare a solemn, sacred fast for myself. I chose the latter. (I just wish I were as good at discerning what the Spirit tells me as I am at discerning what my stomach tells me.)

"Why aren't you eating, Dad?" David said. "This is delicious."

I forced a smile and said, "I'm just enjoying watching you eat."

Which I was. Trying to, at least.

Each week, YWAM Madras held a community meeting with time for worship and teaching. On one such night I was asked to speak, and I spoke on "The Difficult Quest for Truth and Fulfillment in the Twentieth Century," basing my text on biblical references in Ecclesiastes and the seventh chapter of Romans.

I talked about how we live in an age of greed and materialism, wherein unstable leaders rule with frightening weapons; how pollution, corruption, and wickedness are escalating at an alarming rate; how trying to find fulfillment in wealth, pleasure, fame, and a host of activities is fruitless; and how achieving holiness on one's own strength is impossible. I told personal stories of failures and fears. All in all, I painted a fairly bleak picture.

Then I talked about how we can find fulfillment, contentment, truth, love, and hope in Jesus, and how Jesus can empower His followers to wield victory over sin, selfishness, and evil. I concluded my message by offering an invitation to those who wanted to receive Jesus as their Lord and Savior.

After the meeting, a tall, distinguished man approached me. He explained that he was the current leader of the Communist Party in

India, and he claimed to be a true descendant of the Aryan race. He had attended a university in the Soviet Union and now resided in the wealthiest district of New Delhi.

It was not difficult to believe him. Decked out in expensive garments, gold, and jewels, he carried more wealth on his body than the rest of the crowd were likely to earn in their combined lifetimes. Needless to say, I had already noticed him during my sermon.

The man told me that I had a rare talent for portraying the disastrous circumstances facing modern man. He said that he knew of only two other people who could convey our hopeless condition with such competence. These two men were among the richest in the world. Both were Indian gurus; one resided in the United States and the other in Switzerland. Both had amassed their fortunes by presenting messages similar to the one that I had given, but unlike my message, theirs did not offer a solution to the problems.

These gurus, the man told me, make their listeners confident that they know the solution but that it is a secret, something that their listeners must discover through the slow and costly guidance of the guru. People shower the gurus with money and presents in the hope that they will disclose the mysteries of the universe, but the gurus respond only in vague hints. The more unforthcoming these gurus are, the more their audiences lavish gifts on them.

"Right now," the man said, "my assets are worth a few million dollars only. But it has been my great ambition to obtain wealth equal to these two gurus. For a very long time, I have been looking for a man just like you. I have two million dollars in my bank that I will be using to finance your worldwide travel, visiting very, very influential people and staying in the best accommodations. Everywhere you are going, you would be giving this same message that you gave here tonight. However, you must not be giving an actual answer to the world's problems but only be convincing people that you know the answer. We can start immediately and share the profits fifty-fifty."

"Sir, the only reason I talked about the problems," I said, "was to let people know that there is an answer."

"Yes, yes. You were very, very convincing. People will definitely be believing that you know the answer, but you must not give it to them."

I told the man that I pitied him, that even if he had two billion dollars, he would still not find fulfillment. I told him that since I believe that Jesus is the only answer, I would continue to offer the truth of hope, even though I would never become rich as a result. No amount of money could ever purchase the contentment that I have in my Lord.

The Indian DTS students showed tremendous potential for leadership. One of the students was a highly educated young man from the Brahman caste (the highest caste in India, the wealthiest and most educated). His family constantly antagonized him because of his faith. One afternoon, we accompanied him to his parents' home and assisted him in witnessing to his family. A year later, I heard the distressing news that this brave young man had been arrested in Nepal for talking about Jesus.

Another student had suffered terrible physical abuse from her Hindu family. On the day she had left her home to attend the DTS, her father and uncle had thrown boiling water on her. The YWAM staff had rushed her to a doctor, and her wounds were healing. But the ugly words spoken by her father and uncle had cut deep into her heart. She told me how the Spirit of God had been working to heal those wounds and restore her sense of self-worth.

At the end of our week in Madras, David stood before the student body and testified about how God had healed him. The automobile accident should have left significant scars on his arm and forehead; however, not only was David completely healed just one week later, but also his body showed no trace that the incident had even occurred. Even more inspiring than David's testimony was his mature faith. David sparked a spontaneous time of worship, where the Spirit of God moved tremendously upon all of our hearts.

A year later, I met up with the YWAM Madras director, Tim Svoboda, at a leadership conference. Tim told me that he had asked the students in that DTS which speaker had influenced them the most. He was delighted at their answer. In a banner semester that had included some of the world's most sought-after Christian teachers, the person who had received the most votes was ten-year-old David Sanborn.

TWENTY-TWO

Clash of the Cultures

IN MY lifetime, I've met a few geniuses, most of whom descended from India or the surrounding region. It's a beautifully complex culture. Part of the complexity stems from the vast numbers of subcultures. Generally speaking, much of the complexity must also stem from the people's extraordinary combination of intense physical energy and seemingly boundless brainpower. However, the culture has often proved a little too complex for my more limited intellect.

I find it rather ironic that I've been invited to teach there so many times. The students have continuously overwhelmed me with their quick minds and tender hearts, and they often have to guide me in my bumbling efforts to connect outside the classroom.

One afternoon in Calcutta, I really put my foot in it. I walked across town to the YWAM ministry that reached out to the poorest of the poor in the inner city of Calcutta. I was touched to see that one of the new leaders was the former DTS student who had suffered burns from boiling water. Now this woman was reaching out, bringing healing to other hurting women.

From there, I walked to the compound of Mother Teresa's legendary ministry. Just outside the entrance, a middle-aged Indian woman approached me.

"Remember me?" she asked.

"No, I'm sorry," I said, "but I'm afraid I don't."

"Remember? Last night, when you were speaking at the meeting."

"I'm sorry, but you must have me mixed up with someone else."

"You mean you are not the priest who was speaking here? You are looking just like him."

"Well," I said. "I'm flattered that you think I'm one of Mother Teresa's coworkers, because I have the deepest admiration for them. But I'm not a Catholic priest."

"But you are American, are you not?"

"Yes."

"Good," she said. "Then you can be verifying a report another American gave us. He said that in America the vast majority of the population is embracing Hare Krishna as Lord."

Assuming that this woman was Catholic, I assured her that nothing could be further from the truth. I then added, "I personally have met only a couple of Krishna devotees in America. Sadly, both of them were mentally ill patients at George Washington University Medical Center in Washington, D.C."

Wrong thing to say!

"What? We are accepting your mother," she said. "Why are you Christians not accepting our mother?"

The woman then proceeded to yell at me in what I can only assume was the Bengali language. Her shouting attracted a lot of attention, and soon a large crowd gathered. The woman addressed the newcomers, pointing her finger accusingly at me. I stood there, dumbfounded and red-faced, as she skillfully enraged the crowd against me. Easily more than a hundred people gathered around us. I glanced around for an avenue of escape before things could get ugly. When the people started arguing among themselves about what to do, I slipped through the crowd and tore down the road.

After a mile or so, I found safety in a busy restaurant. I grabbed a table and ordered an early dinner. Still a little winded, I breathed a prayer of thanksgiving and quieted my spirit by reading my Bible.

Several hours later, I assumed that the commotion would surely have subsided. Still eager to see Mother Teresa's work, I returned and was shocked to see that the angry woman and about twenty others were still in heavy dispute. I backed stealthily away, disappointed that my foot-in-mouth disease had prevented me from seeing the ministry of one of the world's greatest heroes. I at least had sense enough to realize that caution is the better part of valor, and I returned to the YWAM base.

Despite all the truly delightful aspects of the Indian culture, I've observed that one of the toughest challenges that my Indian sisters and brothers face is their constant battle against the still-prevalent Hindu caste system. I came face-to-face with that struggle on my next trip to Calcutta.

I had spent an evening walking through the impoverished streets of that immense metropolis. It did not take official charts and surveys of the city to surmise that more people lived on the streets than inside the buildings. I was appalled by such severe poverty, especially in the light of a geology article I had recently read that reported that the country of India had more natural resources than the United States.

My thoughts were interrupted by the sight of a tiny, beautiful girl who looked barely five or six years old. The girl had a little rake in her hand that she used to comb through a garbage heap in search of food. She would evaluate the edibility of the scraps by tasting each piece and then putting the good morsels into a pouch. The girl must have been providing for others besides herself.

Another white man also noticed her predicament, but rather than just watch, he did something about it. He went over and handed the girl a 100-rupee note, roughly $2.50 in US currency. The girl stared wide-eyed at the money and then fell to her knees. She began thanking the man and kissing his feet, while her tears washed the dirt from her tender cheeks.

His astonished countenance indicated that the man didn't know that Hindus would generally give no more than one rupee to someone from a lower caste. This way, they could invest toward their own spiritual merit without interfering with the pauper's karma. Giving larger amounts would interfere with the caste system and disrupt the cosmos. It is likely that the little girl had never held more than one or two rupees at any point in her short life.

I was not the only one who had witnessed the man's generosity. A wealthy member of the Brahman caste approached the philanthropist.

"You do not understand what you have done," the Brahman said. "By foolishly giving such a large amount of cash, you are interfering with the child's karma. You see, in her previous life, this girl must have been very, very wicked. This would explain both her present poor condition and her gender. She must be fulfilling her karma as a poor girl so that she may become something better in her next life. You see, I, on the other hand, must have been very, very good and wise in my previous life, which is why, presently, I am wealthy, and a man."

The white man responded in an unmistakable New York accent. "Don't you dare tell me how much I can or can't give, you self-righteous jerk."

The New Yorker's defiance against the Brahman's arrogance impressed me. I approached him and told him how much he had made my day by both his generosity and his defiance. Guessing he was Jewish, I also told him that I was a follower of the Jewish Messiah, Yeshua (the original Hebrew pronunciation of the name of Jesus). At that, I became the new target of his rage. "I'm a Jew," he said, "and you Christians have always abused my people."

Along with the avalanche of harsh words, the man intermingled references to the atrocities done by the Crusaders and the injustice of the Spanish Inquisition. He also said that Hitler, as a Christian, slaughtered over six million Jews.

"Whoa," I said. "You're absolutely right that the Jews were the victims of horribly unjust atrocities in both the Spanish Inquisition and the Crusades. And because the offenders in both cases blatantly went against the teachings of Jesus, the Church that these criminals claimed to represent owes you an apology, at the very least. So as a Christian, I ask for your forgiveness."

"And what about that butchering Hitler? You think a little 'Oh, I'm sorry' will suffice?"

"But Hitler did not even claim to be a Christian," I said. "He strictly adhered to the doctrine of Hinduism, which fits hand-in-glove with his belief in Nietzsche's philosophy of existentialism. The very symbol of Nazism, the swastika, is taken directly from Hinduism, as is the concept of Aryanism. Hitler believed that Germans were the true Aryan race spoken of in the Hindu holy books, the four Vedas. As an adherent to Hinduism, he was a strict vegetarian and a believer in the same caste system that you just encountered with that Brahman."

"Come on, how do you know that's not just a rumor?"

"The testimonies of witnesses attest to the truth. As a matter of fact, Hitler gave orders that the gestapo, his murderous secret police, were not allowed to read the Bible. They had to read and meditate daily on the Vedas. Filling their minds with these Hindu writings enabled the gestapo to rationalize that by killing both Jews and uncompromised followers of Jesus, they might even be doing these people a favor. They believed that perhaps in their reincarnated lives, their victims might be born into a higher incarnation. Hitler condemned Jesus along with the rest of the Jewish race. It appears that Hitler planned to proclaim himself as the true Messiah as he ushered in the worldwide dominance of Hinduism."

"No kidding," the man said. He had softened considerably and was clearly intrigued, so I continued.

"These beliefs," I said, "are in sharp contradiction to God's Word, which teaches that all humans are made in the image of God. No race or gender is superior or inferior. We are all equal in the eyes of our Creator. The idea of an elite race and caste hierarchy is a wicked philosophy birthed in Hinduism. Racial harmony is required for the disciples of Jesus. There is no partiality with God, and He commands His followers to consider others over themselves. He tells us we are given but one life, and at the end of that life is judgment. We will spend eternity with Him in heaven or be separated from Him in hell."

"Huh. So Hitler really wasn't a Christian? Well, I appreciate your enlightening me about that," he said. "I sure haven't had any other enlightenment since I got to this country. I'm changing my ticket to get out of here as soon as possible. As a matter of fact, I'd better get going if I'm going to reach the airline's office before closing time." The man turned to hail a taxi and then said, "Hey, maybe we'll meet again someday. Take care, buddy."

I was sad that this man hadn't encountered the same wonderful Indians whom I had come to love. At any rate, Calcutta was not exactly a prime destination for a picturesque vacation.

One day, while lecturing at the Calcutta DTS, I had to strain my voice to be heard over a commotion that had erupted outside the windows of the classroom. After class, I asked the base director Mike Borden what the commotion was all about. Mike explained that the farmer who lived next to our campus had been bitten by a poisonous snake. Mike had asked the wife's permission to rush her husband to the hospital, a hospital established by the Canadian missionary Dr. Mark Buntain. Dr. Buntain had passed away, but the hospital continued to be one of the best equipped hospitals in all of Asia. Though staffed by very skillful Indian physicians, the local Hindu priest forbade it.

"This foolish Christian does not understand that snakes are gods, and the gods have chosen to bless your husband with a very honorable death," the priest said. "You must not be allowing these Christians to interfere with the will of the gods."

The poor farmer ended up dying, even though he could have easily been saved by an antivenom inoculation. Performing the rites of the farmer's funeral, the Hindu priest explained that the death of someone from such a low caste would normally call for cremation. But the priest ordered that since a snake god had killed the farmer, the corpse was to be thrown into the sacred Ganges River as a blessing to all who would bathe there.

The day before flying back to Thailand, I moved to the inner-city ministry house, since it was much closer to Calcutta's international airport. As I settled into my room, I heard a great deal of screaming and yelling coming from the street. I headed for the balcony to investigate, but one of the YWAM staff grabbed me by the arm.

"You mustn't be going out there," she said. "It is too dangerous for a white man. Let us first find out what is causing the disturbance."

The woman and a few other YWAMers ventured out to assess the situation. A few minutes later, they rushed back and urged me to leave. They explained that some corrupt officials from the Bengali Communist party, the ruling government in Calcutta, had tried to extort money from the shop owner next door. When the shop owner refused to pay them any more money, the officials began beating him. In their anger, they got carried away and accidentally killed the man.

The shop owner's wife and children had fled into the street, screaming and accusing the officials of murder and extortion. A large, angry mob had gathered, but the officials, skilled at crowd control, succeeded in turning the mob against the shop owner's family. The mob was now looting and wreaking havoc in the shop.

I understood that my presence as an American was a hazard to all of us in such a volatile situation. Before I left, we took a moment to pray together. I gathered my things and sneaked down the back stairs and into the alley. By following the instructions of my hosts, I managed to make my way undetected through the back alleys. Within minutes, I was inside a taxi heading toward the Baptist guest house. I was grateful to be safe but deeply concerned for my Indian coworkers.

The next morning at the airport, I had another culturally enlightening experience. Prior to going through immigration, I decided to have one last cup of India's world-famous tea. While enjoying my tea, I saw a young white man with long, unkempt hair. The man was dirty and unshaven, and he wore old, weathered sandals and the characteristic repeat-boutique garb of a hippie. I watched as he handed his ticket to the check-in agent.

The agent glanced at the ticket and then politely returned it to the young man. "Your flight is not until next week, sir," she said.

The young hippie exploded. He threw his large backpack at the agent, barely missing her. "I told the ticketing agent I wanted my flight booked for today," he said. "Now what am I going to do?" He ripped open his shirt. "I'm out of money and don't have any place to stay."

The agent picked up the backpack, handed it to the young hippie, and said, "I'm sorry, sir, but you are booked to fly out next week, and today's flight is full. However, I will be happy to put you on the standby wait list."

Looking angry and dejected, the young hippie slumped down into a chair.

There must be something I can do.

I went over to the man and introduced myself as a missionary. "I couldn't help but notice that you're in a desperate situation. I don't have much, but I want to help you out." I handed him a few US dollars.

"This should be enough to at least pay for food and a guest room for a few days."

"Hey, man, thanks, but I don't need your money. I've got plenty." Seeing my puzzled expression, he said, "When I bought my ticket, the agent told me that this flight was full for a week, so I went ahead and bought a ticket for the first available flight next week. But I know how to get what I want in India. All of that was just for show, a show that'll get me a seat on today's flight. Watch and learn, man. Watch and learn."

Shaking my head, I proceeded to the immigration counter and handed my passport to the official. He eyed me suspiciously and then called over an officer, gave him my passport, and instructed me to follow him. The officer took me to a small, brightly lit room. A senior immigration officer waiting there told me to sit down.

"Where did you stay last night?" the officer asked.

"At the Calcutta Baptist guest house," I said.

"You're lying. What did you smuggle into India when you arrived?"

"Nothing."

"You must not lie to us. What are you trying to smuggle out of India?"

Again I gave the same, honest answer. "Nothing."

"Your luggage is being examined as we speak, so you had better start telling us the truth. Or else."

"I am telling the truth," I said, beginning to worry that I would miss my flight.

"Do not be playing games with us. You will list for us all the people that you have met on this trip to India."

"I couldn't possibly remember everyone, but I'll do my best. Keep in mind, though, that I don't know the surnames of most of the people I met."

After more than an hour of interrogation, the senior officer said, "If you really stayed at the Baptist guest house, can you prove it?"

"Certainly," I said. I reached into my briefcase and pulled out a receipt.

Looking over the receipt, he grunted. "Okay," he said. "You're free to go."

What was that all about? I wondered as I ran to catch my airplane. *These Indians are crazy.*

"Final call for boarding," I heard over the loudspeakers just as I arrived at my gate, where I saw the young hippie preparing to board the plane.

"I see your Raging Bull performance worked for you," I said.

"Like a charm. And I got bumped up to first class." He showed me his boarding pass.

Unbelievable, I thought. *These Americans are crazy.*

TWENTY-THREE

How You Say Dat?

IN OUR attempts to master the Thai language, our family brought a lot of joy and laughter into people's lives (albeit, unintentionally). As I've said before, Thais are among the most gracious people on the planet, so they are usually very patient, and even flattering, when faced with the most appallingly flagrant butchering of their beloved language. But they also love to laugh.

Until quite recently, very few Thais spoke English, so we usually had no choice but to make a mockery of both ourselves and their beautiful but painfully difficult tonal language.

To demonstrate the tonal nature of their language, we often use the phrase, "Mai mai mai mai." Each "mai" has its own unique tone, giving it a different meaning. If intoned properly, it can mean "Does new silk burn?" Alternatively, you can change the tone of the last "mai," and you will thus be making the statement "New silk does not burn." Change each of the tones, and you may end up with the popular phrase "Not silk burn new." Okay, maybe that's not such a popular phrase, but I'm sure that I, for one, have mistakenly said it on occasion.

Thankfully, in our years of speaking Thai, we have yet to enter into any lively discussions about the combustive qualities of silk. That said, we have still had ample opportunity to use the wrong tones in the most inopportune of situations. For instance, in my attempt to express that my audience is "sooay," meaning "beautiful," I have sometimes used the wrong tone, thus telling them that they were "bad luck."

I once addressed a village who had assembled to bid us farewell. I told them how grateful we were for their warm hospitality, and I invited them to visit us at the YWAM base if they were ever in Chiang Mai so that we could reciprocate. At least, that's what I thought I had said. As we began our trek out of the village, my Thai colleagues began to laugh uncontrollably.

"You did it again, Art," one of them said.

"No, that can't be," I said. "I was careful with my tones this time."

"No, you weren't."

My colleagues then proceeded to translate what I had just told the assembly of villagers: "Thank you so much for impregnating us. Please come to the YWAM base anytime that you're in Chiang Mai so that we may impregnate you."

To this day, no one from that village has ever visited the Chiang Mai YWAM base.

Another time I was trying to say, "I enjoyed working in your small village." But I used the wrong tone, thus telling the people, "I enjoyed working in your pigsty."

One day, Ellen was working with a church choir. When the break time was over, she asked the choir to "Maa tii nee," meaning "come here." No one responded, so she concluded that she must have used an incorrect tone. She repeated the phrase, this time using what she thought was the correct tone. She later learned that she'd been right the first time. To the horror of the choir, her second attempt at the phrase was "Dogs, here!" As in many other cultures, "dog"just happens to be one of the worst things that you can call anyone. It was effective, though, because everyone was exceptionally obedient for the rest of the rehearsal.

The Thai word for beef can mean either cow or buffalo meat. Since buffalo meat is ridiculously tough to chew, I once tried to ask a waitress whether the beef used in a certain dish was from a cow or a buffalo. No sooner had I finished asking my question than the waitress turned bright red and ran off with her face in her hands. Four policemen at the table next to mine broke out into roars of laughter.

After several minutes of mocking me with their crude jokes, the cops explained to me that I had used the wrong tone when asking the waitress what kind of meat was in the dish. Instead of saying the word for buffalo, I had intoned a swear word that indicates a certain part of the male anatomy.

Another time, when I was interpreting for a Singaporean preacher, I inadvertently came up with a very original spiritual analogy. The preacher was referencing the Bible verse Zechariah 10:3 to explain to the congregation that God wants us to be like well-trained horses in battle.

"The warrior on the horse," the preacher said, "shouldn't have to focus his energies on yanking the reins this way and that. He should be able to simply give the most subtle nudges with his legs to guide the horse, leaving his arms free to fight." However, I used the wrong tones when attempting to interpret the phrase, "God wants to ride us like a horse." Instead, I later found out that I had mistakenly said, "God wants us to be like dog poop." I'm sure there must be some profound, spiritual insight in that accidental metaphor. I'm just not sure what it is.

Instead of lamenting the shortage of physicians in Thailand, Ellen proclaimed to one group, "One of the major social problems in Thailand is the shortage of sex." Instead of introducing Ellen as my wife, I have often introduced her as my fruit. I often ask for dirt, when I mean to ask for pineapple. Instead of asking where she could buy a ticket, Ellen once inadvertently asked where she could go to prostitute herself. I am sure that I could probably fill the rest of this book with tales of our other tonal bloopers.

During our first few years in Thailand we had such a full load with family and ministry that our language studies were rather patchwork. When we moved to Bangkok, we decided that the time and place were right for us to set aside a few months devoted primarily to language study. Our goal was to pass the "Baw Hoke" exam, which qualifies foreigners to teach at a university level.

The need for this was underscored one day in early 1985 at a meeting for the Evangelical Fellowship of Thailand. I sat next to a Thai university professor, and we got into a conversation during the coffee break. While we were talking, the professor would occasionally chuckle to himself. After several minutes of this, I asked him what he was thinking about that amused him so.

He said that I spoke "naa rock," which means "cute."

I asked him, "Could you elaborate? What is it about my speaking that is so cute?"

He replied, "I can tell that you are an intelligent, educated person, but you speak Thai like a northern Thai country hick."

On the one hand, I was kind of pleased to learn that I had learned to speak so distinctively in the vernacular of the northern Thais. On the other hand, I realized that I really was in dire need of a more formal, scholastic training in the language if I had any hope of connecting with the more educated Thais.

When the next international DTS began, Judy Hayden and Wendy Stonex codirected the lecture phase while Ellen and I attended language school. I still spent the afternoons with the students, since I would be leading their outreach.

I encouraged the students to pray that God would go before us and perform miracles during the outreach. I prayed that God would ruin the students for the ordinary, for them to desire no less than their full destiny and inheritance in serving God wholeheartedly. That prayer would be answered in a way that I was not quite prepared for.

One of the first villages we traveled to was Baan Lao in the province of Chiang Rai. The village chief suggested that we give our presentation at the Buddhist temple. Because the temple abbot was intrigued to hear about our God, he gave us his permission to use the temple grounds.

As we made our rounds from hut to hut, inviting people to our program, we learned that the men generally understood Central Thai, but the women spoke only Lao (Laotian). The local school headmaster kindly agreed to translate our presentation into Lao.

At sunset when we returned to the temple to prepare for our presentation, we found that the abbot had changed his mind. He told us we were not allowed on the temple grounds, and he forbade the villagers from attending the presentation. I wasn't prepared for this abrupt change in his attitude. The use of the temple was his prerogative, but he had no authority to forbid the others from hearing what we had to say.

We obtained permission from the headmaster to use the school grounds, and most of the village showed up. After the presentation, our students made themselves available for prayer and questions. A number of village men immediately gathered around Richard, a Chinese-Canadian student, apparently assuming that he was Thai. I ran to his rescue, since I knew that Richard couldn't speak the language.

To my astonishment, Richard not only seemed to understand the questions but also was answering in perfect Thai. I then noticed a large group of women surrounding Alice, one of our Thai students. I had been stunned by Richard's prowess with the Thai language, but I knew without any doubt that Alice could not speak a word of Lao. I asked the headmaster if he would interpret for her, but it turned out that Alice didn't need any help either. She was speaking Lao fluently.

When we witnessed these fantastic miracles, the team became even more eager to talk with the villagers. Seeing that everyone was doing fine without me, I excused myself and went for a walk.

"God," I prayed, "You say that it is wrong for a parent to show partiality to their children, and You tell us that there is no partiality with You. I don't understand what just happened. For years, we've been trying to learn this language, and we've been laughed at, embarrassed, and constantly humiliated. Why didn't you zap us with the ability to speak the language the way you just did for Richard and Alice?"

After I had spent a while venting, God reminded me of my prayer that He would go before us to perform miracles. God had simply answered my prayer, and now I was complaining about it. Moreover, I'm just a little speck of a man with an even smaller speck of a brain. Who was I to contest the infinite wisdom and love of God?

The next morning after breakfast, we had a time of reporting all the miracles we had witnessed the previous night. After everyone had given his or her praise report, I stood up and humbly repented of my wrongful, prideful accusations of our impartial, loving God. There are some who get ten talents and some who get only one, but "to whom much is given...much will be required" (Luke 12:48).

Besides, that morning, Richard could no longer speak Thai, and Alice could no longer speak Lao. But my comprehension of Thai? Completely intact, thank you very much.

TWENTY-FOUR

Trapped in Paradise

LOREN Cunningham had been encouraging all of YWAM's leaders around the world to attend the new Leadership Training School (LTS) in Hawaii led by his wife, Darlene. We longed to be better equipped, and we were due for a furlough anyway, so we signed up for the Fall 1985 school. We would then spend the first five months of 1986 in Washington, D.C.

Sean and Michelle didn't want to attend two different high schools in one year, so they opted to stay with my parents in Virginia until we joined them in January. David was only in the eighth grade, and he chose to go with Ellen and me to Hawaii.

Other than dealing with the difficulty of being separated from Sean and Michelle, we found that the LTS rejuvenated our spirits. We hungrily soaked up the teachings and were once again impassioned by the vision and foundational beliefs of our mission. We made deep, lasting friendships and learned as much from fellow classmates as we did from the school's world-class faculty and guest speakers.

A couple of weeks before leaving Hawaii, I went to a pay phone near our studio apartment to reconfirm our flights to Washington. Before I had completed my calls, David came running up to me and said, "Emergency, Dad. Mom fell down and hurt herself."

I left everything and ran to Ellen. By the time we got to her, she was hobbling back onto her feet. She looked up at us and said, "Don't worry, I'm okay. I just twisted my ankle. I'll be all right."

David and I helped her to a nearby chair. Once she was seated comfortably, I jogged back to finish my phone calls. Before I got there, I noticed a woman running away from the telephone booth. She was middle-aged and dressed like a flower child of the sixties, with bare feet and unkempt hair. She ran to an old, beat-up Pontiac, jumped in, and drove away.

I suddenly remembered that in the rush to help Ellen, I had left our plane tickets at the phone booth. I rushed over to the booth, only to discover that the tickets were gone. I promptly called Hawaiian Airlines and told them what had happened.

All they could do was to advise me to call the police and report the theft right away. In those days, most domestic plane tickets could be used by anyone, regardless of the name on the ticket. If the police were unsuccessful in catching the thief, we would have to buy new tickets.

We were relieved when Korean Air Lines told us that we didn't need to purchase new tickets from Honolulu to Los Angeles. Only someone holding our passports could use those tickets. However, we would have to replace our tickets from Los Angeles to Washington, D.C., as well as our tickets from Kona to Honolulu. Altogether, we needed over nine hundred dollars to replace the stolen tickets. Because we had a total of only three hundred dollars in our bank account, Ellen, David, and I prayed together.

Then David said, "Dad, I believe God wants us to help the Filipino couple who need three hundred dollars for their airfare home."

Ellen said, "Yes, I can confirm that. I believe God wants us to give away the money we have on hand."

"Wait a minute," I said. "Right now, we're short six hundred dollars. If we give the three hundred dollars away, we'll be short nearly a thousand dollars. We can't afford to give away what little we have. We have to be responsible here."

We prayed some more, and the Lord brought to my mind 1 Kings, chapter 17. In that chapter of Scripture, a Phoenician widow from the town of Zarephath gave her last supply of food to God's prophet Elijah. God then miraculously replenished the food for her and her son and Elijah every day for the remainder of the three-and-a-half-year drought.

Our logic does not always line up with God's. I realized that Ellen and David were right. That evening, I handed over the last of our money to our Filipino friends, just as God had directed us.

The next day, after classes, I walked over to the campus post office and discovered that we had received a check through the YWAM administrative office. The check was for more than a thousand dollars.

I ran to find Ellen and David. After taking a moment to register this amazing phenomenon, they both started laughing. Before breaking out into the dance of joy, however, Ellen asked who had sent us the money. I looked down to see the name, and my enthusiasm vanished.

"This is obviously a mistake," I said. "We don't know anybody named Roland Jones."

I went to the university's administrative office and said, "I think you've made an error. This money must belong to someone else."

The accountant thumbed through his records. "Here it is," he said. "This is the letter that accompanied the check. It's from Roland Jones of Cheyenne, Wyoming. The letter clearly states that the money is to be used for the support of missionaries Art and Ellen Sanborn, YWAM account #7117."

I could not believe my ears. How could this money be for us? This was the largest individual donation we had ever received, and we had no clue who the donor was. I copied Mr. Jones's address and sat down to write him a letter, thanking him for his support and telling him how his donation had been such a timely answer to prayer. I mailed the letter first thing the next morning.

A few months later, after we had arrived and settled into our furlough home in Washington, D.C., the postal service returned the thank you letter that we had sent to Roland Jones. The envelope was stamped

"Addressee Unknown. Return to Sender." To this day, we have no idea who Roland Jones is.

Our LTS ended just a few days before Christmas. We began our trip to D.C. with breathless anticipation, not because visions of sugar plums were dancing in our heads (that actually sounds kind of creepy to me) but because we would soon be reunited with Sean and Michelle.

At Los Angeles International Airport, we had to practically swim our way through the flood of impatient holiday travelers. Finally, we made it to the front of the check-in line at our gate. When the ticket agent looked at us and said, "Next," we hurried to the counter.

Just then an irate businessman butted in and demanded immediate service. Ellen told the agent to go ahead and deal with the man; we could wait. Afterward, the agent took our tickets and instructed us to wait in the seating area. He told us he would call us when he could.

What now?

We watched the other passengers file into the airplane. The final boarding call would soon be announced, and we still didn't have our tickets back from the agent. Just moments before closing the gate, the agent called our names. He handed us our boarding passes, smiled, and thanked us for being so cooperative. We breathed a sigh of relief and wished him a Merry Christmas. As we boarded the plane, I checked the ticket stubs for our seat location. I stopped and grinned. So that's why he had us wait. He had changed our tickets from economy to first class.

Apparently the saying is true, "Honey gets more flies than..." umm...I'm not really sure how the rest of that saying goes. But whatever it is that competes with honey for flies, suffice it to say that the honey wins out. Anyway, this blessing probably had less to do with our sweetness and more to do with God's tender care of His servants. You just cannot outgive God.

Even first class could not compete with the joy of seeing Sean and Michelle again. Just a couple of weeks after our arrival, we found a beautiful, fully furnished house a few miles from the kids' school, available for an unbelievably low rent. Sean could drive his brother and sister to school each day while Ellen and I commuted to Maryland to work at Halpine Church. A few months later, the church ordained me. Presiding over my ordination were ten pastors who drilled me for three and a half hours on my theology. It was pretty intimidating, but at the end of it all, they agreed to give me my certificate of ordination. I marveled at what we'll put ourselves through for a little piece of paper.

By the end of May our family was eager to return home to Thailand.

Before we left the United States, my brother-in-law took me aside. "Art, I'm concerned about your children's education. What grades will your kids be in this September?"

"Sean will be a junior in high school, Michelle a sophomore, and David a freshman," I answered.

"I thought you'd stay in the US now that your children are all in high school. Art, your children are growing up without a computer. Not knowing computers in their generation will be the same thing as being illiterate in our generation."

"Really? Wow! I guess I didn't realize that," I said. "Ellen and I are certainly committed to providing our children with whatever they need to be well-equipped for their future. If that means we need to buy a computer, somehow we'll get one. Still, I do think raising our children overseas, though challenging, is actually going to be more beneficial for them in the long run."

Later that day when I recapped this conversation with Ellen, she said, "How much do you think a computer costs?"

"I haven't a clue, but anything other than 'free' is financially out of reach for us," I said. "We need a miracle."

Our flight home to Thailand allowed for two stopovers. First of all, we stopped in Kauai to visit our friends Mark and Dorien Nakatsukasa. We wanted to take some time to affirm these fellow laborers in Christ, and if that meant enjoying time with two of our favorite people at some of the world's most beautiful beaches on their island paradise, that's what we had to do. (After all, sacrificing for God's kingdom is what we're all about.) Plus, we decided we needed to spend more time with this couple to practice the proper pronunciation of their surname, "Nakatsukasa."

We savored every moment that we spent with our friends, and Mark taught our boys how to surf. We ended the week with an inspiring time of prayer and worship together.

As our family prepared to board our plane, Mark handed me an envelope. "This is a small gift for your family," he said. "You can use this money toward the purchase of a computer."

"How did you know we were praying for a computer?" I asked.

"Before we went to bed last night, we asked God whether He wanted us to give toward your ministry. Dorien and I both received the same figure, five hundred dollars. The thought of designating the funds for the purchase of a computer came to me this morning during my quiet time."

"I only just became aware of our need for a computer," I said. "But Mark, this is too much money. You can't afford this. At least allow me to return four hundred dollars back to you."

"No. Five hundred dollars is what God told us to give." He grinned. "You don't want us to disobey God and miss out on being blessed for our obedience, do you?"

Ten hours later we arrived at our second stopover, Hong Kong, where we stayed at the YWAM base for three days. What a city! At night from the hilltop, the city looked like a brightly lit fairyland. Up close, the city was enough to overwhelm any visitor with its rush of noises, traffic, neon lights, and crowds.

We always enjoyed our time with the YWAM Hong Kong directors, Gary and Helen Stephens. I asked Gary if he had any idea where we could buy a good computer.

"You've come to the right man," Gary said. "How much do you plan on spending?"

"Five hundred US dollars."

"Hmm." He scratched his head. "Realistically, you can't purchase a good computer for less then a thousand dollars. Can't you double your budget?" (In the mid-1980s, even the most basic computers were expensive. You can now see models of those computers displayed at the Smithsonian Museum along with all the other dinosaurs.)

"That's all we have," I said. "There must be a computer out there somewhere for that price."

"No place that I'm aware of, and I know most of the computer shops in Hong Kong."

For the next few days, we went from one computer store to another looking for something in our price range, but to no avail. On the last day, Ellen and Sean set out one last time into the labyrinth of little back-alley shops, while Michelle, David, and I packed for the airport.

About an hour later the phone rang. It was Ellen. "Honey," she said, "we found a little shop that sells IBM compatibles that we might be able to afford. I know it's late, but this is going to take a little more time. How about if we just meet you at the airport?"

With no time to debate, I agreed on a meeting place. The airline allowed me to check in all of our suitcases and gave me all five boarding passes. When it was time to go through immigration, there was still no sign of Ellen or Sean. Michelle, David, and I went ahead and waited in line. When we reached the front, we began motioning people past us.

Barely half an hour before our flight was scheduled to take off, Ellen and Sean came bursting through the airport doors. They weaved their way through the crowds to the immigration checkpoint. In Sean's arms was a large box containing the new computer. We ran to the immigration counter, got our passports stamped, and made a beeline for our departure gate. The doors were just about to close as we scrambled to board the plane.

Once we had settled into our seats, I turned to Ellen and said, "Honey, I'm too old to be running for flights. What took so long? We almost missed our plane."

"It was crazy," Ellen said. "After we negotiated the price, we found out that the guy had to actually assemble and box the computer. Guess how much it cost."

"Got me. How much?"

"Exactly five hundred US dollars," Ellen said with a weary but triumphant smile.

That same computer eventually accompanied Sean to Stetson University, where he received a bachelor's degree in computer science. Just two weeks before buying this miracle computer, we had no clue that we needed one and no means of getting one. Also, it's likely that had we gotten the newest, state-of-the-art computer, Sean might never have become so adept at fixing those crazy machines.

TWENTY-FIVE

Music and Malaysia

E L L E N had been actively ministering to young people in Maryland ever since the mid-seventies, when she started a Good News Club for the kids in our neighborhood and taught Sunday school at Halpine Church. Now, in Bangkok, her ministry to young people really blossomed. She started both an international youth group called Friday Night Alive and a local chapter of King's Kids (a ministry designed by an extraordinary YWAMer named Dale Kauffman to give young people a platform to share their love for Jesus).

By December of 1986, our local King's Kids group consisted of twenty-four children from seven different nations. Since the group was especially gifted musically, Ellen assembled a Christmas show called "Christmas Around the World" that included songs, dances, puppets, drama, and personal testimonies. The King's Kids were invited, along with other presenters, to perform their programs at the American University Auditorium. We learned that the packed-out audiences would include a number of local movers and shakers, including some Thai royalty.

One day while the show was in rehearsals, I visited a dear and highly respected missionary friend who excitedly told me that his mission had raised a hundred thousand dollars to air the first-ever Christmas program on Thai television. The show would air on Christmas Eve in the second-best time slot, 8:00 PM. I told the man how delighted I was to hear such good news.

Then on the opening night of "Christmas Around the World," a local television executive asked for our permission to film the following night's performance, which would air on Christmas Eve in the best time slot, 7:00 PM. He added that his station could not afford to pay anyone.

Ellen smiled. "That's fine."

It thus happened that "Christmas Around the World" became, to the best of our knowledge, the first televised Christmas program in the history of Thailand, and we did not have to raise a penny. As a matter of fact, we could not have made it happen if we had tried. We just don't have that kind of connection (but of course, we know Someone who does).

Ellen encouraged the teenagers in the group to participate in the development of their own program. They did so with great enthusiasm, working together to develop various dramas, songs, and dances. Their finale was a dramatic dance set to a song by Carman called "The Champion." In the song, Carman portrays the heavenly battle between Jesus and Satan as a boxing match. He depicts the crucifixion as a knockout, in which Jesus, having fallen unconscious, rises again before the count of ten to defeat Satan and become the Champion. Carman proclaims at the end, "Jesus is the Champion."

The teenagers presented the program locally to various schools and churches, with very encouraging results. In the summer of 1987, Ellen took the twelve teenage members of King's Kids Thailand on an outreach trip to Malaysia by train. Upon their arrival, the King's Kids were bused directly to their first performance at a large church in Penang, Malaysia. Just before they handed the performance tapes to the church's soundman, they discovered that the master tape for the entire program was missing. They had left it at their last performance venue the night before leaving Bangkok. They were relieved to learn that Michelle had brought along her rehearsal tape.

The rehearsal tape included all the songs from the program—well, almost all. Since the tape had not been quite long enough, the last song had been only partially recorded onto the tape. That one song just happened to be "The Champion." The song now ended with Jesus being knocked out and down for the count. The end. Not exactly the message the kids were going for.

The exciting climax of the song (for that matter, the climax of the entire program) was gone. The group needed a plan B. They listened to the ending a few times to make sure they knew exactly where the tape cut off. After praying and submitting the situation to God, they decided that Ellen would recite the last thirty seconds of the song. The ending would not be nearly as dramatic without the background music, the choir, and a deep, male voice, but it would have to do.

That evening the kids performed before a packed church. Everything went as planned, and toward the end of "The Champion," Ellen leaned over to speak into the microphone. But the music didn't stop. The tape continued to play. Not only were the last thirty seconds there, but also the sound was studio master quality. As the King's Kids finished, the atmosphere was electrified as Carman (or possibly God) declared that "Jesus is the Champion."

Michelle double-checked the tape to make sure it was the same one she had rehearsed with so many times. She took it out of the player and saw all of the unmistakable markings she had made during months of rehearsal.

Throughout the entire trip, at every performance, Ellen would hold the microphone, ready to recite the ending of "The Champion." But the miracle ending was there every time.

At the conclusion of the trip, the kids all returned safely to their homes in Bangkok. I barely had the chance to greet and hug Ellen and the kids before Ellen rushed over to the tape recorder. She carefully pulled out the miraculous little rehearsal tape, which she now kept safely stored in her purse. She had called me from Malaysia to tell me about the miracle, but now she wanted me to hear it for myself.

"Now, honey," she said, "notice how undeniably clearer the last thirty seconds are."

When she played the tape, though, the last thirty seconds were gone. She examined the cassette and saw that, just as before, there was nothing but a few millimeters of clear blue tape where the song cut off. The miracle was no longer needed, and now it was no longer there.

Our time in Bangkok was pretty tough for our children, although King's Kids and the other ministries that Ellen facilitated were wonderful outlets for them, as were the boys' baseball teams, which I helped coach.

On the mission field we often struggled to find adequate schooling for our children. Though Bangkok had a few international schools, it had only one that we could afford, and even that was a financial challenge. On the positive side, the school was a very reputable institution. Most of its staff and students were Asian, but the instructional language was English. As preparation for American and British Commonwealth universities, the school actually had a rule that the students had to speak only English during school hours.

It was easy for Ellen and me to pick out our children among a sea of hundreds of beautiful Asian faces. But it wasn't so easy for our kids to face the prejudice aimed at them by certain teachers and students. I'm sure the staff and student body as a whole had no problem with the color of our kids' skin or their religion, and a number of the difficulties might simply be chalked up to the way that teenagers treat each other worldwide. But when the bigoted words and actions of some of the teachers continued uncorrected, we became desperate to find a solution that would alleviate our kids' misery.

In March of 1987, I called the family together to ask God for direction. We considered every option imaginable, including returning to the United States, but the kids did not want their education to interfere with God's call on our lives. They believed that God would provide a way for us to continue ministering in Asia and still provide them with a solid education. We decided to explore the option of moving to Penang, Malaysia, where the kids could attend a missionary school named Dalat.

I soon learned that Thai Airlines was running a special: two people could fly from Bangkok to Penang for one-third of the normal price, plus three free nights at a hotel. The price and timing were too good to pass up. A week later Ellen and I boarded our plane for the northwest coast of Malaysia.

Penang is not a large island, but in the hour-long drive from the airport, our taxi passed countless hotels. We realized that our free hotel might end up being hours away from Dalat School. As soon as we had checked into our hotel, we asked the concierge whether he knew the location of the school.

"Right over there, sir," he said.

"What do you mean, 'right over there'?"

"Right down there," he said. "Less than a hundred meters away."

Our hotel just happened to be situated right next to the school. At the school's entrance, we saw a sign that announced that an open-house luncheon for pastors was being held that very day. At the luncheon, we met a YWAM outreach team from Honolulu. The team had just arrived in Penang to establish a YWAM base there. We already knew the team's leader, who did not waste any time in asking Ellen and me to pray about moving to Penang to partner with his team. We also immediately felt a kindred connection with the Malaysian pastors we met. The feeling must have been mutual, because several of them offered us open doors to minister at their churches.

Over the next three days, we had one divine appointment after another. It was amazing. When we first arrived on the island, we didn't know anyone, and we didn't have a clue how to even begin to get connected. Now, in just three days, we already felt a part of the community, with several ministry opportunities and offers at our fingertips.

On top of it all, the staff and students at Dalat School greatly impressed us. Ellen and I became confident that this school, with its college-preparatory curriculum and family atmosphere, would be an excellent environment for our kids to spread their wings and grow. When we returned to Bangkok and told our kids all these things, they became equally excited.

In August of 1987, we boarded the train in Bangkok with our belongings once again pared down to ten suitcases and trunks. When we arrived in Penang, we stayed at the new YWAM base until God provided us with the perfect house, barely a five-minute walk from Dalat School.

Once we had completed the move to our new home, I returned to Thailand to lead the next Bangkok DTS outreach. I took the DTS students south to the Thai-Malay border, then into Burma, and back into southern Thailand. We slept on the floors of churches and spoke in villages, schools, and marketplaces. These young believers shared their faith passionately and endured the rough settings like seasoned missionaries.

Toward the end of the outreach, our team was scheduled to speak at a Muslim village near Surat Thani. Since the students were all exhausted, a local pastor accompanied only Chaiyot and me to the village. After I preached, the people invited us to partake of some southern Thai delicacies.

After hungrily gulping down a few bites, I noticed that my colleagues were being cautious about what they ate. Since these men had grown up in this region, I realized that I had better follow their lead. In particular, they discreetly avoided the food offered by an elderly Muslim woman. I had already eaten much of what she had served, and it had tasted delicious. Then I got a glance of her left hand, which was filthy. When we finished our lunch, we thanked our hosts for their hospitality and left the village.

Before the week was out, I was desperately ill. I don't think I have ever been so sick in my life. Feeling as though I was on my deathbed, I urged the team to continue without me. Our generous hostess continually brought me food, but the mere sight of it made me ill. I begged her not to serve me any more food.

She replied, "But Achaan, you must eat, or you won't regain your health."

I had reddish spots on my stomach and a temperature of 106 degrees. After a few days without any signs of improvement, I agreed to visit the local doctor. After examining me, the doctor told me the diagnosis: typhoid fever. He proceeded to take an old needle out of a jar.

"Whoa! What's the needle for?" I asked.

"I must give you an injection," he said.

"Not with that needle you're not."

"You don't have to worry about this needle," he said. "I've used it many, many times. It is tried and true, very strong. It will definitely not break off in your arm."

Not very reassuring.

With as much resolve as my weak body could muster, I said, "There is no way that you're going to inject me with a used needle."

"Look," he said. "Typhoid fever can be fatal. If I don't give you an antibiotic shot, you could die."

I thanked the doctor for his concern but hobbled over to his door and called out to Gampon, who rushed in from the waiting room.

I said, "Okay. Time to go."

The doctor said, "But…"

"We're leaving," I said. "Now."

After I paid the bill, Gampon helped me to the car.

"Achaan," he said, "why wouldn't you allow the doctor to give you that shot?"

"Listen, in this region, I have way too good a chance of getting AIDS from that well-used needle. It would be a lot easier for my family if I died from typhoid than if I died from AIDS. In the prostitution capital of the world, who's going to believe that I contracted the virus at a medical clinic? At any rate, I think my chances of survival are better without the needle than with it."

Gampon resolved to get me on a train to Penang, since we weren't far from the Malaysian border. If I was going to die, at least I could die surrounded by my family and with access to better medical care. The DTS team mournfully carried me onto the train at the Surat Thani station.

I drifted in and out of consciousness during the train ride. Ellen met me at the Butterworth station near Penang. She took my bag, then put her other arm around me to support my weight, helping me off the train and to the car. She then drove me straight to the Seventh Day Adventist Hospital.

After a very thorough examination, my Indian physician said in his distinguished, clipped accent, "You have typhoid fever, caused by the typhoid bacillus."

I had to take a deep breath every few words to manage even a whisper. "Thank you. Please. Just give me a shot. And some medications. So I can return home."

"It's not that easy," he said. "When you contract this disease in Malaysia, you must be hospitalized. You may go home now to get your belongings. I'll make the necessary arrangements with the hospital for you to be admitted tomorrow morning."

"Hospitalized?" I said. "For how long?"

"If we've caught it in time, you may be feeling well in a month or so, but you can't be discharged until we can prove that you haven't become a typhoid carrier. This could take up to six months, or possibly a year."

Isn't it interesting that the last place a sick person wants to be is in a hospital?

"Oh, no," I said. "Trapped. In a hospital for so long. Who's going to pay for this?"

"You'll be responsible for all expenses, of course."

"What if I can't afford to pay?"

"Then I'll make arrangements for you to be admitted to the government hospital." With a mixture of sympathy and disgust, he said, "Have you ever visited that hospital?"

"No. But I've heard some horror stories," I said. "Okay. I'll see you tomorrow morning."

As Ellen drove me home, I said, "Honey, call everyone who's praying for me. I shudder to think about being locked up in a hospital for a whole year." I managed a feeble grin. "Instead of asking God to cover a large hospital bill, let's pray for a quick healing."

The next morning, I felt significantly rejuvenated, and my fever had broken. When we arrived at the hospital, the doctor told us that all the preparations had been made for my arrival.

"Doctor," I said, "I think that God has healed me. Please take another blood test."

"It would be futile to do any more pathology testing. We have all the necessary results from yesterday's lab report."

"Doctor, please, I insist. Before I'm admitted to an inpatient status, I want one more blood test." It's not every day that you beg someone to stick a needle in your arm, but in this case, if I was right, the payoff would be more than worth it.

The doctor yielded, drew more blood, and, after a couple of hours, called us back into his office. "I have the findings from pathology, but there is definitely a mistake in this current report." The good doctor looked more than a little flummoxed.

"Why? What does the report say?" I asked.

"According to this report, you had typhoid, but your body has built up immunities, conquering the disease. The report also indicates you're no longer a carrier, which would mean that you recovered from the typhoid fever a minimum of six months ago. No. This report is suspect. I still want you admitted."

"The current report shows that I don't have typhoid and I'm not a carrier. Therefore, you have no reason to hospitalize me."

"Sir, it's impossible for this last report to be correct. You must submit to another blood test."

I conceded. Once again, I was oddly delighted to offer my arm to the large needle. I had to laugh, knowing that I would be on my way back to Thailand the next day to rejoin Gampon and the rest of the team.

The medical staff repeated the tests, which yielded the same results. The doctor again insisted that something had to be wrong with the tests. The results were not scientifically possible. But after all, *I* had tossed aside the confines of scientific possibility years ago.

TWENTY-SIX

Fighting for Air

WE WERE relieved to discover that English was the language of choice for most Malaysians and we would not need to take time out from ministry to learn a new language. I found that especially reassuring. It was going to be hard enough just keeping my Thai language skills sharp, since Ellen and I would continue to actively partner with ministries in Thailand.

It was pretty easy to get around Malaysia from the start. Even the bills were printed in English. But I often forget that even when speaking the same basic language, communication can still be hazardous terrain.

One day, as I was thumbing through our monthly bills, one particular bill caught my attention: a bill for air. It seemed that we were being charged for breathing. I highly doubted that the locals were charged for the air they breathed. I was accustomed to people trying to take advantage of my ignorance as a foreigner, and I wasn't about to fall for this little scam. I marched straight to the head office of the local Air Department, as specified on the return address of the bill.

I said to the cashier clerk, "Ma'am, I've lived in many countries in my life, and I've never heard of a government having the audacity to charge anyone for air. I refuse to pay this bill."

"Sir, you used the air," she said. "Therefore, you must be paying for it."

"This is just absurd. How can you possibly expect me to pay fifty-three dollars for air?"

"Well, sir, if you didn't want to be paying so much money, you shouldn't have been using so much air."

"Wait a minute. How could you possibly know how much air we've ingested?"

"There is a meter that keeps a record of how much air you are using, and we charge you accordingly."

"You have to be kidding me."

"No, sir. Here in Malaysia, we have the very finest in air technology."

This was beginning to feel like some absurd *Twilight Zone* episode. Since the woman refused to budge, I requested to see her supervisor. A secretary ushered me into a large office on the second floor.

The manager shook my hand. "May I help you? I understand you have a problem with your bill."

Determined to make it clear that I was not the typical, gullible foreigner, I handed him the invoice and said, "Sir, I'm not paying this bill."

"I see nothing wrong with your bill. You clearly used this much air; therefore, you must pay the full amount on the invoice."

"Sir, I find it very hard to believe that you can really know how much air we've used. For one thing, I just spent the last few weeks in Thailand, so I've only been using Thailand's air."

"Maybe you personally did not use the air," he said, "but obviously, someone at your residence did use it."

Was he serious? I tried to keep from grinning as I inhaled deeply and asked, "How much are you going to charge me for the air I'm using right now?"

"What you are presently using will be on your next bill. We are very proud of our air in Penang. It is among the cleanest air in all of Asia. You can use our air straightaway without purifying it, unlike the air of Thailand."

"Sure," I said. "The air in Penang is an improvement to that of Bangkok, but other parts of Thailand have very pure air."

"No, no, no," he said. "In Thailand, one must use only bottled or boiled air."

"Bottled or boiled? Why in the world would I bottle or boil air?"

"The 'air,' or, as you would say in your country, 'water,' is not safe to drink unless you purify it."

"Wait. We're talking about water?"

"Yes, of course. Air. Water. And I personally feel that fifty-three dollars is very little to pay for the high-quality water we provide."

I had wondered why we hadn't received a water bill. Now I realized that in my attempt to prove that I wasn't an ignorant foreigner, I simply proved that I was one.

"I think I understand now," I said. "So, how should I make out the check?"

As I was leaving, I overheard a conversation between the clerk and the manager. The clerk asked, "Sir, how did you get that man to be paying his bill without a fuss?"

"Oh," the manager said, "one just needs to have certain skills when dealing with foreigners."

I drove home and smiled as I replayed the previous scene in my head. When I walked through our front door, ready to tell Ellen my blunder of the day, she was sitting on the couch, crying.

I knelt beside her and took her hand. "Honey, what's the matter?"

Ellen handed me a letter that had just arrived from Halpine Church. I sat down on the couch next to her and skimmed through the letter. Halfway down, the words practically jumped off the page and knocked the wind out of me: Pastor Richard Kline, our mentor, had unexpectedly died from a heart attack. Jim Isom was dutifully filling in as the interim senior pastor until the search committee could find a permanent replacement.

I struggled to maintain my composure. My mind spun through a random montage of thoughts and memories. Pastor Kline was so young, barely in his mid-fifties. I embraced Ellen and joined her in mourning the untimely death of our friend and pastor.

Focusing on our work was difficult over the next few days, but life had to go on. A week or so later, a Malaysian pastor called and asked if I would teach at a church retreat. Six small churches had joined together for a Bible seminar on Pangkor Island off the west coast of Malaysia. The churches had been planning this event for several months, but their speaker had canceled at the last minute.

After praying and consulting with Ellen, I accepted the invitation to speak. There was just one catch. Since the sermon titles for the week-long retreat had already been publicized, I would have to deliver my messages on those same subjects. Reluctantly, I agreed, even though I had never before taught on those topics.

Having had only a few days of advance preparation, I spent every spare moment of the retreat stowed away in my room, preparing lectures for the subsequent sessions. By the third day, though, I was feeling on top of things. I eagerly accepted an invitation to join a boat excursion to a smaller, more remote island.

A dozen of us crammed into a little fishing boat and braced ourselves as the stench of old fish wafted into our nostrils. The old, faithful vessel pushed its way through the waves, announcing its approach for probably miles ahead with the grinding growl of its water pump and the creaks from its expanding wood as the ocean water sifted through the cracks in the hull.

After an hour and a half, we arrived at the secluded island. The skipper dropped us off and promised to pick us up in four hours. Not far from the shores of this beautiful paradise, we could see a turtle sanctuary. In every other direction, all that could be seen was the wide-open expanse of the Indian Ocean. The only other haven between us and faraway India was the island of Sumatra, roughly 150 miles away.

I took a deep breath of the fresh ocean air and shifted my gaze slowly downward from the soft, cloud-streaked blues that gently brushed the sky to the rich blues and greens that sank deep into the ocean. Invigorating breezes whistled through my ears. I noticed that most of the men had brought fishing equipment and had begun casting their lines. The women and children were giddily dodging the surf as they hunted through the vast treasures of seashells that lined the shores.

I dived into the waves. After a few dozen strokes, I noticed that I had already made significant strides. *Wow. I am fast. I'm a better swimmer than ever.*

In my teens, I had spent several summers working as a lifeguard, and I had always been a strong swimmer. But as I now torpedoed myself through the water, I had little doubt that my freestyle speed could match that of an Olympic contender.

I momentarily slowed my strokes to bask in the wonder of my newfound prowess. My puffed-up ego quickly deflated when I recognized that my pace had hardly diminished. I turned to see a blob of floating fish eggs that weren't even paddling but were valiantly keeping pace with me. Something was definitely wrong with this picture.

The current was sweeping me far out into the Indian Ocean, a trip I was not prepared to take. I turned around and began fighting my way back to the shore. My muscles strained against the ocean's forceful tow as I recruited every system in my body to work toward my goal. My legs kicked hard, and my arms reached as deep and swift as my less-than-Olympian frame could manage.

Every few minutes, my eyes strained through the sting of salt water to check my progress toward the island. Though my eyes continued to register that the blur of land was unattainable, I eventually reached the island and crawled ashore, gasping for air.

I barely had time to feel the aches in my weary body when I heard a cry for help. I sat up and surveyed the oversized suction pool that I had just escaped and saw a flailing man in the distance. Aware that I was in no shape to help, I turned to the group standing on the shore.

Still panting, I called out, "Hey, who's going to help him?"

A skinny, little Chinese boy, about nine years old, ran toward the ocean and said, "I'll go." Everyone else looked on helplessly.

I ran after the young hero, stopped him, turned him back to shore, and ordered him to stay on land. I recognized the man who was calling for help. He weighed roughly 250 pounds and stood at about six-foot-three. If this little boy tried to save him, the boy would more than likely end up drowning along with him.

I had no choice. Regardless of my fatigue, it appeared I was the only candidate. I dived back into the water. This time, I was painfully aware that the speed of my swimming had nothing to do with my skill. The current steadily propelled me toward the ocean's newfound human toy. Watching him bob up and down, in and out of the water, I started to panic. What was I doing? How in the world could I get both of us safely back to shore against this current, especially in my weakened state? *Dear God, we need Your help or we're both going to end up drowning.*

I tried to stay positive, but if I had just barely made it back to the shore before, using all of my energy, how could I possibly get back again while dragging a heavy man and using only one arm to swim? As I approached the man, I saw him go under for the third time.

My already-fervent prayers increased in intensity. *God, I'm so tired. You know I don't even have the strength to swim back, much less dive under the water to pull this man up. Please let him bounce back up one more time.*

My heart leapt, this time for joy, as the man burst through the surface with a loud gasp. I knew from experience that a person who has gone under more than once will usually panic, making it much harder for the rescuer amid the fighting, flailing limbs.

"Look," I said to him, "I don't want to have to hit you, so you have to relax. Don't be afraid. I've got you. We're going to be fine."

My words seemed to have the effect I was hoping for. The man immediately relaxed, indicating that he, for one, believed me. I struggled to believe myself that we were really going to make it.

I put my left hand under his chin and began swimming sidestroke for the trip back. I soon noticed a disturbing pattern: I would take one stroke toward the shore, and the current would pull us two strokes back out into the ocean. We were losing ground, and I was only getting weaker.

A rogue thought forced its way into my mind. *If you don't let go of him, you will both die, but if you let go of him now, you might at least save yourself.*

No. I knew where thoughts like that come from, and the thought wasn't from God. *Lord, I'm not going to let go, but I can't do this on my own. Please, Jesus, help me.* But I could not escape the facts anymore than I could escape the current. I was losing any hope of survival. I did not have the strength to swim to the shore, and I definitely did not have the strength to tread water until we reached Sumatra.

Just then, I noticed a large rock protruding out of the ocean. I calculated that by flowing with the current we could maneuver our way over to the rock. We could then rest there and catch our breath before tackling the swim back to the island.

As we drew near the rock, I reached out to grab hold of it. My heart sank as my hand slipped right off the slimy boulder. Reaching for the rock again and again, my hand merely succeeded in pulling away handfuls of green gunk. We were now truly out of options.

Let go of him or die, the rogue voice once again whispered into my mind. *This man is going to die either way. You have a wife and three children. Let go and live. At least you can save yourself.*

I shoved that voice aside again and cried within, *The only voice I'm going to listen to is God's. I am not letting go of this man, but please, Jesus, help!*

As the current dragged us along the side of the rock, my right hand grappled desperately for any kind of hole or notch that I could grip. Just as we were passing the final tip of granite, my hand unexpectedly latched onto a handle in the rock, the only spot on the whole rock that wasn't covered with slippery slime.

It felt as if the handle had been carefully carved to the exact measurements of my fingers. With great effort, we pulled ourselves safely onto the rock and collapsed in utter exhaustion.

As our bodies and emotions recovered from the trauma, we slowly began conversing. I learned that this young Indian man had committed his life to Jesus quite recently. He had changed his name from that of a Hindu god to the biblical name of James. His father, the high priest of the Hindu temple in Penang, had declared James dead and had cut off all communication with him.

After nearly an hour on our granite sanctuary, we still felt weak, but we realized that we had become about as rested as we were going to get under these circumstances, especially as the sun's heat continued to intensify.

We gingerly climbed to the beachfront loft of the rock and slipped back into the ocean. I still had to hold James with one arm, but the current did not put up as much of a fight on this side. We managed a slow, steady progress until shallow waters allowed us to stand and walk the rest of the way.

Back on solid ground, I dried myself and put my shirt on. In the shade of a palm tree, I lay down on the beach, determined not to rise until the fishing boat returned for us. When the skipper returned and I climbed into the boat, this time I was not so repelled by the pungent odors. As a matter of fact, I happily mused, the aroma of dead, rotten fish had never smelled so sweet.

TWENTY-SEVEN

A Wide Reach

SHORTLY after our move to Malaysia, a group of missionaries there asked me to meet with them. At the meeting, they explained that it was against the law to speak about Jesus to any of Malaysia's Muslim citizens.

The group told me about an American missionary family that had recently been deported because they had broken that antievangelism law. If I was to speak to any Muslims about Jesus, they said, I might be putting all of their ministries in jeopardy. They said I must be cautious about even letting people know that I'm a Christian.

I understood their concern, but I asked them, "In all your years of serving in Malaysia, how many people have come to know Jesus because of your witness?"

The collective answer: none. Not a single person. To them, it was not worth the risk of being deported.

I told them I understood that not all ministries are evangelistic, so it would be inappropriate for me to judge them. But as for me and my house, we would ask God to show us how to witness in a way that wouldn't interfere with other ministries or recklessly compromise the safety of the Malay Christians. At the very worst, deportation would be a small price to pay if it meant that people were given the incomparable joy of knowing their loving Creator. I thanked the group for their concern but told them that I would seek the Holy Spirit's guidance and act according to my convictions, just as they must act according to theirs.

I knew of other missionaries in the area who had been open about their faith and had encountered little or no opposition from the authorities, though the threat of imprisonment always loomed.

I studied some surveys and learned that even though Islam was the state religion of Malaysia, less than half of the population were Muslim. Of the remaining 51 percent, 33 percent were Buddhist or Taoist, 10 percent were Hindu, 6 percent were Christian, and 2 percent were Animist. Other than Christianity, the religious divisions predominantly fell into line with the country's three major ethnic groups: Malay, Chinese, and Indian.

Since there were no laws against sharing our faith with the non-Muslim half of the country, we began contacting high schools and universities, requesting permission for our YWAM team to talk about Jesus with the students. To our surprise, not a single school turned us down.

Usually, the principal would announce during school assembly that we had prepared a Christian presentation for them and that it was therefore unlawful for any of the Muslim students to stay. After the Muslim students had filed out of the auditorium, we would see them gather at the open windows, intently taking it all in, eager to find out why they were not allowed to hear about Christianity.

As we discussed what we had observed at the schools, we became more and more convinced that God had some creative strategies we could use in speaking with the Muslims. We asked God what we should do with the piles of Christian tracts in Bahasa Malay and English that were gathering dust in our office. After a time of prayer, one of our team members came up with the idea of stamping all of our publications with the notification, "For non-Muslim eyes only."

One by one, our YWAM women would approach women cloaked in black burka and ask, "Are you a Muslim?"

"Yes," the women would reply.

"Oh, I'm sorry," the YWAMer would say, "but you're not allowed to read this."

The YWAMer would then set the tract down near the women and walk away. Curiosity took care of the rest.

With this approach, we kept legally aboveboard. If any of the Muslim police officials had stopped us, we could have confidently said, "It is clearly printed on the tract that this literature is intended for non-Muslims only, and we told them that they were not allowed to read it. What more could we do?" In the end, we never even had to use that defense.

Malaysia had two distinct divisions of cops. The first division was the regular police, who took the more traditional law-enforcement duties, such as controlling traffic and arresting criminals for theft and drug dealing. The second division was the religious police, who had the authority to arrest and imprison anyone caught in activities forbidden by the Qur'an, such as committing adultery, peddling pornography, or preaching the gospel.

One day, I was entering the YWAM lecture hall when a cop approached me. He identified himself as a Religious Police Officer and said he knew who I was. He scowled at me in an obvious attempt at intimidation.

"We are watching you," he said.

"I'm so glad," I said. "I have no secrets. Please, come inside. How about a hot or cold drink?"

Taken aback, the cop started fidgeting. He mumbled something and then hurried away. I never saw him again.

For the most part, we encountered civil, professional behavior in our interactions with the Malaysian authorities. We often faced more opposition from international sectors. I recall when we were trying to get a visa for one of our Malay friends so that she could attend a DTS in the United States. The woman had her acceptance and all of the necessary paperwork, but the immigration official at the American embassy refused her request for a student visa. When I asked why, he said, "I happen to think we should respect that if a person is born Muslim, she should die Muslim. How dare you convince her to go to a Christian school. Her visa is denied." Thankfully, Singapore had a DTS starting about the same time. The woman went to it and had a terrific experience.

In 1988, we took one of our DTS teams on the overnight ferry from Penang to Medan, Indonesia, where we worked out of a small church in a predominantly Muslim neighborhood. For the first ten days, we went door to door inviting the Muslim community to attend our evening meeting at the church.

About 250 people attended that first service. After songs, testimonies, and dramas, I presented the message, pushing through a barrage of loud and rude remarks from the audience. We spent most of the next day again inviting our neighbors to the evening's events. I asked Adrian, a Chinese Malay in his late teens, to give that evening's message.

"Just to warn you," I said, "this is a tough crowd. I've been preaching for many years, and the crowd last night was one of the hardest I've ever faced. Don't let them discourage you. Just speak from your heart, and God will do the rest."

That evening almost 350 came, packing out the auditorium. Adrian gave a simple, heartfelt message. To my amazement, thirty Muslims rushed forward at the end to receive Jesus as their Lord. Among them was an elderly Muslim woman who turned to the crowd and said, "Most of you know me. You know that I was almost blind. This morning, three of these young Malaysian Christians came to my home to invite me to church. Before they left, they prayed for me. When they left, I realized that I could see without my glasses. For the first time in years, I can see!"

Our whole family embraced our life and ministry in Malaysia with passion, just as we had done in Thailand. Whether Malay, Chinese, or Indian, the people earned a treasured place in our hearts. Between ministering in local schools and churches and directing and teaching in YWAM training schools, we certainly never had reason to complain of boredom.

I still spent about half of every year taking students on outreach to Thailand. Half of that time, whenever school holidays allowed, Ellen and our kids came to minister alongside me. Even after returning to the States for university, our kids would return to assist us with the mission work, whether that meant digging ditches and building outhouses or preaching from their already extensive understanding of the Bible.

Ellen's mother, Liz, even came in the summer of 1989. We had planned to spend June and July in northern Thailand, and I assumed that Liz would want to stay in a nice, air-conditioned room in Chiang Mai while the rest of us trekked to the villages. We had friends who could keep her entertained, and we could spend time with her between trips to the villages. But she was determined to trek right alongside us, no matter how remote the destination.

In one village, our hostess had a room that she hadn't been able to use for several weeks because a horde of bees had built a honeycomb that took up an entire corner of it. No one in the village had any experience with bees, but when Liz saw the beach ball-sized honeycomb, she promptly went to work. Recognizing that these were honeybees, she drew up blueprints for a wooden beehive and commissioned one of the young men in the village to build it.

Next, Liz recruited David, Michelle, and Sean to assist her in removing the bees from the bedroom. "The bees get agitated if they smell fear," she said, "so just relax and know that they have no intention of hurting you. If you do get scared, get out immediately. I don't want them stinging me because they smell your fear."

First, they used smoke to draw most of the bees out of the honeycomb. Then, without any special protective covering, Liz took a knife and began cutting the twenty-pound nest from the wall, bees swarming all around her. She instructed our brave children to spray the bees with a gentle mist of water to calm them. Once Liz had fully severed the honeycomb from the wall, she and the kids placed it into the newly constructed beehive.

Only one bee stung her, and even then, Liz paid no heed to the pain. "Oh, sorry, that was my fault," she said. "I moved too quickly and scared the poor little fella."

When the honeycomb was safely in the hive, Liz said to our hostess, "There you go. Now you'll have all the honey you could possibly want. Remember, bees aren't our enemies. They're a gift from God."

A crowd had gathered, and everyone applauded, giggling with delight at the fearlessness of this extraordinary white woman who so defied her age.

Next on her agenda, Liz set her sights a little higher. It was one thing to build a house for some honeybees, but now she wanted to build us a house near hers in Florida as an inheritance. I didn't doubt her intentions, but a lot of people had made a lot of promises over the years, and not many had actually followed through. Liz, however, wasted no time. She took Ellen shopping at a teak factory, where she bought a truckload of beautiful, hand-carved teak furniture.

Once she had filled out all the paperwork to have the furniture shipped to Florida, Liz said, "I certainly don't have anywhere to put all this furniture, so now I have to build you a house, just to have someplace to put it all."

When Ellen's mom returned to the United States, she did design and build us a house. And when I say that she built it, I mean that literally. The friends who helped her build it tell me that she kept pace with the young men, hanging from ladders and rafters with power tools.

My own mother had always been one of our strongest supporters, but my father and I had never been very close. But in 1986, shortly after our last furlough, he began to write me letters that grew progressively warmer.

In 1990, I started counting the days until I would see my father again, since we were preparing for our first furlough to the United States in four years. I had so many questions that I had never been able to ask him. More than that, I was looking forward to the chance to connect with him in person, the way we had begun to connect through our letters.

That April, just three short months before our furlough, I returned to Penang after leading an outreach to Thailand. Ellen met me at our front door and whispered, "Honey, I think you'd better sit down."

"What's wrong?" I said. "You look as though someone died."

"Your sister Margie called from Wyoming last week. I tried to contact you through Chaiyot, but you were evidently in a remote village."

I didn't want to hear the next words.

"Honey," she said. "Your dad had to be hospitalized for a broken arm associated with his cancer. He had a heart attack, and he didn't make it."

I was stunned. I knew my father had cancer, but the last I heard, he was doing fine. After all these years, my dream of developing a closer relationship with him was gone. I would never see him again.

Ellen and I walked to the beach, where hand in hand we paced for a few hours. My heart welled up with pain and frustration.

"Why God? I don't understand."

The Lord comforted me by reminding me that my dad had devoted his life to Jesus just after our furlough in 1986. I now began to understand how Frank's parents must have felt when their son died during our first outreach in Honolulu a decade earlier. I needed to weep, and I needed to grieve, but I also needed to remind myself that I *would* see my father again. Just not in this life.

The pain made me even more aware of the amazing gift God had given me in my children. My relationship with them had never faltered. While we watched other teenagers go through periods of rebellion and rejection of their parents, our children had remained our best friends.

During our three years in Malaysia, all of our children finished their high school years having had great experiences and the highest standard of education at Dalat School. The teachers excelled at their jobs, but more important, they were solid role models for our children.

In June of 1990, Sean and Michelle came home from Colorado Christian University to attend David's high school graduation in Penang. Sean and Michelle were both in the process of transferring schools because of their majors. Sean would be studying computer science at Stetson University, and Michelle would be studying premed at Wheaton College. David also would get his music-theater degree from Wheaton.

After graduation, David joined Ellen in packing up the house while Michelle joined Sarah, her best friend from Chiang Mai, on an elephant trek through northern Thailand. Sean and I headed off to Surabaya, Indonesia, where I was scheduled to teach at a DTS.

When we arrived at the bus station in Surabaya, I was puzzled that no one came to the station to meet us. Several weeks earlier, I had sent them all the details of our arrival. After waiting for a little while, we set out on our own to try to find the YWAM base. Since I had been there three times before, I was confident that I could find the training center. After two and a half hours of wandering through congested city traffic, we finally found it. We walked in, grateful to be relieved of our heavy bags.

The leader of the base came out of her office, looking rather astonished to see us. "Art, didn't you receive our letter? The DTS has been postponed."

I shouldn't have been too surprised. This was not the first time the region's postal system had failed us. Over the years, we had lost quite a substantial number of letters and checks in the mail. I told her I had not received the letter.

"I am so sorry. We have plenty of room if you and your son would like to stay for a while, but there is no school in session," she said. "Oh, wait a minute. Now, I don't know if you would be interested, but there is a pastor from Manado who is working among the Javanese people. He is holding an evangelistic crusade this week and asked YWAM for help. When he called, I told him that we were all already overextended."

"Tell him that help has just arrived," I said.

Sean and I were fascinated to learn about the Javanese people, reportedly the largest Muslim group in the world and virtually unreached with the gospel. The pastor from Manado told us that he was thrilled to have us and put us to work right away. We preached every night that week and saw a total of seventy-one Muslims delivered from oppression to freedom in Christ. Sean and I had no doubt in our minds that God was in control of our schedule. I was so grateful that I had not received the letter informing me of the DTS postponement.

It now occurred to me that someday—in heaven, perhaps—I would understand why my dad had died just months before our scheduled furlough. Meanwhile, God has given me more than enough reason to trust that He never does anything without a wise and loving motive. Not everything that happens in this world is His will, but "we know that in all things God works for the good of those who love him, who have been called according to his purpose" (Romans 8:28, NIV).

On the trip back to Penang, I told Sean about how Bob Fitts had recently come to Penang to do a concert. Not only is Bob an amazing singer and musician, but also he's a real man of God and a dear friend. When he visited our home in Penang, I had asked him if he would be able set aside some time to teach our students about worship.

"Sure, Art, I'd be glad to," Bob said. "But rather than simply teaching, I'd really like to lead them in a time of worship. What we should do is have the students gather on the highest peak in Penang and just worship God and pray His blessing over the city."

"Sounds great," I said.

That Monday we all gathered at the top of Penang Hill, and Bob led us in a wonderful time of worship. He told the students that when we pray and worship Jesus, God's almighty power is released. Even though we cannot always see it with our earthly eyes, we can learn to see with our spiritual eyes how the demonic strongholds are torn down through worship.

The next day we saw in the newspaper that at the exact time that we had been worshipping on Penang Hill, the huge, bottom-heavy, gold-plated idol at the foot of the hill—the well-guarded "Goddess of Mercy"—had somehow fallen over. The high priest in charge of the shrine said in the interview that this was a very bad omen. He couldn't imagine that this several-ton idol could have fallen over on its own, and he said there must have been some spiritual attack.

Excited that God had given us an earthly glimpse into the strongholds that He was knocking down in the spiritual realm, we decided to go up to Penang Hill again the following day. This time, we sent an open invitation to the churches, welcoming anyone who wanted to join us. Since Bob Fitts has a pretty strong international fan base, when the word got out that he was leading worship, several hundred people managed to get off work to join us at the top of the hill.

Worshipping the Lord that day, we did not even need to see the physical results of our worship. We knew, deep in our spirits, that God was unleashing His healing power upon our island and tearing down oppressive strongholds.

The following day, the students checked the newspaper to see whether there had been a physical sign to mirror what God was doing in the spiritual realm. There on the front page, we saw that not only had the Goddess of Mercy inexplicably fallen over yet again but also this time the idol's head had cracked. Again, it happened in the same hour that we had been worshipping above it on the hill.

We further read that the local snake temple had experienced a momentous loss. Over the past several years, more and more snakes had assembled at the temple dedicated to their worship, and every year, more and more human worshippers received the "honor" of losing their lives to these deadly "gods." But on this day, snakes began leaving the temple in droves, as if running (or slithering) for their lives. The priest of that temple declared this, too, to be a "very bad omen."

The Hindu priests did not know what to do to get their serpentine gods back. The Buddhist high priest, however, acted without delay to have the Goddess of Mercy fixed. The priest reportedly put a call out to the greatest artists of the land (all the king's horses and all the king's men) to come and help put their multimillion-dollar goddess back together again.

I thought they should also have considered giving their goddess a new, more appropriate name: Humpty Dumpty, perhaps?

TWENTY-EIGHT

Those Crazy Americans

SINCE our children had spent so many years in Asia, they faced pretty serious culture shock when they returned to the States to attend university. I remember calling Sean a few weeks into his first semester.

"How's it going, son?" I asked. "Are the subjects difficult?"

"The class work is easy, Dad," he replied. "The hardest part is memorizing the *TV Guide* so I seem like I've got a clue."

Before starting university, each of our kids attended the Narramore Foundation Reentry Camp for Missionary Kids. At the camp, the kids got a crash course in "American Culture 101." The camp was a huge help.

David could have really benefited by taking the course before he had even landed on American soil. Upon his arrival in Los Angeles, he was supposed to call the foundation and arrange for his transportation. After collecting his luggage, he did something he had done only a handful of times in his entire life. He made a phone call.

"Hello," said the voice on the other end, "This is the Narramore Foundation."

"Hi," David said. "This is David Sanborn."

"No one is available to take your call at this time—"

"Could you just leave a message for me, then?"

The "person" on the other end interrupted him. "So please leave your name—"

"This is David Sanborn."

"Number—"

"I'm at the airport."

"And—"

It's amazing how you can have a zillion thoughts in the amount of time it takes to say the smallest word. *Wait a minute. This has to be some kind of machine. Wow. A machine that answers the phone for you? This place must be ridiculously wealthy.*

The voice continued, "A brief message—"

Confident that he now knew how to respond, David began recording his message. "I need—"

"After the sound of the beep."

Wait a minute. When he said the word, beep, *was that the beep? Or is there going to be a different beep after he said the word,* beep?

David decided to just plow through. "This is David Sanborn, and I'm at the airport—"

"Beeeeeeep!"

Oh no. Was that beep signaling the end of my time to record a message, or was it signaling the beginning?

By now, David was completely disoriented. "Uh…okay," he said, "so, um…I'm here."

David hung up the phone. Then he did something that he was much more accustomed to than making phone calls. He spent the night at the airport.

David assumed that the answering machine would be used only if no one was in the office. He didn't try the number again until the following morning, at which time he talked to a live human being. Everything worked out in the end.

In July of 1990, Ellen and I returned to the States for our furlough, and we divided our time between our supporting churches. The new pastor at Halpine was completely different from Pastor Kline, who had been a scholar's scholar. The church had changed a lot, but it was not the only thing that had changed.

Microwaves and computers were now standard equipment in nearly every home. Instead of four choices of television channels, there were now more than a hundred. Even the choices in the grocery stores were overwhelming, with whole aisles dedicated to just shampoo or breakfast cereal.

We had been in the United States barely three weeks when Grammy Award–nominated songwriters Jimmy and Carol Owens telephoned us. They asked us to join them full-time on the staff of their new School of Music Ministries International (SMMI). The goal of the school was to set up short-term courses and seminars around the world to train worship leaders in musicianship and to train musicians in worship.

Earlier that year, during May and June, Ellen had staffed SMMI's inaugural session, which was held in Singapore. During those six weeks, she had been home only on the weekends, taking the train to Singapore each Sunday night and returning to Penang each Saturday morning. She was also recording her album *Refuge* at the time. It was a grueling but rewarding time, and she kept her sense of humor in high gear. For example, one morning at the school, a respected American vocal coach led the students in a vocal warm-up exercise.

"Repeat after me," the coach instructed. "Mee mee, mee maa, mee moo, mee mia."

A Thai musician could not contain his laughter. He caught Ellen's eye, and Ellen began to giggle, too.

"What's so funny?" the instructor said.

"I am so sorry. We didn't mean to be rude," Ellen said. "It's just that in the Thai language, you just told us, 'I have a bear, I have a dog, I have a pig, I have a minor wife.'"

Since Ellen's experience with SMMI had been so positive, we contacted Loren about linking with the Owenses' music ministry. YWAM was our family, and we didn't want to join the Owenses if it meant having to leave YWAM. Loren gave his blessing, as did our supporting churches. Our next step was to set up an international home office for

SMMI in Texas. In addition to administrating the schools, Ellen taught voice while I provided spiritual discipleship. The Owenses, with their warmth and humility, quickly earned our love and admiration.

During the next few years, we earned our fair share of frequent-flyer miles, operating SMMI in Australia, Malaysia, Hungary, and countless other places. We lived out of our suitcases an average of ten months each year. In the interim periods between SMMI sessions, we continued to teach at YWAM bases and lead outreaches in Southeast Asia.

We were very grateful to Ellen's mother for building us a house, which meant that we at least had a home base for our family. To this day, when people ask where we live, we reply, "Well, we have a house that lives in Florida."

People also commonly ask us, "With all of your traveling, where do you like to go for vacation?"

Our reply is always the same: "Home."

Even our own kids had trouble keeping track of us. In January of 1993, Sean had graduated from university and was working as a computer programmer while staying at our "house that lives in Florida." We had been in Australia for a few days before calling home.

"Where have you been?" Sean said. "I have been worried sick."

When we apologized, he graciously agreed not to discipline us. "Just don't let it happen again," he warned.

Later that year, Alan Lim, the dynamic director of YWAM Singapore, asked us to consider making Singapore our home base. Alan was confident that we could still continue our various ministries while aiding him with his vision for Singapore. This seemed right to us, and the Owenses agreed that we could limit our involvement with SMMI to Asia.

The new pastor of Halpine Church was unhappy about our decision to continue on the mission field. He had wanted us to return to Halpine as associate pastors, but when the elders voted to continue our support, he accepted the decision.

As usual, we received full support from the pastors of our other main supporting churches, Pastors Dan Duis, Charles Schmitt, and Derrel Emerson. That meant a great deal to us, since we have such tremendous respect for these three men of God. We told Alan that we would move to Singapore in 1994.

Sean had graduated from Stetson University in December 1992, but the ceremony was held in May 1993. We watched from the balcony as Sean walked down the aisle to receive his degree. Despite the solemnity of the occasion, we all burst out laughing when we saw the top of his graduation cap. There in large letters were the words, "WILL WORK FOR FOOD."

At Michelle's graduation the same month, Billy Graham gave the baccalaureate address. He said that in his graduation ceremony at Wheaton College fifty years earlier, he hadn't heard a thing that the speaker had said. All he could think about was a date that he had with a cute girl named Ruth. Some of the graduates laughed.

Mr. Graham then told the graduates that they would probably not remember who spoke at their baccalaureate. We all laughed.

After graduation, Michelle began preparations for medical school. *Time* magazine reported that 1993 had become one of the most competitive years in US history for medical school applicants, and we were all elated when Michelle was accepted into the school of her choice, St. George University School of Medicine in Grenada. This had been a lifelong dream of hers.

One day, Ellen received a call from the school's administrator. "Mrs. Sanborn," the administrator said in her thick New York accent, "the reason I'm calling is to let you know that we have set your daughter's application aside."

"But I thought she was already accepted," Ellen said.

"Academically, yes, but we need to clear up some financial issues. Mrs. Sanborn, do you realize that our school costs thirty thousand dollars a year?"

"Yes."

"And you still have one son attending Wheaton College, which I am assuming is about fifteen thousand a year. Is that correct?

"Yes."

"Well, I have your tax returns from the past two years, and I see that you listed your annual income as fifteen thousand dollars. Is it possible that you accidentally left off a zero?"

"I can understand where you're coming from, but there's really no need for concern." Ellen went on to explain that our daughter had diligently pursued her goal, that she hoped to become a medical missionary and work with the poor and needy, and that God, who had always taken care of our every need, would honor the fact that Michelle's motives for becoming a doctor were pure.

Ellen then told the administrator some of our stories of God's miraculous provisions and said that Michelle was not just low maintenance, she was no maintenance; that she would happily take the cheapest, most crowded accommodations; and that food would not be much of an expense for her, since she always traveled with her rice cooker and Thai spices.

"If money is the only obstacle to Michelle's becoming a doctor," Ellen said, "we have nothing to worry about."

The administrator seemed at a loss for words. Finally, she said, "Your daughter does qualify for graduate student loans, and I see here that she has a scholarship with the Christian Medical Foundation. With her lifestyle, that will lower expenses. But even after all that, she will still be short at least five thousand dollars, which is a third of your yearly income."

"Yes, I understand," Ellen said.

"I have to tell you, I've never talked to anyone like you before. Let me submit Michelle's name for a private student loan the school sometimes grants. It has to be repaid, but maybe she'll qualify."

"That would be wonderful. Thank you so much for all your help."

Two weeks later, our whole family was in the kitchen when Michelle received another call from the school. We watched for her reactions during the phone call but just couldn't decipher either her doe-eyed poker face or her polite poker voice. When she hung up, we crowded around her.

"Did you get the loan?" Ellen asked.

"No, they turned it down," she said.

"Oh," we groaned.

Ellen said, "It's okay. You've come this far. I'm sure God will supply somehow."

"Hmm." Michelle nodded. Then, with a twinkle in her beautiful blue eyes, she said, "Actually, they did mention one other thing. The board has decided to start a new scholarship fund, and I am the first beneficiary. It's five thousand dollars a year for the next four years."

Later, after granting the scholarship to Michelle, the board decided to give it a name: The Italian-American Scholarship. Now, we have Native American ancestry, Irish ancestry, Scottish, Dutch, Norwegian...you name it. We are regular, all-American mutts. But Italian? Who knew?

TWENTY-NINE

Dancing in Hungary

AMONG more than a dozen schools that we led for SMMI, the six-week school we held in Budapest, Hungary, was particularly memorable. The Berlin wall had just come down, and this formerly Communist country was struggling to find its way. We had fifty students from ten Eastern Bloc nations. We were saddened to see just how much prejudice existed between the various ethnic groups, but in time, the students learned to love and appreciate each other.

We also had fun with the English language. Since our family has so often had to live out of a suitcase and with limited income, it has been difficult to have hobbies like collecting stamps or dolls. Or money. Instead, our family collects accents.

One day, Ellen was talking and joking with two Russian musicians when she unconsciously started speaking with a Russian accent.

"Vat can I do?" she said (meaning, of course, "What can I do?").

"Vat did you say?" one of the young men asked.

"Vat can I do?"

"You speak Russian phrase," he said.

"I did?"

"Ya."

"What did I say?" Ellen asked.

"Vodka naj doo," the young musician laughed, "is Russian phrase, meaning, 'Let's go find some vodka.'"

One day, a couple of our students—a Hungarian girl and an American girl—were discussing the Bible. The American complimented the Hungarian on her deep maturity and understanding of the ways of God.

"How long have you been a Christian?" the American asked.

"Only two years," the Hungarian replied.

"Only two years? But you have such a deep relationship with Christ."

"Well," the Hungarian said, "maybe it is because every morning I worship the Lord by playing the violin, and I belly dance before the Lord."

The American unsuccessfully tried to conceal her astonishment.

The Hungarian said, "In America, you have very good belly dancers in your churches, no?"

"Not that I've ever heard of," the American replied. "To tell the truth, I really can't imagine seeing such a thing in most American churches. But Hungary is a very different culture. I'm sure the Lord is very pleased when you worship Him with your cultural dance."

"But I know for a fact you have the belly dance in your churches— many American women who belly dance before the Lord all over America."

"I could be wrong, but I really don't think so. Not that there's anything wrong with it…"

The conversation went back and forth like this for several minutes, until the Hungarian said, "But you know. You put on your belly shoes and—"

"Oh, wait," the American said. "You mean ballet shoes?"

"Of course. Belly shoes. To do the belly."

"Oh." The American burst out laughing.

I was intrigued to learn that Hungary was considered "the Breadbasket of Eastern Europe." The reason for this moniker, I decided, must be that all they had to eat was bread. The young man who made all the arrangements for the school unfortunately paid the caterer in advance, and the caterer took advantage of the situation. Even the local students complained about the food. Apparently, uncooked pork fat is not generally considered a local delicacy. However, there was a lot of bread. A lot.

Since we had such a large group, we ate in two shifts. One day as we led the second group toward the dining hall, we met the group that was just leaving, led by our guitar instructor. The instructor's four-year-old son, Nathan, looked up at us as we approached, his eyes wide with horror. He shook his head in a manner ominously slow for one so young.

"Go back," Nathan said. "Go back, I tell ya. It's green. It's greeeeeen!"

We should have heeded his warning. The vision (and taste) of that food still haunts my dreams. I'll take fried crickets and boiled silkworms in Thailand any day over that food.

A few days later, we were hanging out in the dilapidated youth hostel that served as our dorm. Little Nathan came through singing a song that Karen Lafferty had led the night before at our weekly concert. The correct lyrics of the song are

Ain't it grand to be a Christian, ain't it grand. Yee haw!
Ain't it grand to be a Christian, ain't it grand.
On Monday, Tuesday, Wednesday, Thursday,
Friday, Saturday, all day Sunday,
Ain't it grand to be a Christian, ain't it grand. Yee haw!

But little Nathan was singing, "Amy Grant is a Christian, Amy Grant. Yee haw!'"

Of course, we couldn't help but laugh. Some of our local students asked us what was so funny. When we told them of the child's mistake, one of them said, "Oh, no. We all sang this."

"Yes," another student said. "Karen Lafferty obviously know that we had wonder whether Amy Grant was Christian ever since she sang that 'Baby, Baby' MTV video. So Karen clear up the question by make us all stand up and sing 'Amy Grant is a Christian, Amy Grant. Yee haw.'"

We would regularly set up our band equipment to perform in the local parks and other public places. After one such performance at a shopping center, a man approached us and introduced himself as the manager of a local television newscast.

"It is so bizarre," he said, "to see modern-day Hungarians who have been educated in Marxism being so receptive to a myth. I must film this, with your permission."

"You have our permission to televise us," I said, but then I went on to explain that Jesus is not a myth, that it's a historical fact that He lived, that He still lives, and that, unlike Marxism, Jesus' teachings bring truth and freedom, not bondage.

The man returned the next day to film us. Although we did not see the program when it aired, our students told us that it was possibly the first time in fifty years that Christians had a voice on national television.

When we returned to the hostel that evening, Ellen asked me if I had her purse. It didn't take us long to turn our tiny room upside down looking for it. We were particularly concerned because her purse contained not only her credit card and driver's license but also our passports. The next day we asked the students to pray that we would retrieve the purse. Their cynical responses disappointed us.

"Prayer is a waste of time," one said. "This is Budapest. If anyone finds your credit card, he will keep it. And your passport? Even more so."

American passports could fetch a healthy price on the black market.

One young man said, "If you actually get your purse back with everything intact, I will believe in miracles."

I told them, "You guys need to know that God cares about even the smallest of details in our lives."

When we finished classes that afternoon, I asked Ellen when was the last time she remembered having her purse.

"I definitely had it at McDonald's," she said.

I took her hand. "Let's go. We can just get there before closing time."

The McDonald's was a fascinating structure. It had formerly been a train station, and its veneer attested to its former glory. All except for the alien golden arches that had landed on the roof.

When we arrived at McDonald's, we searched the whole restaurant and consulted the manager. The purse was nowhere to be found. We prayed the whole way home and determined to go to the American embassy first thing in the morning to report our missing passports.

The next morning, we arrived at the embassy before it opened and were the first in line. As soon as the doors opened, the guards ushered us in, and we informed the embassy official of our loss. The official handed us some forms to fill out which we promptly completed and handed back to her. She glanced at the top of the first page.

"Your name is Ellen Sanborn?" She reached under the counter, pulled out a purse, and handed it to Ellen. "Is this yours?"

"Praise God," Ellen said and began rummaging through her bag.

"How did the purse get here?" I asked.

"That nice Hungarian man who was just ahead of you in line. He said that he'd found it on the subway."

"What man?" I asked.

"Didn't you see him?" she said.

We had been the first ones in line, the first ones through the door. But before I had a chance to say anything, Ellen said, "Honey, everything's here: credit card, cash, plane tickets, and our passports."

I couldn't wait to see the students and tell them that prayer is never a waste of time, that God does indeed care about even the smallest of details in our lives, and that Hungarian is apparently the mother tongue of angels.

THIRTY

Back to Asia

WE CONTINUED to lead a number of outreaches to Thailand throughout the 1990s. We especially enjoyed leading outreaches for the Primary Health Care School (PHCS) of the University of the Nations. Those teams gave us very practical opportunities to minister to both physical and spiritual needs.

The PHCS students separated into two teams and alternated between ministering in Bangkok and ministering in northern Thailand. In Bangkok, the students operated a mobile clinic, attending to the seven hundred children who lived at Pakkred Handicapped Children's Home (an orphanage for both mentally and physically handicapped children). They managed to identify and treat a variety of illnesses, from scabies to conjunctivitis, while giving and receiving a lot of hugs.

I led each of the teams in during their time in northern Thailand. I took the first team to a large, orderly Karen Village in the Mae Hong Son province. The village was named Musekee, which means "friendship"

267

in Karen. There, we were hosted by Te-Te, a missionary from the Mizo tribe of India.

Te-Te had three children of her own but took care of another seventy teenage girls. This allowed the girls to attend high school safely away from the wealthy pimps who came to the region to buy girls for prostitution. Musekee had the only high school in the region, making it an ideal location for Te-Te's ministry.

The founder of the village, Pastor Bonnee, welcomed us along with his oldest son, Timothy, who was the chief of Musekee. Timothy and his wife, Esther, spoke English fluently, as did Te-Te. All three were a huge help in translating for both clinic and Bible-teaching ministries.

The director of the PHCS, Janet Ditto, visited each of her Health Care teams to ensure that everything was going smoothly. After her visit with us in Musekee, I drove her to Chiang Mai so that she could catch her train to Bangkok. I also needed to buy more food supplies in Chiang Mai.

With a few hours to spare before catching her train, Janet accompanied me to the market. "Art," she said, "along with the regular food supplies, why don't you bring the team back something really exotic?"

"What would you suggest?" I asked.

"How about a snake? I'll bet none of them have ever eaten a snake before."

"Sounds good," I said.

We found some snakes at the market, but they were more than just raw. They were still breathing. If it's possible for food to be too fresh, live, squirming vipers would surely apply. Staring at these deadly serpents, I was not particularly salivating with delight. The snakes definitely seemed to be, though, as they stared back at me with their beady little eyes.

The customer ahead of me in line picked out a snake, which looked more testy than tasty. The grocer placed the venomous creature inside a clear plastic bag, which he tied at the top with a rubber band.

I told Janet, "I'm sorry, but there's no way I'm carrying back a live, poisonous snake in my backpack."

"Can you think of something else?"

"I know just the thing," I replied. "I spotted them as we first entered the market." We walked back to the market entrance, where I pointed out the cuisine I had in mind. "What do you think?"

Janet laughed. "Excellent! I wish I didn't have to leave this afternoon, because I would love to see their reactions when you show them their supper. I want to hear the whole story next time I see you."

After I had taken Janet to the train station, I drove straight back to Musekee. It was nine o'clock at night by the time I arrived. A very hungry team came out to meet me.

"Tonight," I announced to them, "you are in for a real gourmet treat, a true Thai delicacy. You're about to taste something on a completely different level from anything else you've ever tasted before."

"I don't care what you brought us," one young man said. "I am so hungry, I could literally eat a horse. Hurry, get out the food and let's eat."

I pulled out a two-kilogram bag of boiled beetles, termites, and grasshoppers.

The young man said, "That's not food. That looks more like fish bait. What have you done with our food?"

I opened the bag, grabbed a handful of bugs, and placed them on a few empty dinner plates. "Come on, guys, you don't know what you're missing out on," I said as I began popping the critters into my mouth.

"Oooo, he isn't kidding," one of the girls said. "He actually expects us to eat insects for dinner."

The team leader stood up. "I think God has called me to fast tonight."

Before long, though, all the guys on the team had eaten at least one insect, as had a couple of the girls. After about fifteen minutes, I figured I had gleaned about as much fun as I could in honoring my promise to Janet.

"It appears tonight's appetizer is not very popular. Perhaps the main course will be more to your liking." I pulled out a bag of roasted chicken and sticky rice.

"All right!" the team leader said. "That's more like it."

Silence enveloped the room as the students all began scarfing down their food. I took the bag of boiled insects over to Te-Te's girls' dorm. Substantially more appreciative of the treat than had my team members been, the teenage girls devoured the bag's contents.

Early the next morning, we set up four examination rooms, one for each of our four interpreters. One boy presented with a dirty, rusted fishing hook that had gone right through his left thumb. The students removed the hook and bandaged the boy's thumb. The boy was quite brave until the health-care student gave him a tetanus shot. At that point he started crying, partly out of pain and partly, I think, because he thought we had betrayed him by sticking another sharp object in his arm the moment after we had taken the hook out of his thumb.

Next in line, an old woman came in and sat down. When I asked her what ailed her, she said, "My throat hurts."

"Ask her to describe the pain," the health-care student requested. I translated the question.

"Oh, no, I don't feel any pain in my throat right now," the old woman said.

"Then tell me," I said, "when do you feel the pain?"

"When I swallow chicken heads."

I paused for a moment and pursed my lips to keep from grinning.

"What did she say?" the student asked.

"She is saying that her throat doesn't hurt right now," I said. "It hurts only when she swallows chicken heads."

"Art, stop joking around. What is she really saying?"

"I'm not joking. That's what she said. I'm astonished that you would think that chicken heads are a laughing matter."

"Come on, Art. You expect me to believe that this woman swallows chicken heads? No way. Seriously, tell me the truth."

"I'm telling you the truth," I said.

Clearly, this student had skipped the most fundamental of all medical classes, "Solutions to Chicken-Head Swallowing 101."

I turned to the patient and gave her some nonprofessional advice. "Auntie, God didn't make our throats big enough to swallow anything as big as a chicken head. I'm afraid you'll have to stop eating the chicken's beak altogether and cut the rest of the head into small pieces before eating it."

"Yes, what you say is good," she said. "I will give it a try."

That afternoon, when we took our lunch break, I saw that the villagers had blessed us with their favorite meal, chicken-head-and-foot soup (I call it "foot-n-mouth soup"). The team had trouble believing me when I tried to convince them that I had not put our hosts up to it. Imagine thinking that I would do something like that! Ever the loving father, I warned the students not to eat the heads whole lest they mysteriously develop sore throats.

In January of 1994, Ellen and I moved to Singapore. First on our agenda was to lead YWAM's School of Frontier Missions (SOFM) there. All twenty-eight of our students were delightfully eager. In our first week, we had an unusual bonding experience—we all gave blood. Not the typical icebreaker, but it certainly was effective.

An Indonesian woman had come to Singapore for advanced cancer treatments. In the course of her treatments, she required several blood transfusions. The hospital told her that she had to either pay cash or find some people willing to give enough blood to replace the supply used to combat her cancer.

The woman decided that she knew just where to go to find people willing to give their life blood—the local YWAM base. Alan Lim told her that he would bring a group of staff and students the very next day. After our morning worship, we all went to the hospital to give blood on behalf of the dying woman.

We were rather amazed to learn that out of the whole group, only Alan and I had the same blood type, the usually common A-positive, as the woman. The rest of the group were still able to give blood to credit the woman's account, but only Alan and I were able to give blood directly for the treatment of the woman's cancer-riddled body.

Before leaving the hospital, we all gathered around the woman and prayed for her. Just two days later, her doctor announced that her cancer had inexplicably gone into remission. Given a clean bill of health for now, she was discharged from the hospital. But before leaving, she gave witness of the miracle to her hospital roommate, who consequently decided to dedicate her own life to Jesus.

When we heard the good news, Alan said, "Huh. We give blood, and the next thing you know, the woman's healed. Art, you and I should go into business together, selling our blood as a miraculous healing potion."

"I think I'll keep my blood to myself, thank you very much," I said. "A pint every now and then is one thing, but I don't think either of us has enough extra blood to start a franchise. Of course, we both know that Jesus is the One who's really responsible for this healing."

"You can say that again," Alan replied.

A Singaporean student named Esther believed that she was called to be a missionary to Cambodia. She had enrolled in our school on the recommendation of her pastor, who had promised to support her but wanted her to first receive more training at the SOFM.

Everything was going as planned until Esther received a disturbing telephone call from her aunt, a devout Buddhist. "You are a disgrace to the family," the aunt said. "How dare you go off to Cambodia, leaving your mother all alone."

Esther was sadly aware that her mother had coerced the aunt into making the phone call. Even though Esther's mother was Christian, she was against Esther's plans to minister in Cambodia. Esther's mother was a wealthy woman and certainly did not need any financial assistance from Esther. She simply did not want to live alone in her house, and she didn't want anyone other than Esther living with her.

When Esther told us and her pastor about her dilemma, she received a host of conflicting opinions. The one thing everyone could agree on, however, was to lift Esther up in prayer.

Just days later, Esther testified that God had answered her prayers. She and her mother slept in the same room, and late the night before, Esther had awakened to see her mother fall out of bed. Esther's eyes had then shut again out of exhaustion, but Esther told herself, "No, you can't go back to sleep. You must force yourself to wake up and help your mother back into bed."

When Esther compelled her heavy eyelids to open again, she looked across the room and saw her mother lying peacefully on her bed. Rationalizing that she must have been dreaming, Esther closed her eyes and went back to sleep.

At breakfast Esther told her mother, "I had the strangest dream last night."

"Tell me," her mother said. "What was your dream about?"

"I dreamed that you had fallen out of bed. But then, when I opened my eyes, I saw that you were peacefully lying on your bed."

Esther's mother turned pale at first, but after a moment's reflection, she smiled and began laughing. "I did fall off the bed," she said. "I, too, thought it was all a dream. I saw angels catch me before I hit the floor, and they lifted me comfortably back onto my bed. Now I know it wasn't a dream but that it actually happened." She bowed her head for a moment and then looked up again at Esther. "Angels are watching over me. I guess I don't need you to stay with me, after all. God has assigned an angelic host to take your place."

Esther's mother then called the aunt who had rebuked Esther for wanting to leave. She said, "My daughter has been called by God to help the Khmer people. She must do what she needs to do to fulfill the destiny God has given her. I will be fine. I don't need Esther to take care of me. God Almighty has commissioned His angels to take care of me."

It was clear that God had an important calling on Esther's life, and as long as Esther was obedient to that calling, He would take care of the rest. (Esther has been serving in Cambodia ever since.)

The three-month lecture phase flew by. For practical, hands-on application of their studies, the twenty-eight students were then commissioned to various countries, from Siberia to Cambodia, each for a minimum commitment of two years.

When the Frontier Missions lecture phase ended, Alan Lim pleaded with us to direct a School of Intercession. He had received permission from Paul Hawkins, the founder of the program, for us, along with an adequately trained staff, to direct a session of the school. Alan told me that a great hunger existed in Singapore for teaching on intercession and spiritual warfare, and he felt strongly that Ellen and I were to direct the three-month program, starting no later than September.

"I don't know," I told Alan. "That doesn't leave us much time to prepare. Plus, we're overseeing another session of SMMI starting in October. I honestly don't see how we could do both at the same time."

Alan eventually convinced me, however. I determined to find a way to host both schools simultaneously. It was a stretch, but the two schools' subjects were fairly complementary, allowing us to bring in guest speakers who could teach in both programs. Ellen and I had to personally teach during only a few weeks of the School of Intercession. After we committed ourselves to this crazy juggling act, we wondered whether we should have been committed...into a very different type of institution.

One evening that October, Ellen was having dinner with students from both schools. "I almost forgot to tell you," she said suddenly. "Our daughter, Michelle, just delivered her third baby. Isn't that amazing?"

"That's fabulous," one of the students said. "That's...oh, wait a minute. I didn't even realize your daughter was married."

"Oh, no, she's not," Ellen said. "She hasn't found the right guy yet. Plus, she's so busy with these babies, she doesn't have much time for a social life."

"The baby that she just delivered," another student said, "was it a boy or a girl?"

"I don't know," Ellen said. "She didn't say."

"What's the baby's name?"

"No idea. I didn't ask."

Another student asked, "How much does it weigh?"

"She didn't really give me any of the details, and I didn't ask. Poor Michelle has enough on her plate without her mom bugging her about every baby she delivers." Ellen smiled, picked up her tray, and said, "I'd better get going. See y'all later."

Just as she had reached the door, Ellen stopped in her tracks, turned around, and made a beeline back to the table.

"You do realize that my daughter is in medical school?"

After taking a moment to let it sink in, the bewildered students burst out laughing. "Oh, so Michelle assisted in the delivery of the baby."

"That's right. What did you think I meant? On second thought, don't answer that." Ellen laughed. "I know exactly what you were thinking."

Our students in the School of Intercession did extensive research on prayer needs for the country of Singapore. After gathering all the information, we decided to concentrate our prayers toward an area of northern Singapore called Yishun. The primary religions in Yishun were Buddhism, Confucianism, Jainism, Taoism, Hinduism, and Islam. The first and only surviving Christian church in the region, Yishun Christian Church (formerly known as St. Peter's), had been founded by the British army decades earlier, and it had only a tiny congregation.

In the early 1990s, Yishun's total population was just under 56,000, less than two percent of the country's three million total population. Our research revealed that Singapore averaged roughly four hundred suicides and sixty murders per year. Out of that national average, the tiny province of Yishun was responsible for almost half of all those murders and suicides.

A deep enough exploration of history can usually reveal the roots of a problem, so we investigated Yishun's history. We learned that at the beginning of World War II, British troops lined all of Singapore's shores facing the open sea and boasted that the island was absolutely impenetrable. To their surprise, though, the Japanese troops hiked through the perilous Malay jungle and crossed over into northern Singapore at Nee Soon (now called Yishun), an area with very little fortification. The battle was over before it began, and the Japanese took control of the island.

There in Yishun, the Japanese set up their headquarters and their notorious, horrific prison camps. From 1942 to 1945, the Japanese army performed genocide on the inhabitants of Singapore at Yishun. Even after the Japanese retreated in 1945, it seemed that the spirit of death continued to rule over the previously peaceful Yishun province. For half a century since then, Yishun had regularly led the country in murders and suicides.

We knew that God longed to take control of the area and turn it around for His glory. As Hudson Taylor, the pioneer missionary to China, had once said, "When we work, we work. When we pray, God works." We thus focused our prayers against the spirit of death over Yishun, taking long walks through the streets, praying blessing upon the people, and worshipping Jesus. We started our prayer walks in October. By December, a number of churches from other Singaporean districts had joined our little band of prayer warriors.

The school session came to an end at Christmas of 1994. Those of us who stayed in Singapore continued throughout 1995 to pray that Jesus, the Spirit of Life, would reign over Yishun. We knew that we might not see the result of our prayers in our lifetime, but we knew that God was able to use our prayers to make inroads here on earth ("as it is in heaven"). As long as the Holy Spirit put it on our hearts to do so we would continue to focus our prayers toward Yishun's need for new life.

We were discouraged when Singapore's 1995 statistics matched those of 1994, with over four hundred suicides and over sixty murders. Again, Yishun led the way in both categories, but we determined to continue. As the Scriptures say, "The effective, fervent prayer of a righteous man avails much" (James 5:16).

Then, in 1996, for the first time in decades, a new church actually succeeded in drawing a growing congregation. Quietly, with no great fanfare, the Spirit of God began touching the hearts of the people, and the end-of-year statistics reflected a change more extraordinary than we had imagined. Singapore's national suicide rate had been cut by more than 30 percent, down to 271, and the murder rate had dropped more than 80 percent, down to 13. Most significant of all, Yishun, the little territory that had led the nation in murders and suicides for more than fifty years, had dropped considerably in both categories. Yishun's total count of suicides and murders for 1996? Zero.

THIRTY-ONE

Dream Team

IN SEPTEMBER of 1995, we directed a Crossroads DTS in Singapore. We wanted to keep the number of students down to a manageable twenty-five, but we received more than eighty applicants. Alan Lim urged us to consider accepting more students than we had originally planned. After a lot of prayer over every applicant, we settled on thirty-nine students.

Our little group of staff and students represented five continents, and our times of worship and fellowship became rousing celebrations of the beautiful kaleidoscope of cultures that God had created. Almost half were Singaporean, but the other half came from South Korea, Malaysia, Indonesia, Thailand, Burma, Germany, America, England, South Africa, and New Zealand.

The students were all loads of fun and extremely zealous for God. Ellen and I called them the Dream Team. Time would reveal how appropriate that name was. In the years since, these students have all persevered in outstanding service for Christ.

One of the last speakers in the school term was Gary Stephens. We had known Gary for about fifteen years and had deep respect for his work as the director of YWAM Hong Kong. Alan invited Gary to speak in our weekly community meeting. Gary spoke about his wife, Helen, and her ministry as the director of an orphanage in mainland China. He shared some very touching stories about how God was miraculously providing for these abandoned children. By the time Gary had finished speaking, those of us in the audience were running out of tissues.

Alan thanked Gary for speaking and then addressed the rest of us. "I'm very inspired by the work that Helen's doing, and I want to give to this ministry. We are going to take up an offering. One hundred percent of the collected money will be given to Gary for the support of Helen's ministry to the orphans. Before passing the offering plate, we'll pause for a few minutes so that you can pray and ask God how much He wants you to give."

After a couple of minutes of prayer, Ellen asked me how much I felt we were to give.

"I feel led to give all that's in my wallet, ten dollars," I said.

Ellen replied, "I believe God wants us to give one hundred dollars."

"How much money do you have?" I asked.

"Not a dime."

I figured the facts could clarify God's will here. "I have ten dollars, and I believe we're to give it all."

"Hmm…" Ellen said, "Can you at least pray about whether God wants us to give a hundred dollars? I feel very certain that that's the amount He wants us to give."

"But we don't have a hundred dollars. How can we give what we don't have?"

"You never know what God's going to do, right? How many times before has God told us to look beyond our wallet for His direction?"

I agreed to pray again about it. At least then I would be able to steer Ellen in the "right" direction, graciously revealing to her what God was really saying. After all, we all make mistakes in hearing God's voice at times, so she need not feel discouraged by the fact that she was wrong.

I got down on my knees and prayed, "Okay, God, You know I have only ten dollars in my pocket. I ask You, how much do You want us to give?"

God often speaks to me by giving me scripture verses. Over the years, I had learned to pretty well discern the difference between my own imaginative thoughts and the "still, small voice of God." At this moment, I knew without a doubt that God wanted me to look up Luke 8:8. I opened my Bible to that verse and read, "'But others fell on good ground, sprang up, and yielded a crop a hundredfold.' When He had said these things He cried, 'He who has ears to hear, let him hear!'"

I swallowed my pride, closed my Bible, tore a blank piece of paper from my notebook, and wrote, "We owe you $100." I signed my name on the note, which I then handed to Ellen. When the offering plate reached us, Ellen dropped the IOU into the plate. She didn't say a word but just smiled one of those melt-my-heart smiles, and I gazed in awe again at this amazing woman I had married.

When Ellen and I returned to our apartment, we discovered an envelope that had been slipped under the door. I picked up the envelope, which was addressed "To Art and Ellen." I tore it open and pulled out a one-hundred-dollar bill. No letter of explanation, just a lonely hundred dollars looking for a home inside my wallet.

Ellen and I both stared at the envelope a bit stunned, and then Ellen said, "Quick, run to the administration office before it closes and retrieve our 'IOU.'"

I did just that. Then on my way back to our apartment, it occurred to me: I still had ten dollars in my wallet.

A few days later, Alan asked all the staff to pray about helping David Cole's family financially. Since it had been quite a while since the Coles had visited their home country of New Zealand, they had planned to fly home to spend Christmas with David's parents. Their travel agent had quoted a price for the tickets on Malaysian Airlines, provided they bought them before the deadline. Even though they came up with the money for the tickets before the deadline, Malaysian Airlines was now completely sold out. The Coles would have to fly Qantas Airways, which cost 50 percent more.

Ellen and I prayed that God would meet the Coles' needs and that He would provide us with some money that we could give to them. The following evening, Ellen was checking our e-mail in the office. Someone came by and placed a folded sheet of white paper next to the computer. Since we received a lot of memos that way, Ellen didn't think anything of it at the time.

When she had finished in the office, Ellen picked up the piece of paper. The outside fold read "To the Sanborns." Ellen unfolded the paper, and there, wrapped inside, was a one-hundred-dollar bill. She returned to our apartment and showed me the money. We both knew that this was the answer to our prayer. In the same way that a human parent will give his little child money to buy his brother a birthday present, God had given us this money to bless the Coles.

Our apartment had three bedrooms. We subleased two of the bedrooms to four single YWAM men for a hundred dollars each per month. In all, it covered almost half of our monthly rent, and it gave the guys an affordable home with the bonus of some surrogate parents. One terrific young man had been unable to cover his part of the rent for three months. When he came to us and apologized for getting so far behind, we joined with him in praying that God would provide for this three-hundred-dollar debt.

A few minutes later, I received a telephone call from the pastor of a nearby church. The pastor told me that their scheduled speaker for the evening's service had cancelled because of an emergency, and he wondered whether I would consider filling the pulpit at such late notice. I told him I would be happy to.

Just a few hours later, after I had addressed this congregation, the pastor thanked me and handed me a sealed envelope. When I got home, I opened the envelope and found a thank you note and an honorarium of three hundred dollars in cash. There was no doubt in my spirit about what to do. Smiling at the way God answers prayer, I put the cash into another envelope, sealed it, and addressed it to the young man who owed us rent money. Then I slid it under his bedroom door.

The next morning our quiet time was interrupted by a sudden outburst of whooping and hollering. "Praise God," the young man said. "I have the rent for all three months. God answered our prayer!"

This fortnight of fun with funds was not yet over.

The DTS lecture phase would conclude in just a few weeks. We needed to finalize our plans for the DTS outreach to northern Thailand for one month, followed by a month on the island of Java, Indonesia. Factoring in travel and living expenses, we calculated a total cost of $1,500 per person. That meant that Ellen and I needed to come up with $3,000 so that we could lead the outreach.

Little by little, Ellen and I received funds that we assumed would go toward our outreach fees. But time after time when we prayed about it, God directed us to give the money toward the outreach fees of a number of our students instead. We knew that the students needed the money more than we did, since many of them came from impoverished backgrounds. When the deadline arrived, Ellen and I wondered how God was going to provide the $3,000 for us to lead the outreach.

To our astonishment, we discovered that our outreach fees had been paid in full. Three thousand dollars had been deposited into our outreach account, and not a dime of it came from our own pockets.

That was not all, though. The YWAM accountant informed us that all of the students had met the deadline for their outreach fees. When we reported the good news to the students, they all excitedly gave testimonies that echoed our own. Apparently not one of the students had put any money toward his or her own outreach fees but had, across the board, given all he or she had toward each other's outreach fees.

Thrilled about this demonstration of God's fun and free style of accounting, I decided to tally up the amounts that we had all deposited toward each other's accounts. I was stunned to learn that every one of us would have been short by 25 to 50 percent had we kept our money for ourselves. God had miraculously made up the difference as we followed him in obedience.

Joe Harbison, the former director of YWAM Thailand, was now living in Penang, Malaysia, as Director of Compassion International for Southeast Asia. Because he had some business to attend to in Singapore, he stayed an extra day to visit Ellen and me. We took him shopping.

We told him how God was continuing to miraculously provide for our needs, starting with how God had paved the way for Michelle to get into medical school and finishing with the events of the last couple of weeks with the DTS.

"Man, I miss that," Joe said.

"You miss what?" Ellen asked.

"I miss having to trust God alone for my daily bread. Compassion pays me a good salary. Plus, they pay for our housing, they pay for our kids' education, they provide for all of our needs. I know that it's God who's providing through them, but I miss the days when it was essential to daily pray and trust God for all these things, to live completely by faith. Y'know, I actually envy you guys."

We had never really thought about it like that before. We tended to consider this lifestyle more of a hardship than a luxury. But that night, Ellen and I thanked God for the privilege of living by faith, for a life in which trusting God was the indispensable focal point of our daily survival.

We marveled at how, by His Spirit, we can actually find joy and gratitude in the very things that would ordinarily tempt our flesh to worry and complain. That was the thing that most impressed us about our DTS Dream Team. When God asked them to make sacrifices, they did so in a spirit of love and joy and thankfulness.

On the mission field, if you're not flexible, you'll simply break, but a good attitude will see you through the most frustrating of circumstances. Our Dream Team got a little taste of that on outreach, and each member of the team met the challenges with a full measure of grace. For example, in Thailand the team had to endure a full ten days with nothing to eat but rice and cabbage because of an outreach facilitator who had performed a disappearing act. After that, Ellen and I promised to do whatever we could to eliminate cabbage from their diet for the rest of the outreach. But they didn't complain.

Nor did the team complain when we arrived at the train station in Yokejakarta, Indonesia, and things did not exactly go as planned. The train was scheduled to depart at 10:00 AM. The vans that were supposed to take us to the train station did not pick us up until 9:15 AM, but our Indonesian hosts assured us that we were only a few minutes from the train station and the train was always late anyway. We arrived at the train station at 9:30, a good half hour before our departure time. By 10:20, the train still had not arrived.

I was accustomed to this lack of punctuality from years of living in Southeast Asia, but I figured the stationmaster might have a clue as to how long we would have to wait. I asked him what time the ten o'clock train to Jakarta would arrive today.

The old stationmaster looked at his watch and replied, "The ten o'clock train for Jakarta has come and gone."

"Sir, that can't be true. We've been here, waiting, since nine-thirty this morning. No train has come into the station for the last fifty minutes."

"Today the ten o'clock train arrived at nine twenty-three and left at nine twenty-seven." He pulled out a cigarette and lit it.

"How could the ten o'clock train come and leave before nine-thirty?"

"Oh, this is Indonesia," he said.

I had heard that statement of explanation before. Once on a flight from Jakarta to Medan, I had asked to be seated in the nonsmoking section. As soon as the plane took off, all the other passengers in the nonsmoking section lit up their cigarettes in unison. When I complained to the flight attendant, she simply said, "It's okay. This is Indonesia."

But now, with a team of forty-some people waiting for a train that was not going to come, this explanation did not suffice.

"Sir," I said, "there must be a reason. Why would the train leave more than half an hour before its scheduled time of departure?"

The stationmaster took another puff from his cigarette and said, "The ten o'clock train to Jakarta has been late every day for a month, so today it made up for all the lost time."

Of course. Why didn't I think of that? That makes absolute sense. That is an absolutely logical solution. *I'll bet their office is going to be flooded with letters of commendation because of that brilliant executive decision.*

I held my tongue except to ask, as politely as possible, "When will the next scheduled train leave for Jakarta?"

"The next train will be here at one o'clock," he said.

"Will you take our first-class tickets from the ten o'clock train and trade them for first-class seats on the one o'clock train?"

"Since it wasn't completely your fault that you missed your train, I'll trade them for third-class seats on the next train."

"Oh, no, I've experienced the third-class cattle cars and won't do that again if I can help it. This team's been through a lot, and I don't think they have the energy to stand on a train for eight hours. I must insist on getting what we paid for, first-class seats."

"There are only third-class seats on the one o'clock train," the stationmaster said.

"Okay, then, when does the next train with first-class seats arrive?"

"Tomorrow morning at ten o'clock."

"You have only one train per day that has first-class seats?"

"That's right," he responded. "We have one first-class, one second-class, and one third-class train per day."

"What time does the second-class train arrive?" I asked.

"Tonight at seven thirty."

"Well, okay. Put us on the second-class train, then. Any chance of collecting a refund for the difference between the amount that we paid and the price of the second-class tickets?"

"No refund. I'm sorry, but those are the rules. You can't expect me to change the rules, can you?"

"Why not?" I said. "After all, this is Indonesia."

THIRTY-TWO

God's Pro-Vision

T H E assistant leader of our Dream Team's outreach, Roy Christian, took care of the team for the first couple of weeks of January 1996 while Ellen and I flew to Australia. Our wonderful friends Kevin and Jan Craik had invited us to be the keynote speakers of their annual Christian Music Seminar in Cooma, Australia. We realized that it would also be an ideal setting to get together with our kids for a belated Christmas.

It had been years since we celebrated Christmas with our kids on the actual date of December 25, but we always made a point to celebrate the holiday together whenever we could, whether before or after December. This year, Ellen and I were leading the outreach in Thailand, Sean was working as a computer programmer in California, Michelle was doing medical student rotations at hospitals in England, and David was working as an actor and singer in Florida. Australia seemed as good a place as any for us all to meet up.

At the seminar, Sean got the best Christmas gift of all. A beautiful and delightful Aussie girl named Anne Kershaw caught his eye. And his heart. Five months later, they were engaged and set their wedding date for September 2. Ellen and I could not have been more pleased with this godly young woman.

After we joined up again with our Dream Team, we received a letter from the senior pastor of Halpine Church who explained that more deep cuts had to be made from the missionary budget and they would need to further decrease our monthly support. We wrote back, releasing the church from their commitment to support us. The original promise for our support had been made to us by Pastor Kline. After the death of Pastor Kline, our dear friend Jim Isom had served as interim pastor and had renewed Halpine's commitment to us. (Jim Isom and his wife, Judy, now serve as full-time missionaries with YWAM Europe. We never connected very well with the pastor who had taken Jim's place as Halpine's pastor for the previous seven years.) We said that we did not want to be a burden to Halpine, and we believed that God, as the true Source of our provisions, would get us through this financially difficult time. A few weeks later, Halpine's elders wrote back to us, reassuring us that they would not reduce our monthly support by more than ten percent in 1996. They also told us that the senior pastor had resigned.

In March of that year, I went to Washington, D.C., and stayed with my mom for a couple of weeks so that I could visit our supporting churches. When I attended Halpine's morning worship service, I was stunned to discover that the membership, which had once reached the thousands, requiring several Sunday services, had dwindled to a total of forty members. This auditorium that had once boomed with seven hundred joyful voices at a time now echoed with the eerie silence of an ancient tomb.

That evening, I phoned Ellen and asked her, "Honey, are you sitting down? The elders of Halpine have asked if we would consider becoming their interim senior pastors. I believe God wants us to say yes. We could wrap up our commitments in Asia this summer and start at Halpine in early autumn. Then I imagine it will take them a few months to find a permanent senior pastor. The thing is, they've been so burnt by the past few years of church leadership, I believe that they'll close their doors unless we agree to come and serve them for a while."

After praying about it, Ellen agreed. Together again in Singapore a couple of weeks later, Ellen and I took a few days to fast and pray for wisdom on how to best contribute to the needs of Halpine's wounded congregation. We were comforted to discover that the Holy Spirit had directed us both to the same scripture reference: Zechariah 1:18–21. In these verses, an angel tells Zechariah that four horns have scattered God's people. The Lord sent four carpenters (in some translations, craftsmen) to terrify and cast out the four horns. We believed that the carpenters symbolized the Spirit of Jesus.

Ellen and I asked God what, in our present situation, the four horns represented. God revealed to us both the same thing. The horns were the earthly spiritual strongholds brought into Halpine by the four primary sins of the previous leadership. The four spirits were greed, deception, immorality, and personal kingdom building (in other words, selfish ambition).

We asked God how to "terrify and cast out" these strongholds (as Zechariah had phrased it). Again, we both received the same answer: by coming in the opposite spirit. We faxed the following conditions to the elders at Halpine:

To come against the spirit of greed, we will not accept the budgeted pastoral salary. We will instead maintain our missionary support salary. This will mean that we won't have enough money for housing in the D.C. Beltway area; thus the congregation will have to house us in their homes. By both refusing a salary and living with congregational members, we believe our lives will also then be open books, thereby averting any strongholds of deception and immorality. We cannot very well keep secrets if we we're constantly either at the church or in a church member's home. Furthermore, to come against the spirit of personal kingdom building, Ellen and I will not accept the position of permanent senior pastors. Any changes we make in rebuilding and reaffirming Halpine's foundations will be for the congregation and their future leadership, not for ourselves.

Both the elders and congregation unanimously accepted our offer. We confirmed that we would begin our assignment at Halpine in September.

Next on our agenda was to finish preparations for our seventh annual School of Music in Singapore. One of the school's guest instructors was Australian singer/songwriter Geoff Bullock. One evening after Geoff had performed, Ellen and I invited him out for dinner. We wanted to take him to one of the canal-front, open-air cafes at Boat Quay, one of the most romantic, picturesque spots in Singapore.

We hopped into a taxi, and I asked the driver to take us to Boat Quay. "But," I said, "don't drop us off at the bridge."

The taxi driver insisted that the bridge was the best drop-off point for Boat Quay.

"No," I said, "we want to go to the other side of Boat Quay. Please take us to the Overseas Union Bank, the one that has a large statue of a man with a hole in his stomach."

"I don't know that one," the taxi driver said.

"That's okay. Just drive toward the Singapore River, and I'll guide you to our stop."

"Okay-lah," he said.

From the front seat of the taxi, Geoff turned around to Ellen and me and said, "You're both from America, right?"

"Yes, we're Americans," I said. "Why do you ask?"

"I'm curious about the American singer Whitney Houston. Do you know her?"

"We know Whitney Houston's music," Ellen said, "but we've never met her personally, if that's what you mean."

"I was hoping that maybe you knew her. I'd like to know if she's a Christian or not. In interviews, she seems to imply that she's a Christian, but her actions don't seem to line up. The news reports that she's a cocaine addict, and I thought that since you're from America, you might know the truth about her."

Ellen said, "Lots of Americans come from Christian subcultures but have never personally accepted Jesus as Lord. Also, the press is notorious for twisting the truth and printing unfounded gossip about celebrities.

It's hard to know the truth about someone just from what you read in the papers."

The taxi driver asked, "What about Madonna?"

"I believe I can answer that question," Geoff said. "Madonna makes it very clear that she's not a believer in Jesus."

The cab driver insisted. "What about Madonna?"

"I agree with Geoff," Ellen said. "Madonna has actually spoken out against Christianity."

These answers did not seem to satisfy our driver, though. "No, no," he said. "What about Madonna?"

"Sir," I said to the driver, "are you asking about the singer Madonna?"

"No, not Madonna. MaDona. I let you off at MaDona."

"Oh," I said, "you mean McDonald's?"

"Yes, of course-lah. MaDona!"

"Umm, right. Sure," I said. "McDonald's will be fine."

Our next few months continued to brim over with nonstop ministry, between teaching all over the globe and leading outreaches in Southeast Asia. At the end of the summer, we joined our kids in Florida to finish preparations for Sean and Anne's wedding. Sean and Anne had asked me to perform the ceremony, which was one of the greatest honors of my entire life.

After the wedding, Ellen and I flew to Rockville, Maryland, to begin our season as the interim pastors of Halpine Church. The first thing I wanted to change was the church's financial management policies. I wanted to establish a rule that the senior pastor would never be responsible for handling the money. He should certainly have a say in how the money was to be spent, but to keep him free from both accusation and temptation, he wouldn't actually handle the money.

Furthermore, the accountant would need to keep clean and clear financial records for strict accountability. After we set up the books, a professional accountant came in to manage them. We also hired an outside accounting firm to audit the books annually.

Another key part of the constitution that I wanted to change was the rule for voting in a new senior pastor. I felt that the vote for a new pastor should not be passed merely by a simple majority but by at least a two-thirds majority. When I made this proposal to the congregation, they prayed about it and decided that the vote should be changed to a 77 percent majority.

Once that was finalized, we put together a pastoral search committee. We received several resumes, but three of the applicants were of particularly high caliber. We brought them, one at a time, before the congregation. All three received votes of over 67 percent, but none received the new requisite of 77 percent.

A few times the elders secretly called a referendum to have us elected as the permanent pastors, to which the congregation voted unanimously. Ellen and I agreed, however, that God had made it clear to us that we were not to accept the position. We thanked the congregation for their vote of confidence but told them that out of obedience to God, we would not under any circumstances accept the position.

Over the next two years, Ellen and I lived with six different families, staying in various basements and guest rooms and preparing and waiting for the church to choose a new pastor.

One day, a revelation struck me. I realized that this season of ministry was the fulfillment of one of the most tangible visions I had ever received. It had come to me one evening back in 1977 while I was praying in our basement recreation room. It was like sitting back and in my mind's eye watching a film clip.

In the vision, I had seen myself preaching from the pulpit at Halpine Church and visiting homes and hospitals, ministering to and praying for members of the congregation. The awesome, Holy Presence of God had never felt so close. The day after I had had the vision, Pastor Kline had announced that the church had a position opening for an administrator.

I had prayed, "Lord, is this You? You gave me a vision that I would be working at this church, and now, the very next day, I find out that they're looking for an experienced administrator."

After the service, I asked Pastor Kline, "Would you mind answering a frank question?"

"Of course not," he said. "Fire away."

"Is this administrative position available for anyone to apply? I know that you have always wanted to groom John Bayles for the ministry and that he would be your first choice, but I had a unique vision last night. That, as well as my experience as an administrator, has led me to think that I should apply for this position."

"By all means," he said, "please do apply."

A week later, after interviewing the candidates, Pastor Kline called to tell me that the position had been given to John Bayles. "Art," he said, "it is true that I do want to mentor John for the ministry, but I am equally convinced that the church should not delay or interfere with your call to the mission field."

When I hung up the phone, my mind spun in confusion. Maybe the vision was not from God after all. "And, Lord, You've still not released us to go to the mission field. I just don't understand. What do You want me to do? I'm willing to serve You, but are You saying that maybe I'm not up for the challenge?"

Less than three years later we had joined YWAM, and I had realized that Pastor Kline was right, that our future really was on the mission field. Through the years, though, I had still occasionally wondered what that vision had meant. Now, after nearly two decades, God had brought the vision to light, and it was not until months after taking the pulpit that I even realized it.

It was not easy rebuilding the foundations of this church from the ground up. But God continually strengthened us, and the congregation was quite hospitable.

After one of my first sermons at Halpine, one of the parishioners came up to me and shook my hand. "The best sermon I ever heard," he said, "the absolute best sermon I ever heard…"

Okay, remember to stay humble. Of course, that was a pretty fantastic message, but just remember, the glory goes to God. All the glory for making me so brilliant goes to God.

"I tell ya, without a doubt, the best sermon I ever heard," he said, "was given by this preacher that I saw on TV."

As he went on and on about this preacher that I really needed to watch and learn from, I realized I wouldn't need to work too hard at keeping myself humble, after all. These people seemed more than happy to accommodate.

In 1998, the church family finally appointed a permanent senior pastor. This man, who received exactly 77 percent of the votes, was none other than the Reverend John Bayles—the same John Bayles whom Pastor Kline had chosen to mentor twenty years earlier.

In the early 1980s, John had relocated his family to Boston, Massachusetts, so that he could study at Gordon-Conwell Theological Seminary. After earning his master's degree in divinity there, John had moved his family back to Maryland. He had established Grace Fellowship in Germantown, Maryland, and later merged Grace Fellowship with Living Word Fellowship. The newly joined congregation was christened "Amaranth Fellowship."

Back in the 1970s, around the same time that I had received my vision for Halpine, John had received a vision for Halpine, and he always wondered how and when God would bring it to pass. Now, as he witnessed the unveiling of that vision, John wanted to continue to be a pastor who unites God's Church in a world where division and divorce have become so prevalent.

John united Amaranth and Halpine into one church. Since Amaranth was already two churches in one, Halpine was now actually three in one. For John, accepting the position at Halpine was tantamount to receiving his covenant inheritance.

For Ellen and me, it was time to return home to the jungles of southeast Asia and leave behind the perilous jungles of Washington, D.C.

THIRTY-THREE

No Fear

T I A came from the White Hmong tribe, but she had a tender heart for the mostly unreached, poverty-stricken Blue Hmong. A few years after attending our Thai Discipleship Training School back in 1987, she married an American named Bruce Taylor, and the couple both devoted their lives to helping the Blue Hmong. They eventually moved to a village located on Doi Inthanon, Thailand's tallest mountain.

One of the village's five or six hundred residents was a famous maw phee. This witch doctor had a reputation for being able to put powerful curses on people. Even famous Thai politicians had given him money to place curses on members of opposing political parties. The maw phee's name was not only famed but also feared. It was common knowledge that he had total control over the chief of the village, and with so many visitors paying for curses, he was by far the village's wealthiest resident.

The maw phee must have seen the Taylors as a threat to his operations, because he went to great lengths to make it clear to them that they were not welcome. Once, for example, the Taylors returned home to find that their pet dog had been tortured and killed. Everyone in the village knew who was responsible. Another time, the Taylors' pigs were stolen, and again, there was no mystery about the identity of the instigator. At school, the Taylors' four children (two boys and two girls) faced an unusual amount of abuse and persecution from both their teachers and their schoolmates.

The Taylors bought some land on which they planned to one day build a church. The chief, reportedly at the behest of the maw phee, forbade them from building a church on this property, which was located on a high point of the village. The maw phee wanted no god elevated higher than his idols. A church would be allowed only on one of the lowest levels of the village.

As Tia's former teachers, Ellen and I had always been impressed by Tia's talents and heart for service. It saddened us to see the persecution her family faced, and we wanted them to know that we believed in them. We determined to support them in prayer and to periodically bring teams to serve and assist them.

On my last trip to the Taylors' village before breaking my neck in Hawaii, I hosted an outreach team from the University of the Nations. The Taylors had built a Hmong-style home on the land originally intended for the church, and they now graciously welcomed the team to spread their sleeping bags all over the house.

While the team settled in, I went out into the village to invite everyone to attend our evening service, which would be conducted by this international team from Kona, Hawaii. As I passed by the maw phee's temple, I heard an unusual amount of noise ringing from his gongs and bells.

I paused to watch. In front of his large idols, the maw phee was jumping and leaping, his long robe fluttering all over the temple hall as he ran back and forth hitting the gongs and bells. I watched in amusement for a good twenty minutes at this amazing aerobic workout that could give Richard Simmons a run for his money.

When I returned to the Taylors' home, I told Tia, "I've been watching your notorious witch doctor. For a man of his age, he is in superb physical shape. Does he normally exert so much energy in the worship of his demons and gods?"

"Oh, no," Tia replied. "He is doing all of that because he saw you come into the village earlier today."

"Because of me? But I've never met the man. He doesn't even know me. Why would he be doing anything because of me?"

"Art," she said, "do you remember when you brought us that YWAM team last year?"

"Yes."

"Do you remember how the team spent a number of hours every day after breakfast worshipping God and praying for the village? Everyone would pray and, in the Name of Jesus, demand the departure of all the evil spirits that brought cursing and fear."

"Yes."

"After your team departed last year, we learned that the maw phee had lost all of his demonic power."

"Really?"

"Yes, every one of the spirits that he had invited into himself was gone. Without these spirits he could not place a hex on anyone, so he had no more customers for his curses. He has spent the past year performing rituals to entice the evil spirits to return. And he must have been successful, because yesterday he finally had his first paying customer all year."

I laughed. "No kidding."

"So," she said, "when he saw you return to the village, he became very angry. Now he is doing whatever he can to keep you from having the same effect you had last year. He has also ordered the people not to attend our service tonight. He has announced that he will place a curse on anyone who comes. I'm afraid that only the twenty-some Christians from our village will show up, but that's it. Everyone else is too afraid."

"We'll see about that," I said.

I told the team what Tia had said and asked them to pray. While the team prayed, I went out and began speaking to the villagers. "Your maw phee's own words testify that our God has far more power than his evil spirits. Therefore, if you never want to be afraid of the maw phee and his evil spirits again, you come tonight."

That night, the entire village showed up for our meeting.

The next morning, as I was whistling carelessly along the winding, dusty village thoroughfare, I passed the maw phee's temple. The maw phee was all decked out in his priestly robes, banging his gongs and ringing his bells, jumping and leaping through the thick fog of incense that wafted out into the street. Outside the temple wall, I noticed a gory sight. A rooster with its feet tied by a rope was dangling about ten inches off the ground, helplessly flapping its wings. Another rooster viciously pecked away at the helpless rooster. Both birds were covered with blood.

Knowing that blood and torment were ingredients for the maw phee's rituals, I walked onto the temple grounds. Holding back the attack rooster with my left hand, I took out my pocket knife with my right hand and cut free the tortured bird. As my knife cut the rope, I heard the sound of a vast, synchronized gasp behind me.

I turned around and to my surprise saw that quite a number of the villagers had gathered around. They were clearly terrified on my behalf. This made me terrified for me, too. I followed their collective gaze toward the temple entrance and saw the enraged face of the maw phee, his inflamed, piercing eyes fixed on me, the impudent intruder who had dared to defy him.

Breathing heavily, the maw phee began running toward me, his fists tightened as if ready for a fight and his eyes steadfastly locked on his prey. His mouth was moving slightly as if muttering a curse under his breath. My heart, desperate to break free, began pounding madly at the wall of my chest. I did not need a medical degree in psychiatry to discern the man's intentions. I had to get out of there, and fast.

Then I remembered what I had said to the villagers just the day before—that Jesus was more powerful than this maw phee's evil spirits, and that if they gave their lives to Jesus, they need not be fearful of the maw phee. How could I retain any integrity if I now gave in to the fear that gripped me? I stood my ground, even though I did not have a clue as to what to say or do.

I whispered a prayer, "God, help. What am I going to do? Lord, You promised that You would give us the right words to speak by Your Spirit when we are brought before governors and kings. How about angry witch doctors?"

Just as the priest approached, I suddenly knew what to do. I went on the offensive. With all the breath that I could muster, I yelled in his face, "Pra Yesu rock khun," which means "Jesus loves you."

The maw phee stopped dead in his tracks. Stunned, he stared at me for a moment, then lowered his head in defeat, turned around, and scurried back to his temple. Clearly frustrated, he immediately resumed his "Sweatin' to the Banshees" workout, gongs, bells, and all.

The maw phee's business and income declined dramatically over the next few years. Both of his wives divorced him, and he sold his temple to a woman from Bangkok and moved out of the village. By the year 2000, more than a third of the members of the village had become Christian, one of whom was elected chief. The new chief has proven to be a capable, conscientious, and honest leader.

The thing that especially intrigued me about my encounter with the maw phee is that he somehow understood the power of Jesus even more than I did. The Bible says that the demons believe that God is who He says He is and shudder in fear of Him, though they have refused to submit to Him (James 2:19). How much more should we, who serve Him, recognize the reality and supremacy of His power?

At the Bangkok train station, I once picked up a very energized outreach team from Singapore. As I helped them load their bags into the truck, they told me what had just happened to them. Their train had stopped for several hours in Kuala Lumpur, and they had decided to make the most of their time. They began performing skits and trying to reach out to people in the middle of that booming railway station. But no matter how earnest they were, no one was interested in talking with them. They even got the stiff shoulder from people who were waiting around with nothing to do.

Rob, the team leader, told me what had happened next. "Art, you know how you always say that when all else fails, just start singing God's praises? Well, I gathered the team together and suggested that we pull out the guitar and just focus on Jesus, singing songs of worship to Him. We were singing "Our God Reigns," and I told the team that when we got to the end of the chorus, I would count to three and then we should all shout out that Jesus reigns."

The rest of the story was pretty astounding, but there were certainly enough witnesses to testify to it. Rob told me that when he counted to three and the team began to shout, all the electricity in the railway station shut down. In the cavernous silence of that blinded railway station, all that anyone could hear was "Jesus reigns!" echoing throughout the terminal. Then, as abruptly as it had shut off, the electricity came back on.

All eyes were now focused on the outreach team. Scores of people asked them who was this Jesus, who had the power to shut down one of the world's busiest train stations. The team was able to minister to a number of broken, hurting people and see them radically changed through the power of Jesus.

And of course, that is the point. God will shut things down to get our attention, but He is really in the business of building things back up.

Which brings us to the final chapter.

THIRTY-FOUR

Back to the Ending

I WARMED up for this last chapter by jogging ten miles. Yesterday, I did three sets of fifty pushups. It sure helps to have been miraculously healed.

It wasn't one of those instant, lightning-zap type of miracles like some of the other miracles I've chronicled in this book. It has been gradual but steady. Little by little, I'm getting more feeling and more movement. To this day, I'm still discovering miraculously restored sensations in my body pretty much every month.

I am now a walking miracle. Nearly ten years after my accident, I am a medical mystery, a scientific enigma, a physiological conundrum, a real-life...you get the idea. And, oh yes, I recently beat both of my sons in basketball (of course, they were so afraid of hurting me, they played me with almost no defense). But that's just one of the many things I have done in my past few years of physical freedom.

To share all that's happened since I left the hospital in Honolulu would take more typing power than I have in even these supernaturally recharged fingers of mine. But I will do my best to give you the basic gist.

Back in February of 1999, our trip from the rehab hospital in Hawaii to our home in Florida was quite a challenge. We were surprised to discover that neither the Honolulu nor the L.A. international airport had individual, handicap-accessible restrooms. Ellen convinced the airport cleaning personnel to set up a "Do Not Enter" sign so that she could assist me into the women's restrooms. We stayed away from the men's restrooms altogether.

So it's come to this.

Would I ever again experience the warm and friendly ambience of a men's restroom? Well, okay, maybe that didn't actually bother me so much. But I was still a little nervous that some woman would disregard the "Do Not Enter" sign.

Getting me from the wheelchair to my seat on the airplane took a lot of creativity and strength on the part of David and Ellen, but they managed admirably. On the upside of that trip, the airline food tasted genuinely gourmet after months of hospital food.

The journey was worth it, though, to arrive home at last. Sean and Anne and Michelle were all there to welcome us, and we celebrated the fact that God was working an extraordinary miracle in my body. I was now able to stand up from my wheelchair and lean briefly on my walker. Since that should have been medically impossible for me, we believed that God had more miracles on the horizon.

As a quadriplegic, I would be allowed to park in handicap parking spots. Or so I thought. When we presented all the medical evidence of my spinal cord damage and broken neck (including my doctor's signed recommendation for the permit) to the local officials, they refused to grant me my handicap parking tag. Had I known they weren't going to grant me a parking tag, I might have thought twice about breaking my neck. The officials probably thought that since I wasn't in any position to be driving anywhere, I certainly would not need the tag.

At any rate, on April 7, 1999, I managed to walk a dozen steps with my walker, and I never returned to my wheelchair again. I would sooner drop down on the floor than have to go back to the wheelchair, although one night, I accidentally did just that. I woke up and decided to get myself a drink of water. Not wanting to disturb Ellen, I chose not to turn on the bedside lamp. Not wise. The walker's back legs were tilted up off the ground, so when I shifted my weight onto the walker I tumbled headlong to the floor, crash landing on the one part of my body that had full feeling, my head.

As you can imagine, that disturbed Ellen a lot more than a little light might have. Even from downstairs, David heard the clatter and got up to investigate. Just when the doctors had been considering removing my neck brace, that little trip ensured that I would have to wear the brace for another two months.

An orthopedic surgeon would be regularly monitoring my pain medications, but our insurance company refused to cover any outpatient physical therapy in Florida. We decided we'd better find a way to afford a professional physical therapist at least twice a month, but for the daily exercises, David became my personal therapist.

David is not a trained physical therapist, but as a professional actor, he can play the part. As a matter of fact, he played the part so well that even my muscles were fooled. He did study up on the subject as much as he could, but in the end, he consoled himself with one thought: No one could accredit my miraculous recovery to the work of an ace physical therapist. Instead, it would be all the more obvious that God was responsible for this miracle.

Since I had now attained at least pseudoindependence with the walker, I felt it was time to join a gym to advance my physical therapy. Ellen found an affordable exercise center nearby, called the Candlelite Health Spa, a funky-fun, fully stocked gym, painted green and orange, with loud seventies rock 'n' roll playing in the background.

The muscleman who owned the gym met us at the counter. Thinking I'd impress him by proving that I could be one of the guys, I stood up from my wheelchair and held onto my walker for dear life.

"I'd like to sign my dad up for a membership here," David said to the owner.

The muscleman looked at me. My bulging, foam neck brace nicely complemented the fact that I was supporting myself with an oh-so-stylish walker.

"Is that your dad?" the owner asked.

"Yup," David replied.

"Well," he said, "it's your money, kid."

By May, I felt ready to try walking on my own without any assistance. Putting my walker aside, I zeroed my focus toward Sean, who sat just three steps away. Since I still had no feeling in my legs, it took all of my concentration to keep my left foot firmly planted while summoning my right foot up for that first step.

Sean did not make it any easier for me. As I began the epic journey toward him, he began saying, "Come to son, Dada, you can do it, Dada…" Despite having to contain my laughter, I did successfully walk the three steps unassisted.

I turned to Ellen, who was watching, and said, "Honey, you're going to need to get one of those baby books and turn it into a 'hubby book.' You know, so that you can record those landmark dates when 'Hubby took his first step' and 'Hubby stopped wearing diapers' and 'Hubby fed himself without any help.'"

Just five months after my accident, I switched to walking with a cane and put the walker aside permanently. When I practiced walking without any assistance, I would occasionally fall, but as long as I didn't fall on my head, it didn't hurt. Having a numb body does have its benefits.

Once I could bend over and stand on my own, I decided it was time to begin some weight lifting. On my first day, I hobbled over to a spot between two no-neck giants and their ludicrously overstacked barbells. I crouched down and picked up my one-quarter-pound broomstick, just as my professional therapist had prescribed. After several moments of struggling and straining, I finally prevailed, with the broomstick proudly displayed above my head. I rather doubt that I impressed either of these guys, but at least I felt like a member of the weight-lifting brotherhood.

Little by little, I made attempts at brushing my hair, bathing myself, and brushing my teeth unassisted. Ellen would help me squeeze the toothpaste onto the toothbrush, but I managed, completely on my own, to brush the toothpaste—all over my face and even in my hair. Despite my lack of dexterity, I did succeed in getting some of the toothpaste on my teeth.

When I tried feeding myself, Ellen would cover me with a sheet, since only one in five spoonfuls made it safely inside my mouth. With a bib that size, we decided we would wait awhile before eating out at a romantic restaurant.

One day, I asked Ellen to put shaving cream on my face and hand me my razor. Hesitantly she did as I asked but pleaded with me to reconsider. After I had finished shaving myself and Ellen had begun applying little Band-Aids all over my face, she said, "Why don't you leave the shaving to David and me for now?"

"Nope," I said. "I am determined to do it."

"All right, suit yourself," Ellen said. "I'll just have to go to Sam's Club and stock up on some of those refrigerator-sized boxes of Band-Aids."

In September of 1999, just nine months after I had broken my neck, we returned to Kona, Hawaii, to lecture for a week at the University of the Nations. Afterward, we flew to Honolulu for an appointment with my surgeon, Dr. Bernard Robinson. I left my cane in the waiting room and walked into his office, unassisted. You'd have thought Sean Connery had just walked into his office. It took the good doctor a moment of just staring at me before he could speak. "You're walking?"

"Of course," I said. "Didn't you think it was possible?"

"Honestly, considering the extent of your injury, I did not expect you to ever walk again. I thought you would need major support for the basic amenities of living for the rest of your life."

"But Dr. Robinson, you're the only medical professional, other than my daughter, who gave me any hope or encouragement that I might walk again."

"I'm a doctor," he said, "so I know that it's impossible. But I'm also a Christian, so I believe that with God anything's possible. Can you walk on your toes?"

I did as he asked.

"Good. Now try walking on your heels."

Did that too.

"Your orthopedic surgeon in Tampa has kept me apprised of your case, but..." He shook his head. "She did, at least, tell me that you can lift your arms over your head, and she said that she encouraged you to try lifting a broomstick over your head, then progressively adding more repetitions and more weight. Are you at the point yet where you can lift one or two pounds over your head?"

"No, Dr. Robinson, I'm not lifting one or two pounds—"

"That's okay," he said. "Don't be discouraged. With your injury, it is unrealistic for you to be able to use your arms at all."

"I'm not lifting one or two pounds," I said. "I'm now lifting one hundred pounds over my head."

"That is amazing. You have worked hard, and I salute your tenacity."

"Thank you, but there are a lot of guys with the same injury who have worked at least as hard as I have. From the reports, I would venture to guess that Christopher Reeve probably works even harder than I. But with all the prayers that have been going up on my behalf, I think that Jesus, not my tenacity, gets all the credit for this miracle."

"No arguments here," he said.

"Dr. Robinson, what I want to know is, when will sensation return to my body? I still have very little feeling from my neck down, and my perception and equilibrium are way off. I'm driving again, but if I were ever stopped by the police and asked to walk a straight line with my eyes closed, I don't think I could. I can't touch my nose with my fingers if my eyes are closed, either. Just as long as they don't ask me to drive with my eyes closed, I'm fine, but how much longer will it be until my body is fully restored?"

"Let me be frank," Dr. Robinson said. "For your body to ever regain these normal functions is not medically possible. You fractured C-3 and C-4 in your neck, and your spinal cord was severely damaged. But that said, 90 percent of what you are already doing is medically impossible. Just keep praying and working hard. I would not be surprised if you miraculously received full function some day."

The next day, Ellen and I went to the Honolulu YWAM base to visit the Lehmanns, the Darroughs, and some of the other friends who had encouraged me in the hospital. The YWAM base had a basketball net, so I decided it was at last time to try some hoops. I picked up a basketball and threw it toward the basket. The ball, unimpressed by my loud grunt, limped a couple of inches in the air and then fell to the ground, just barely missing my feet.

Hmm. Maybe I'm not quite ready to try out for the NBA just yet.

It seemed my slow-twitch muscle fibers were building back up, but my fast-twitch muscles needed some work. So I added push-ups to my weekly exercise regimen. That first day, I discovered that I could do an entire set...of one push-up. So I did three sets of one. That same week, I began moving around cane-free for one hour every day. With every step, my movements became less awkward, and I looked less and less like an impersonation of Frankenstein's monster.

In November of 1999, Ellen and I made a pastoral care trip to Asia, visiting Singapore, Malaysia, and Thailand. It was truly an emotional time for me to see so many friends, when less than a year earlier, I had been told that I would never see this part of the world again.

On our way back from Asia a month later, we had a week-long lecturing engagement in Honolulu. While we were on the island, we visited the Rehabilitation Hospital of the Pacific, where we were greeted with hugs and tears. We learned that the young Hawaiian man who had been in therapy with me there (and who had virtually the same injury) had also visited the hospital that same morning for the first time since his discharge. When I asked how he was doing, a therapist said, "Wonderful. He gets around in an electric wheelchair and is able to use a few of his fingers."

"But for God's help," I said to Ellen, "that would be me."

As we met with these professional health-care workers who had made up my whole world just ten months earlier, I was amazed to discover that most of them were shorter than I am. From my perspective from the bed and wheelchair, they had all looked like giants. That realization made me slightly more confident.

I told the guys on staff, "I'm ready to challenge you to some hoops now."

Tony, always alert, said, "Art, you said we had until March of 2000, and this is only December. You need to give us more time to practice."

In September 2000, Ellen and I again lectured in Hawaii for a week. When I visited the rehab staff and challenged the guys to a one-on-one basketball game, every one of them refused.

"Art," Tony said, "if any of us win, what are we going to say? 'We beat a spinal cord patient?' But, even worse, what if you win?"

When other patients heard that I had been a patient on that floor, they knew I must have been in a wheelchair. As a result, many of them asked me to pray for them. It was a privilege to do so. I also encouraged them that in or out of the wheelchair, my source of true life and contentment was found in Jesus Christ alone.

In January of 2000, I went running outside for the first time. I had to be extra careful, since I still couldn't feel my legs or body, but I managed to jog stiffly for five minutes before stopping. In March of that year, I jogged one full mile. It took half an hour. In October, I jogged three miles, though it took me nearly an hour.

Inspired, Ellen decided to go jogging with me. After twenty minutes, she stopped and said, "That's enough for me. I'm going back home."

The next day, she complained that every muscle in her body ached. "Doesn't your body hurt?"

"I don't know," I said. "I still can't feel most of my body, so if it does hurt, it certainly doesn't tell me."

Many physicians, upon hearing my story, have asked me the same question: "If you cannot feel, how can you walk?" The first couple of times, I answered them, "I don't know." Sometimes, I would say, "Wait a minute. Which one of us went to medical school?" But now I simply smile and say, "Because I'm a Christian. I don't walk by feelings. I walk by faith."

Even now, almost ten years after the accident, when I get especially tired, I have to focus on thinking through every step. After a lot of intense training, though, I'm now agile enough to actually run and chew gum at the same time. However, with my numb hands, buttoning my shirt and tying my shoelaces continues to be a challenge. As a result, I have acquired a much greater appreciation for the wonders of Velcro. Since my legs are still mostly numb, I have to remember to check them every evening for cuts and bruises. One day, I noticed a little bruise on my left shin. "I wonder where that bruise came from."

Ellen said, "I wonder if I did that this afternoon at lunch when I was kicking you under the table."

"You were kicking me under the table? Why were you kicking me under the table?"

"Well," she said, "you were going on and on, complaining to our friends that someone had given us this stupid video, which was one of the worst movies you had ever seen."

"Well it is. It's a terrible movie, and I wanted the Johnsons (not their real name) to avoid the mistake of renting it."

"Right, well, I was kicking you in an effort to get your attention because, honey, the thing is," Ellen lovingly placed her hand on mine, "the Johnsons gave us that video in the first place."

After I got over the delayed embarrassment, Ellen and I brainstormed for some new strategies of covert communication.

On another occasion, a group of friends had just finished praying for me, and one of the women said, "I am so sorry, Art. I don't know what my son was thinking."

"Sorry for what?" I said. "What did your son do?"

"Apparently," she said, "he wanted to see whether you were telling the truth about having no feeling in your body, because while we were praying for you, he kicked your legs a few times, and when you didn't flinch, he turned to his brother and said, 'Yup. He definitely can't feel 'em.'" The boy was right. I did not feel a thing.

A group of children once asked if they could pray for me and ask God to restore feeling to my legs. Touched by their compassionate hearts, I said, "It would be an honor."

That night as I lay in bed, I realized that for the first time in over two and a half years, I could feel exactly where my right leg was. I still didn't know where my left leg was, but as long as I knew where my right leg was, I figured the left leg could not be far away. Plus, if I was ever captured and tortured by some terrorist group, I could just follow Brer Rabbit's lead and tell them, "Brer Terrorist, sir, go ahead and inflict pain to any part of my body you want. But please, Brer Terrorist, whatever you do, don't hurt my poor, little left leg."

A few weeks later, I was punching my left leg to see if I had any feeling, but I still had none. Then I punched my right leg, and to my horror, I couldn't feel that either. I panicked, thinking that my body had started to regress, but when I looked down, I realized that my wallet was in my right pants pocket. I pulled out my wallet, punched my right leg again, and involuntarily cried out, "Ow!"

Ellen said, "Art, you could feel that? That's so wonderful." She shouted to the next room, "David! Dad just hit his leg, and he can feel the pain. Isn't that wonderful?"

"No other word for it." I winced. "Really...wonderful."

Ellen winked at me. "You really should stop beating yourself up, though. If you want someone to hit you, just let me know, and I'll be happy to oblige." I seriously doubt, however, that she could bear to hit me, even if I pleaded with her.

One day, I sat down and closed my eyes for a few minutes. When my nose started to itch, I ordered my right hand to scratch my nose. But there was no response. Alarmed, I opened my eyes to investigate and found my hands tightly clasped together. I summoned my hands to unclasp, and they obeyed, leaving my right hand free to scratch my nose.

For the first couple of years after leaving the hospital, I didn't have the ability to measure my grip. When I looked down, I would realize that I had either squeezed my hand into a tight fist or not at all. So whenever I tried holding a Styrofoam or paper cup, the cup would end up crumpling under my viselike grip before I could get it to my mouth. That also made drinking out of a glass very risky business. For countless hours, I practiced picking things up with a firm but gentle grip. It was pretty tricky trying to grip lightly without dropping the object.

To this day, though I have regained almost full feeling in my arms and partial feeling in my hands, my hands still have a tendency to curl up like claws. To counter this, I often deliberately force my hands to stay stretched out. I'm sure on-lookers just think I'm trying to impress them with my Mr. Roboto dance movements.

One Sunday, I met someone new at church. When I shook his hand, his face began puckering in obvious pain. I looked down and saw that his knuckles were turning white under my overzealous grip. I quickly let go and apologized, claiming that I was a quadriplegic and could not feel how tightly I was squeezing my hand. Somehow, I don't think he believed me.

A woman once approached me and said, "Somebody told me that you broke C-3 and C-4 and partially severed your spinal cord."

"Yes, that's right," I said.

"But you're walking."

"Thanks to Jesus," I said. "I'm walking proof of the power of prayer."

"I'm a nurse at the local rehabilitation hospital, and I know for a fact that if you really had that injury, there is no way in the world that you would be walking. You are a liar," she said and abruptly walked away.

That left me a little rattled at first, but upon reflection, that encounter actually became a source of affirmation. Anyone who has a personal relationship with Jesus knows that He can do all things. Jesus could have completely healed me moments after my accident, but if He had, who would have ever believed that I had really broken my neck? Now I have MRI films that were taken both before and after my operation, in addition to all the other hospital records that verify my injury.

After my daughter's internal medicine residency with the University of Florida, she served with the US Air Force for three years. During her third year, Michelle was stationed in South Korea, where she met and fell in love with Moon Lee, a brilliant orthopedic surgeon. His hands are worth more than their weight in gold, and so is his heart. A few months before their wedding in 2003, I showed Moon my medical files.

"Wow," he said. "These are really your MRI films?"

"Yes, they are," I said.

"These films show a very serious injury. Your recovery is remarkable; I'm surprised you're walking."

"As I've said many times, it's a miracle."

In September of that year, Ellen and I were flying from Chicago to Tampa. When I boarded the plane, I noticed a distinguished-looking African-American couple a few rows from us.

I whispered to Ellen, "Isn't that my surgeon, Dr. Robinson?"

"No, I don't think so," Ellen said. "Looks a little like him, but I can't imagine a renowned surgeon like Dr. Robinson traveling in economy class."

"You really don't think it's him?"

"Remember, honey, it has been more than four years since we last saw him. I could be wrong, but I really don't think so."

Exiting the plane in Tampa, I caught up with the couple and asked the gentleman, "Excuse me, sir, are you Dr. Bernard Robinson?"

"Why, yes. What is your name?"

"I'm a former patient of yours. You performed surgery on my neck almost five years ago, in December of 1998. My name is Art Sanborn."

"You're Art Sanborn? Wow, look at you. I heard that you were back doing missionary work, living your life just as you had before your injury. I can see now that these reports were not overstatements." After introducing us to his wife, his eyes started to water, as he said, "Art, I want to thank you."

Why would he thank me? He was the one who operated on me and saved my life.

Seeing my confused expression, he said, "We have three children—two daughters and a son. Our son was born perfectly healthy, but both of our daughters were born with a rare, terminal blood disease. Our oldest daughter died from this disease. But seeing the miracle that God worked in your life really strengthened my faith. We started praying with increased intensity for the life of our youngest daughter, and our church also rallied around us with fervent prayers for her. Now she is in graduate school in California, and she is fine. I shudder to think of what would have happened to her had we not prayed with such faith. So thank you for your testimony."

Ellen and I are now back into the full swing of our lives, seeing God work His wonders. Recently God provided millions of dollars for a Broadway-scale production of *Judah Ben-Hur* in Singapore. This musical, written by Ellen and David, is based on the epic story of Ben-Hur. I administrated the finances. As God would have it, even with all the investments that came in, there wasn't quite enough for David, Ellen, or me to get paid at all. Oh, well. That just means we get to continue living by faith. Perhaps I'll write more about all of that in my next book.

In the devastating aftermath of 9/11, as well as the fairly recent tsunamis, hurricanes, and earthquakes around the world, we have seen a lot of people become emotionally crippled. For many, those catastrophic events simply brought to the surface the pain that already resided in their hearts. Ellen and I have more recently had the chance to reach out with the love of God to thousands of Muslims as well as to thousands of others from a variety of backgrounds.

I want to reach out to those who are hurting with the message that Jesus longs for them to receive His healing power. We simply have to be willing to receive it and to trust Him to work His will in our lives. This may mean that physical healing will need to wait in order for spiritual healing to occur, whether to us or through us.

Over the years, people have heard of the events of my life. Then, upon meeting me, they have often said, "But...you are so ordinary. There is nothing special about you, and yet God really worked all those miracles in your life?" That's exactly right. I'm just a very ordinary guy who serves an extraordinary God. People often call me "a walking miracle" and sometimes even "the miracle man." But I'm no miracle man. I just serve a miracle-working God.

All God asks of us is that we allow Him to work in our lives. That cannot happen as long as we are running our lives *our* way. That being the case, I guess it's easier for a guy like me. I don't have so much going for me that I can deceive myself into thinking that I can do it on my own. With me, it's painfully obvious that I need Jesus. I want to see all these weary, wounded people renewed and made whole, but I know that the only unfailing source of peace and purpose is Jesus.

In a single moment, with one toss of a wave, we can lose all our ability to function. In a heartbeat, we can lose those whom we love. But if we make Jesus our Lord, He will reveal Himself to us in the most life-infusing ways, and nothing can rob us of that joy. God loves us even more than we love ourselves, and He intimately knows our needs. But He will not interfere against our will. He is just waiting for us to invite Him into our lives.

When I was in the hospital, unable to do anything for myself, I would occasionally get my eyes off God and onto my problems. I would start to wallow in self-pity until I once again turned my focus back onto Jesus and began worshipping Him. He would hear my cry and come to my side, once again filling me with the inexpressible peace and joy of His presence. I can honestly, experientially testify that I would rather be stuck in that intensive care unit with Jesus than to have success in every earthly area of my life, including relationships, without Him.

It is a shame that even believers of Jesus so often put their hope and security in the crutches of the world. As a result, they will inevitably come crashing down if the rug is ever pulled out from under them. But God has proven to me time and again that "those who wait on the LORD shall renew their strength; they shall mount up with wings like eagles, they shall run and not be weary, they shall walk and not faint" (Isaiah 40:31).

A number of people have said to me, "Against all odds, you're walking. Isn't it amazing? The brain just has a power that we don't even understand."

The first time I heard this, I couldn't help but laugh. When my friend didn't even break a smile, I said, "Wait, you're serious? You're attributing this miracle to the power of my brain? You are obviously unfamiliar with my brain. If my brain had the ability to work scientific wonders, I would have seen signs of it long ago. This is the same brain that had to take Spanish One twice in high school, barely scoring a passing grade even the second time around. This brain did not fare much better when I studied beginning Hebrew while attending university.

"In the many years it took me to learn Thai, I am positive that my brain holds the record for the most stupid mistakes. I mean, once this brain of mine was responsible for telling a group of university students that Jesus was crucified on a pair of trousers instead of a wooden cross. And then there was the time I meant to lead everyone in a prayer to the Almighty God of the Universe. But instead, I found out later that I had led them all in prayer to the Fat Woman on the Bicycle.

"If no brain has ever succeeded in rebuilding its own network of nerves," I continued, "there is no way in the world that *my* brain is going to be the first to do so. My brain has trouble enough keeping up with average brains, much less confounding all scientific understanding. Let's give credit where credit's due. The One who is rebuilding my nerves is Jesus, the same One who created them in the first place."

I recently repeated that last little anecdote with a group in Thailand. I was happy to give them some laughs at my expense, but then I brought home the point of my message—that God alone is responsible for this miracle. Then, with the deepest of reverence, I asked them all to bow their heads and pray…to the Fat Woman on the Bicycle.

About the Author

ART SANBORN had a thriving career as an administrator for George Washington University Hospital in Washington, D.C., until 1979, when he and his wife Ellen and three young children—Sean, Michelle, and David—gave away nearly everything they had in order to dedicate their lives to the poor and needy. In the decades since, they have served with YWAM in Southeast Asia, where they helped to plant twelve churches, led over sixty outreach teams, and directed twenty-five missionary training programs. Art and Ellen are currently pioneering a church and YWAM training center in the Tampa Bay, Florida, area. Art is also a frequent lecturer at universities, churches, and conferences around the world.

International Adventures

Lords of the Earth, by Don Richardson
Engulfed in the darkness of Irian Jaya's Snow Mountains lived the Yali—cannibals who called themselves "lords of the earth." Missionary Stan Dale dared to enter their domain. 1-57658-290-6

Peace Child, by Don Richardson
God opened a way for Don and Carol Richardson to share the gospel with the Sawi people of New Guinea—cannibals who admired Judas's betrayal more than Jesus' sacrifice. 1-57658-289-2

Bruchko, by Bruce Olson
The astonishing true story of a nineteen-year-old's capture by the Stone Age Motilone Indians in a South American jungle and the impact he had living out the gospel among them. 1-57658-348-1

A Cry from the Streets, by Jeannette Lukasse
A dramatic story of rescue and restoration unfolds when a young couple goes to live among the street children of Brazil. 1-57658-263-9

Imprisoned in Iran, by Dan Baumann
Wrongly accused of espionage and thrown into the most infamous high-security prison in Iran, one American man witnessed the powerful triumph of God's love over fear. 1-57658-180-2

Torches of Joy, by John Dekker with Lois Neely
In one generation, the Dani people of Irian Jaya took the dangerous leap from the Stone Age into the twentieth century, discovering the gospel of Jesus and their destiny as His helpers. 0-927545-43-8

The Man with the Bird on His Head, by John Rush and Abbe Anderson
A converted atheist on a medical mission may be the mysterious messenger predicted by the prophecies of a Pacific cult and the key to reaching an island with the gospel. 1-57658-005-9

Living on the Devil's Doorstep, by Floyd McClung
From the hippie trail through Kabul, Afghanistan, to the infamous red light district of Amsterdam, a young couple steps out in faith with the message of hope. 0-927545-45-4

Against All Odds, by Jim Stier
The story of one man's dedicated passion for the people of Brazil is a compelling reminder that God restores broken lives and broken dreams. 0-927545-44-6

Tomorrow You Die, by Reona Peterson Joly
Facing the ultimate risk, two women obey God's call to bring the gospel to the people of Albania. 0-927545-92-6

Dayuma: Life under Waorani Spears, by Ethel Emily Wallis
The story of the five missionary martyrs in Ecuador comes full circle in the breathtaking true story of Dayuma, who left her tribe on a desperate odyssey into the unknown. 0-927545-91-8

Adventures in Naked Faith, by Ross Tooley
Stories from the Philippines bring a challenge to a deeper, tested faith that will change believers' lives and the lives of those they encounter. 0-927545-90-X

Totally Surrounded, by Christina Di Stefano Davis
Surrounded by militant rebels, witch doctors, and the Philippine jungle, one woman relentlessly proclaimed the transforming power of God. 1-57658-165-9

Christian Heroes: Then & Now

Adventure-filled Christian biographies for ages 10 to 100!

Readers of all ages love the exciting, challenging, and deeply touching true stories of ordinary men and women whose trust in God accomplished extraordinary exploits for His kingdom and glory.

Available from YWAM Publishing
1-800-922-2143 www.ywampublishing.com
Also available: Christian Heroes Unit Study Curriculum Guides